Japanese Swords and Armor

日本刀

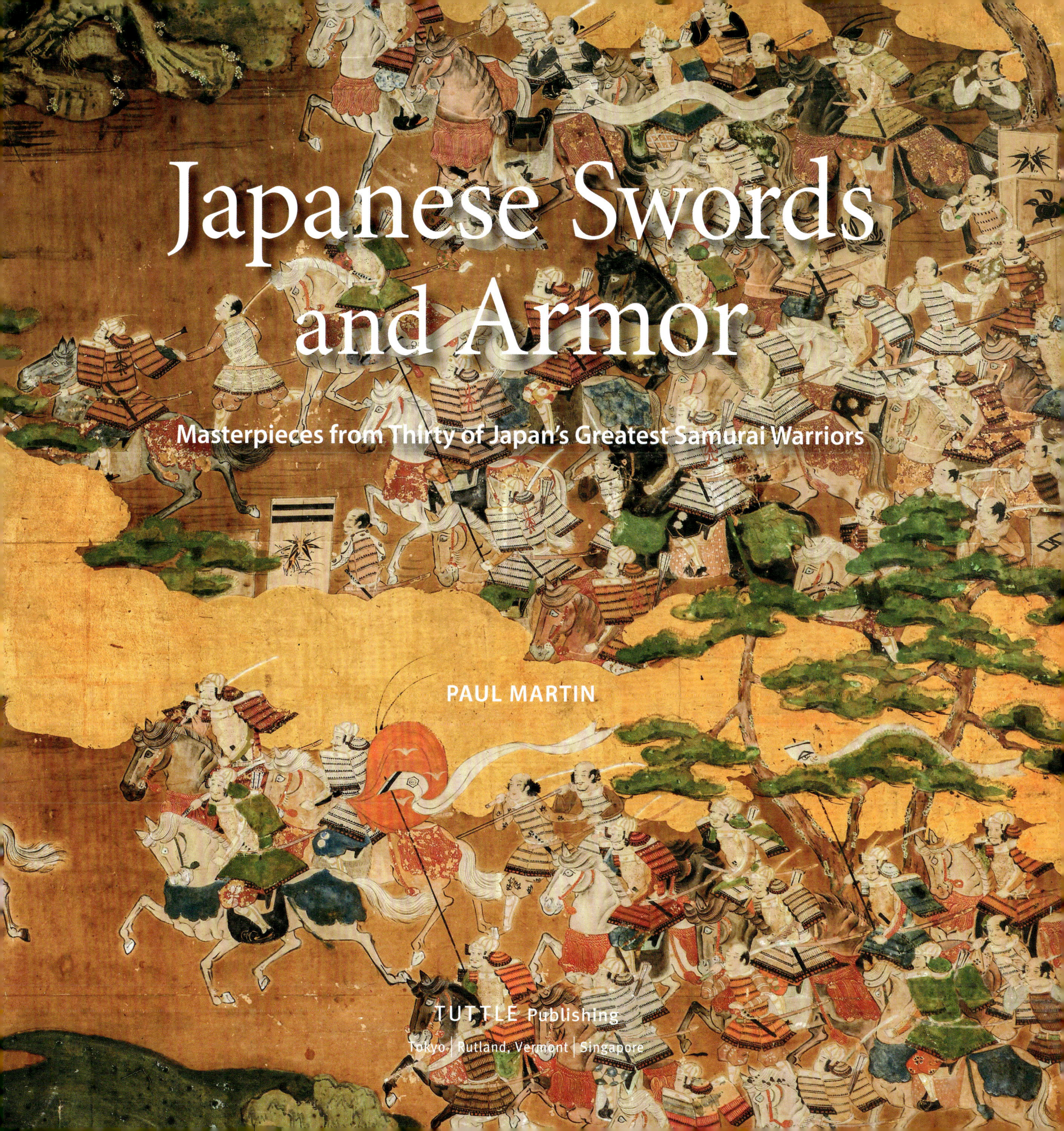

Japanese Swords and Armor

Masterpieces from Thirty of Japan's Greatest Samurai Warriors

PAUL MARTIN

TUTTLE Publishing
Tokyo | Rutland, Vermont | Singapore

CONTENTS

目次

Page 1
Tachi signed "Tomonari Saku" and probably belonging to Taira no Noritsune, 12th–13th c., Important Art Object (see pages 62–63).

Pages 2–3
Kanō School, two-panel screen depicting Minamoto no Yoshitsune and his soldiers defending the Takadachi Castle (1187), ink, color and gold leaf on paper, c. 1624–1634.

Right
Utagawa Kuniyoshi (1798–1861), *Battle on Mount Yoshino*, c. 1851.

浄妙山
水迺屋
溪垣真清
壽室諸實
四方歌

Katsushika Hokusai (1760–1849), *Minamoto no Yoshitsune and Benkei fight on the Gojō Bridge (Kyōto)*, c. 1820.

Preface
はじめに

The subject of the samurai and tales of their heroism has beguiled generations of westerners and Japanese alike. The culture of the samurai arose around the sword, so it is no coincidence that the rise of the samurai class and the origins of the curved Japanese sword happen at around the same time.

People who are interested in samurai tend to be broken into several different groups. Those who enjoy samurai history. Those who like samurai armor. Those who like Japanese swords, with further subdivisions of people who collect and appreciate the blades themselves, and people who prefer to collect the sword fittings. The lines are not clear-cut, as there are many people who cross between two or more of those groups.

This book is not a definitive work on samurai, but hopefully an entry level book that encourages more people to take an interest in samurai history and culture, or encourages people who are already interested in samurai to look beyond their own specific interest and take a deeper interest in other areas of samurai culture by introducing swords, fittings and armor that were owned and loved by well-known samurai.

Some of the items featured in this book have somewhat tenuous links to their famous owners. However, just like the origin myths of Japan and actual history, it is sometimes difficult to extrapolate fact from fiction.

I am very grateful to all of the people who have lit my way on this journey. Any mistakes are entirely my own.

Paul Martin
An auspicious day in the second month, 2023

The Samurai Warrior Class and the Aesthetics of Arms and Armor

武士及び武器と甲冑の美学

The samurai warriors of Japan have a unique place in the world. Of course, warriors of all countries are prized for their bravery and loyalty, but the samurai were unique for several reasons.

Not only were the samurai prepared to give their lives in combat at any moment, but they were also ready to commit ritual suicide (*seppuku)* either on the orders of their superiors or in repentance for serious misconduct to save their family's honor or even to follow their lord in death. This as well as refined code of etiquette and other complicated rituals that would later come to define Japanese decorum.

In the west, the phrase, *the pen is mightier than the sword,* appears to insinuate a disparity between education and martial prowess. However, for the samurai a philosophy of *the pen and the sword in accord* (Bunbu Ryōdō), was adopted as the samurai were expected to be educated, read classical literature, and write poetry. This also is connected with ritual suicide as there are many occasions when they would pen a death poem with their final thoughts or view of the transient world.

In their desire to become like their aristocratic social superiors, the sophistication of the samurai developed in many areas including the popularization of the tea ceremony, calligraphy and art. They took great pride in their appearance. In the Heian period (794–1185), warriors would imbue their armor with fragrant incense and apply make-up in case their heads were taken and in the late Edo period (1603–1868) their tastes had become so extravagant that the term Samurai Dandyism has been coined, a trend that was even incorporated into tales that featured female samurai.

Left
Hirose Choko (1884–1917), hanging scroll, *Yakko no Koman*, color on silk, c. 1910.

Right
Yashima Gakutei (1786–1868), *The Poet Warrior Minamoto no Yoshiie* (1039?–1106), from the series *Six Immortal Samurai Poets*, 1825.

武家六歌仙
源義家
岳亭筆

Anonymous, hanging scroll, *Minamoto no Yoshitsune*, ink and color on paper, 19th c.

The samurai cultivated a deep sense of artistic appreciation in combination with the Japanese reverence of nature. The sliding panels of warrior residences and castles were often adorned in paintings by specialist schools of artists. As you would expect of a societal caste with such an appreciation of the aesthetic, this appreciation was not limited to paintings, pottery and fashion, but would also influence the design and appreciation of arms and armor. Samurai armor were in made in flamboyant colorful designs with intricate, delicate fittings. Even the weapons contain an intrinsic beauty in the steel that reflects the Japanese appreciation of nature.

The most iconic and famous of these is the Japanese sword. However, contrary to most people's conception, they were not used as much as people think. They were prized functional art that you would not want to use unless your life depended on it. There have always been much more practical weapons that could be used at a greater distance from the enemy. The blades made by famous makers were passed between elite families as gifts, as part of dowries in marriage, as rewards from lords to retainers for loyal and courageous acts, and even to lords from retainers as a symbol of their allegiance.

The Japanese long sword comes in two main types: tachi and katana. As well as long sword blades, there are *wakizashi* (short swords), *tantō* (daggers), *naginata* (halberds), and *yari* (spears). Nowadays, all of these bladed weapons come under the umbrella of *nihontō,* or Japanese swords. However, out of all of those weapons, the most commonly used in battle was very likely the *yari*, and even before that was used the bow would probably be the first weapon of engagement. The *yari* uses less steel in its manufacture and is affixed to a long pole creating a greater distance between the user and the enemy. It can be used as a thrusting or slashing weapon.

The refined polishing and appreciation of the intrinsic qualities of the folded and differentially hardened steel of Japanese swords is a custom unique to Japan. The various combinations of the crystalline activities in the steel have a specialist terminology that reflects the Japanese affinity with nature. Many also have decorative carvings that illustrates the beliefs of a spiritual connection between the of gods of Japan and the sword.

Although, in later periods a terminology was used to describe the different levels of cutting ability of various sword makers blades, none of the terminology used to describe the shapes of blades, the grain pattern structures in the steel, the patterns of the hardened edge or the crystalline structures within has any connection to the effectiveness of cutting ability. Conversely, it is all very poetic and romantic.

Early sword fittings were rather practical, but even by the Nanbokuchō era (1336–1392), rather decorative fittings with applied colors appear reflecting images of the seasons and other philosophical themes, such as the transience of life. Once Japan was unified by the end of the 16th century, specialized schools of highly decorative fittings makers began to appear. The techniques and designs become increasingly sophisticated until end of the samurai era in 1868, when power was restored back to the Emperor and Japan embarked on an accelerated path to modernization.

The samurai class was officially abolished at the start of the Meiji era (1868–1912), creating a steep decline in the need for swordsmiths and fittings makers, with many turning to other crafts. However, not to be extinguished, small numbers of specialist craftsmen have managed to continue the arts of the samurai into the present day.

Right
Yukihiko Yasuda (1884–1978), hanging scroll, *Battle of Uji*, color on silk, c. 1903.

Opposite
Eitatsu Koyama (1880–1945), hanging scroll, *Uesugi Kenshin*, ink on silk, 1930.

The Rise of the Samurai
武士の台頭

The samurai became the de facto ruling class of Japan for 800 years. The perfected curved Japanese sword had not long come into existence, and the bow was the primary weapon.

Following the Genpei war (1180–1185), the power of the state was transferred from the imperial family to the warrior class. The emperor became a mere puppet of a section of the warrior class who were the most powerful at the time. However, during these times of disturbance and rebellion, which established the distinctions between the classes, there was much development in the arms and armor of the warrior class.

Warriors of the Warring States Period (Sengoku-jidai)

戦国時代の武士

Following his success in over-throwing the Kamakura Shogunate and returning Emperor Godaigo to power in the Kenmu Restoration (1333–1336), Ashikaga Takauji was appointed *shōgun* in 1338, establishing the Ashikaga Shogunate. However, as Emperor Godaigo's unpopularity increased and the various clans grew in autonomy and power, the Ashikaga Shogunate eventually collapsed and widespread fighting took place between various clans for control of lands.

Beginning with the Ōnin War in Kyōto 1467, Japan entered an extended period of civil turmoil that lasted for over a hundred years. During this period there were many warriors that rose to fame. However, it was not only a period of courage and bravery, but also one of deceit and betrayal. Additionally, the arrival of Europeans and the introduction of the gun eventually tipped the balance of power that led to Oda Nobunaga coming to the fore.

The Three Great Unifiers of Japan

三英傑

Above left
Utagawa Yoshitora (att. c. 1836–1887), *Oda Nobunaga of Owari province*, from the series *Sixty-Odd Famous Generals of Japan*, 1866.

Above center
Utagawa Yoshitora (att. c. 1836–1887), *Mashiba Hisayoshi* (*Toyotomi Hideyoshi*) *of the Settsu province*, from the series *Sixty-Odd Famous Generals of Japan*, 1866.

Above right
Utagawa Yoshitora (att. c. 1836–1887), *Tokugawa Ieyasu, the first* shōgun, from the series *Heroes of Mikawa*, 1873.

Opposite
Utagawa Yoshitsuya (1822–1866), *The Shuten-dōji of Mount Ōe*, 1858 (detail).

After over a century of civil warfare, three warriors, Oda Nobunaga, Toyotomi Hideyoshi and Tokugawa Ieyasu are credited with the unification of Japan and the final great peace. Following his success at the Battle of Okehazama, Nobunaga began to unify Japan and rebuild the devasted capital of Kyōto. However, he was betrayed by his vassal Akechi Mitsuhide, and died at Honnō-ji (Temple) in 1582.

His loyal vassal, Toyotomi Hideyoshi, quickly avenged his death and took up the reigns by forming a group of regents to continue unification. However, following Hideyoshi's sudden death in 1598, Tokugawa Ieyasu saw his opportunity to seize power. Finally, after emerging victorious at the deciding Battle of Sekigahara, and securing his position at the Siege of Ōsaka Castle, Ieyasu set up systems that allowed the Tokugawa Shogunate to rule Japan for the next 265 years.

敦賀尉碓氷貞光

The Heroes of the Bakumatsu Era

幕末の志士

After a long period of peace in Japan, and 200 years of isolation from the rest of the world, Japanese society was becoming dissatisfied with the feudal systems, and the role of the samurai class. Even within the samurai class, lower class samurai confined by the feudal system were ready for change.

Then in 1853, Commodore Perry arrived from America in large black steamships, and demanded that Japan open its doors to the west and allow free trade. In its 200-year peaceful seclusion, Japanese indigenous arts and culture had developed to a high degree. However, military technology had stagnated, leaving the Japanese with antiquated swords and muskets.

In a division between warriors who wanted to preserve the samurai status quo, and others who wanted to embrace the technology and ideology of the west, a final civil war erupted that would eventually see the abolishment of the samurai class.

Above
Utagawa Yoshimori (1830–1884), *The Honnō-ji Incident*, 1869.

Next spread
Tsukioka Yoshitoshi (1839–1892), *The Kagoshima Rebels Leaving Camp for Battle*, 1879.

Page 20
Kanō School, two-panel screen depicting Minamoto no Yoshitsune and his soldiers defending the Takadachi Castle (1187), ink, color and gold leaf on paper, c. 1624–1634 (detail).

村田三介
村田新八
池上四郎
別府新助
篠原國幹

西郷吉之助隆盛

麑嶋暴徒出陣圖
頃ハ明治十年二月中旬
鹿児島縣の士族暴発
し其勢凡二万有余総
大将西郷隆盛副将篠
原桐野を始め村田逸見
池上其他の隊長伍列を
正し三太郎峠の雪を
分け道を岐して正奇
の両軍肥後熊本へ繰出
せ勢ひ最も廣大なりしと
逸見十郎太
池邊吉十郎
桐野利秋
西郷小平
児玉八之進

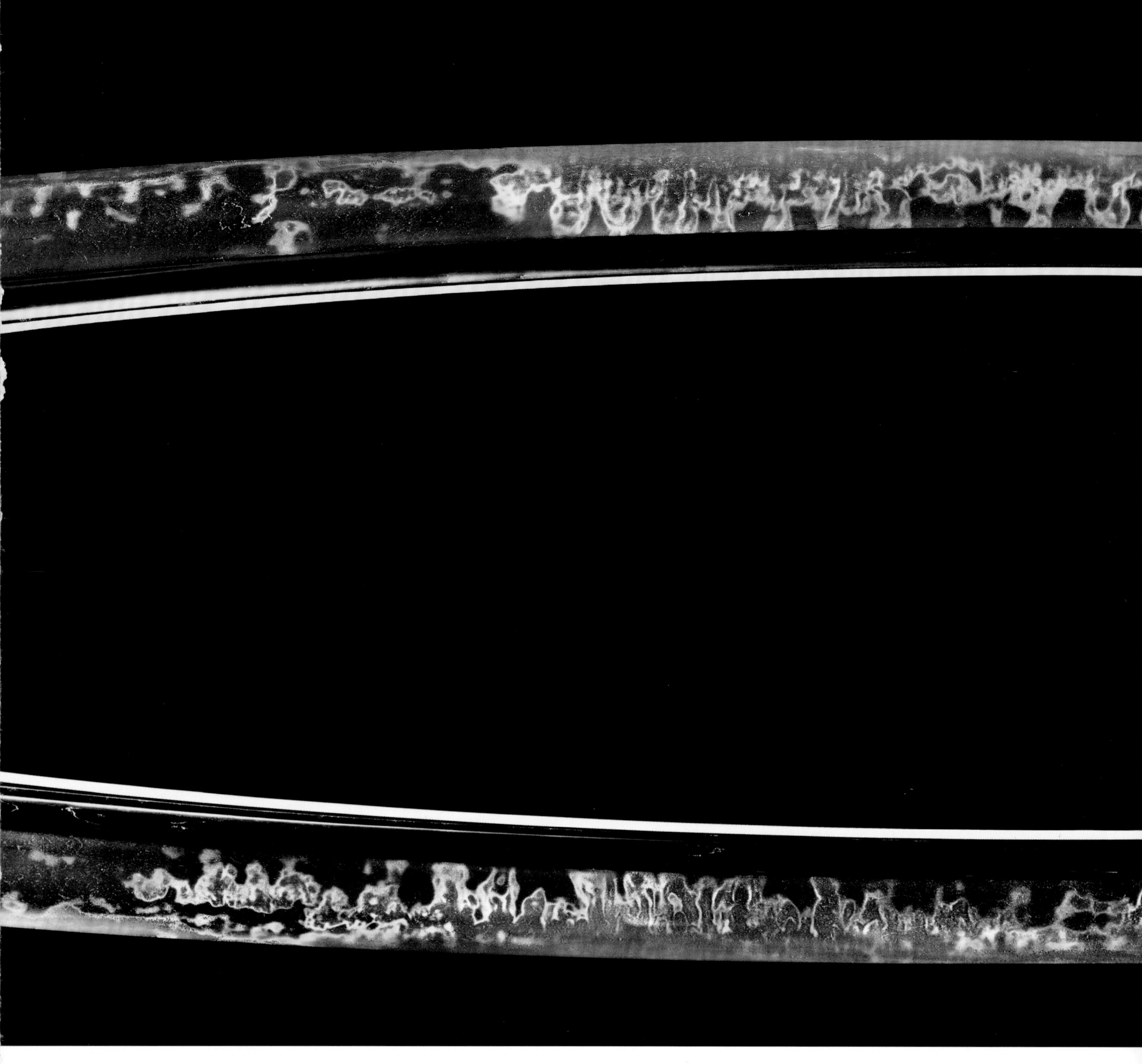

● UNSIGNED **ATTRIBUTED TO THE ICHIMONJI SCHOOL**
OTHER NAMES **YAMATORIGE, SANCHŌMŌ**

CUTTING-EDGE LENGTH **79.5 CM (31⁹⁄₃₂ IN)**
CURVATURE **3.4 CM (1⁵⁄₁₆ IN)**

TACHI
太刀

92.5%

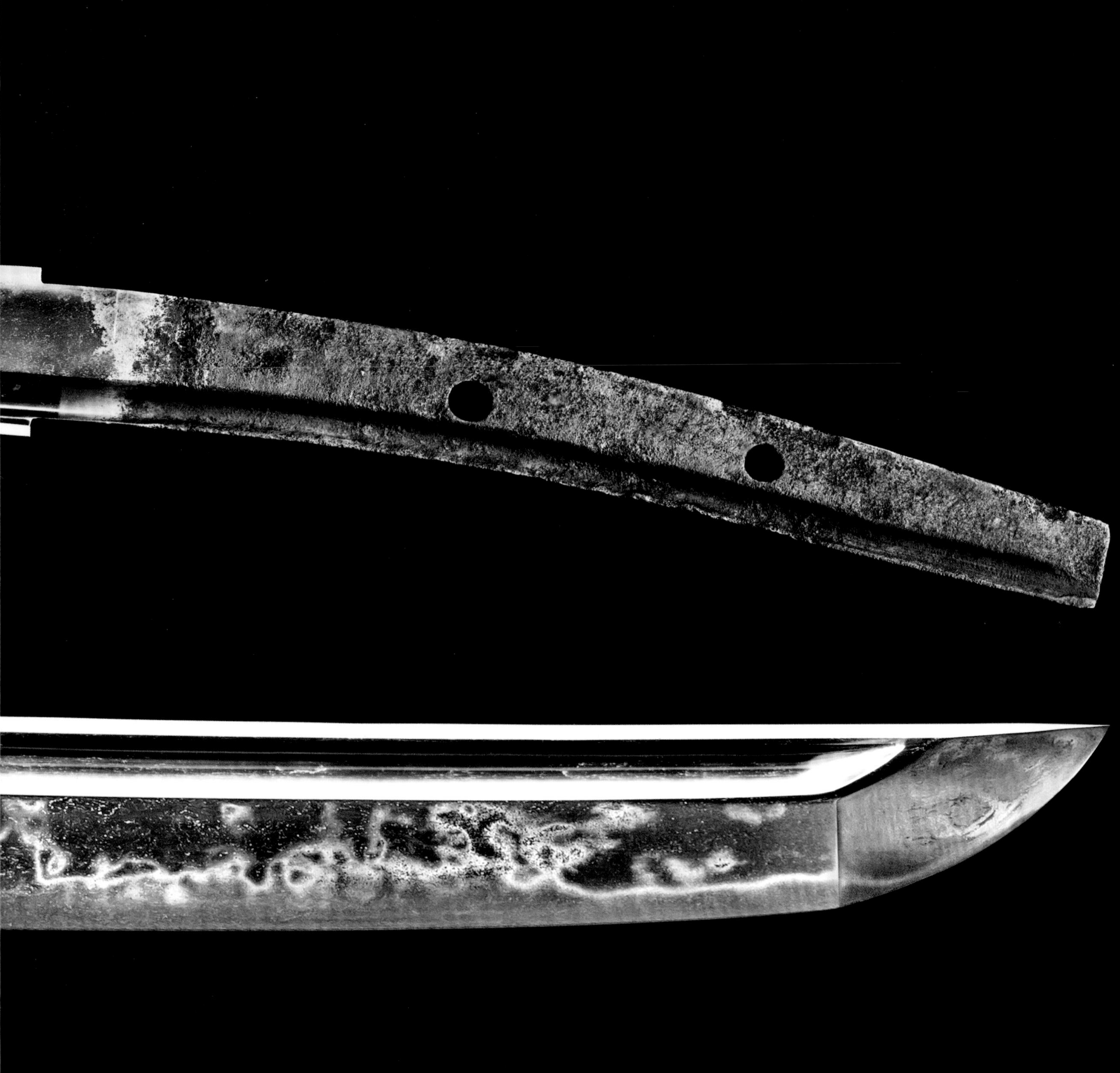

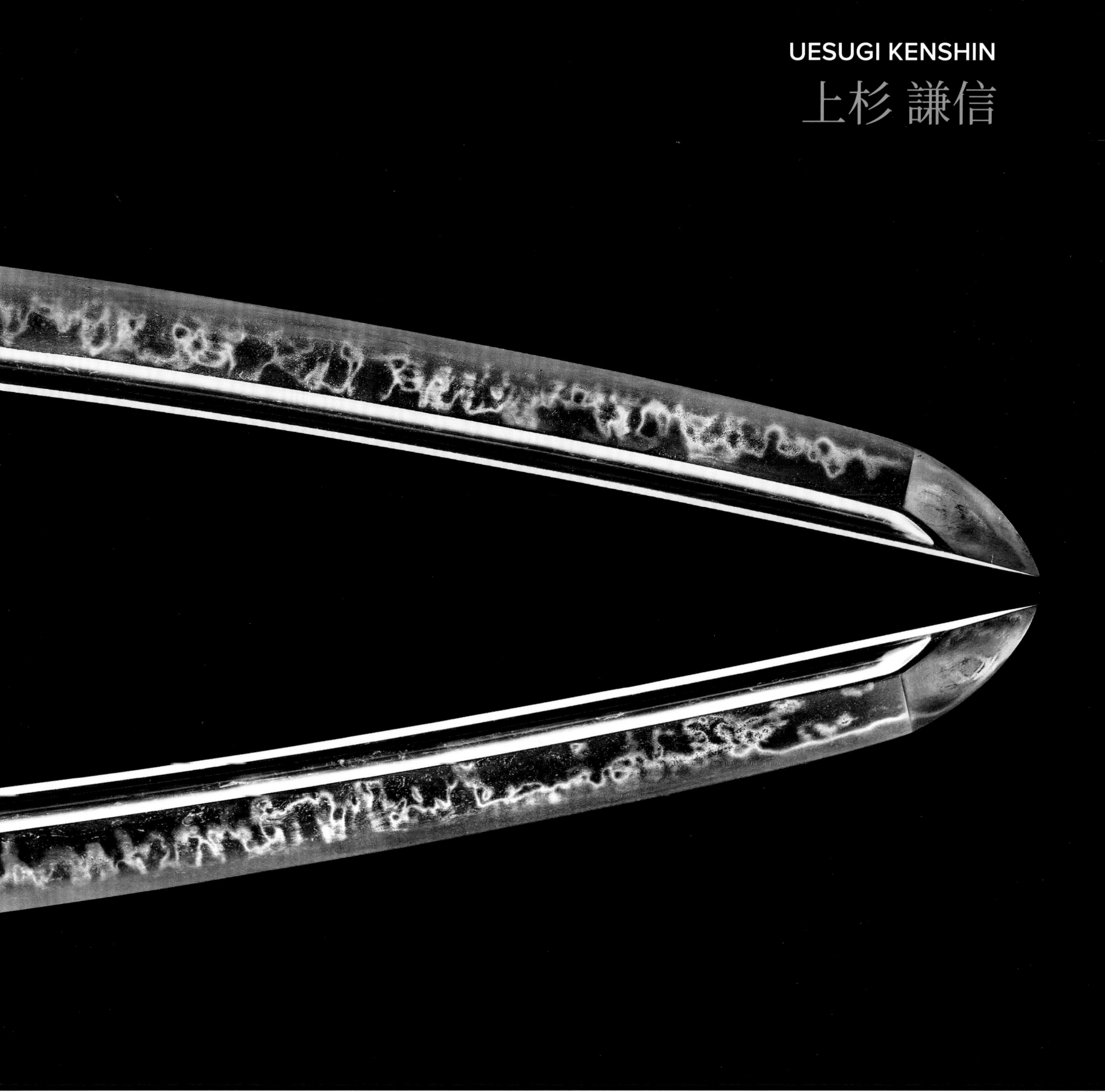

UESUGI KENSHIN
上杉 謙信

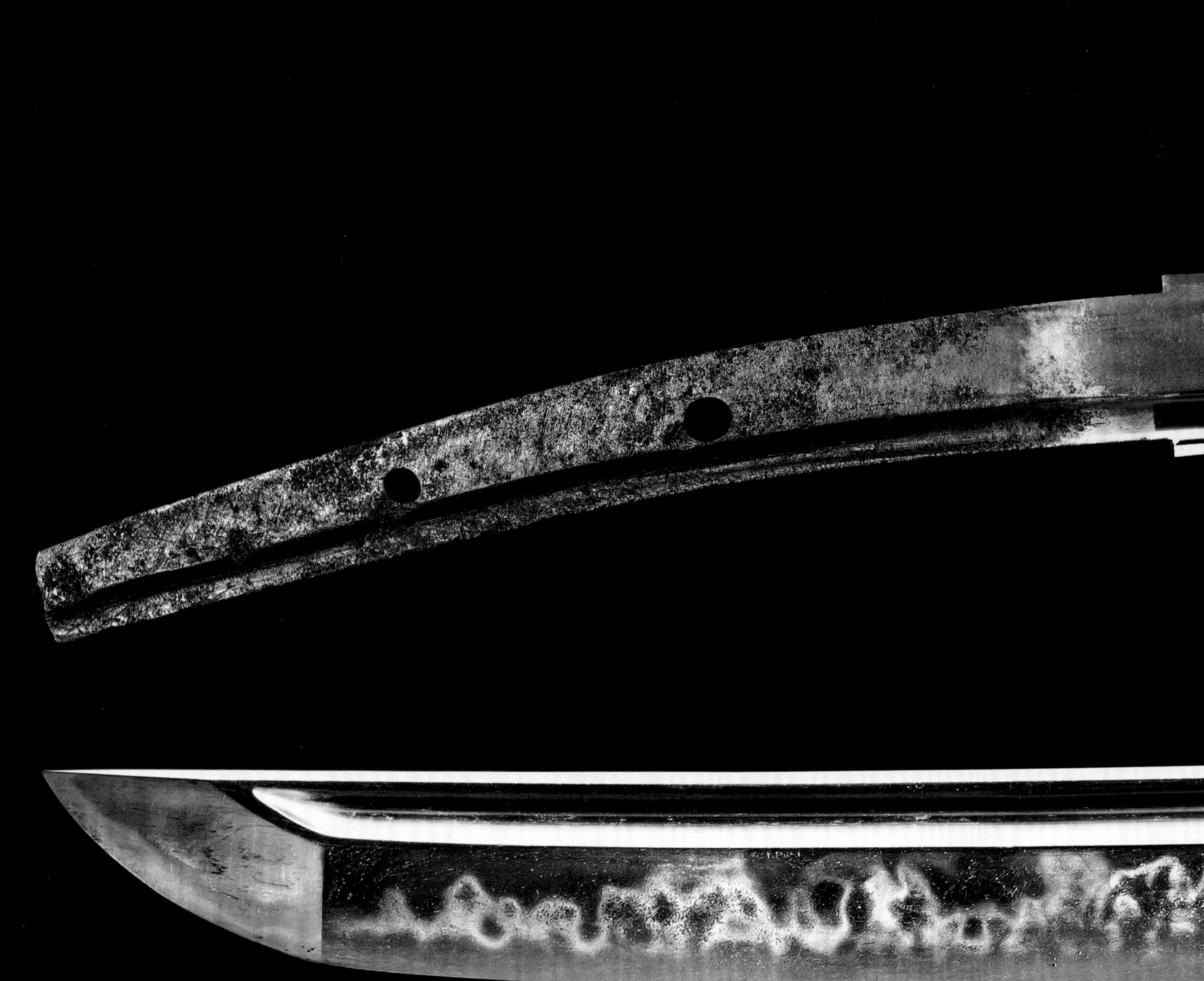

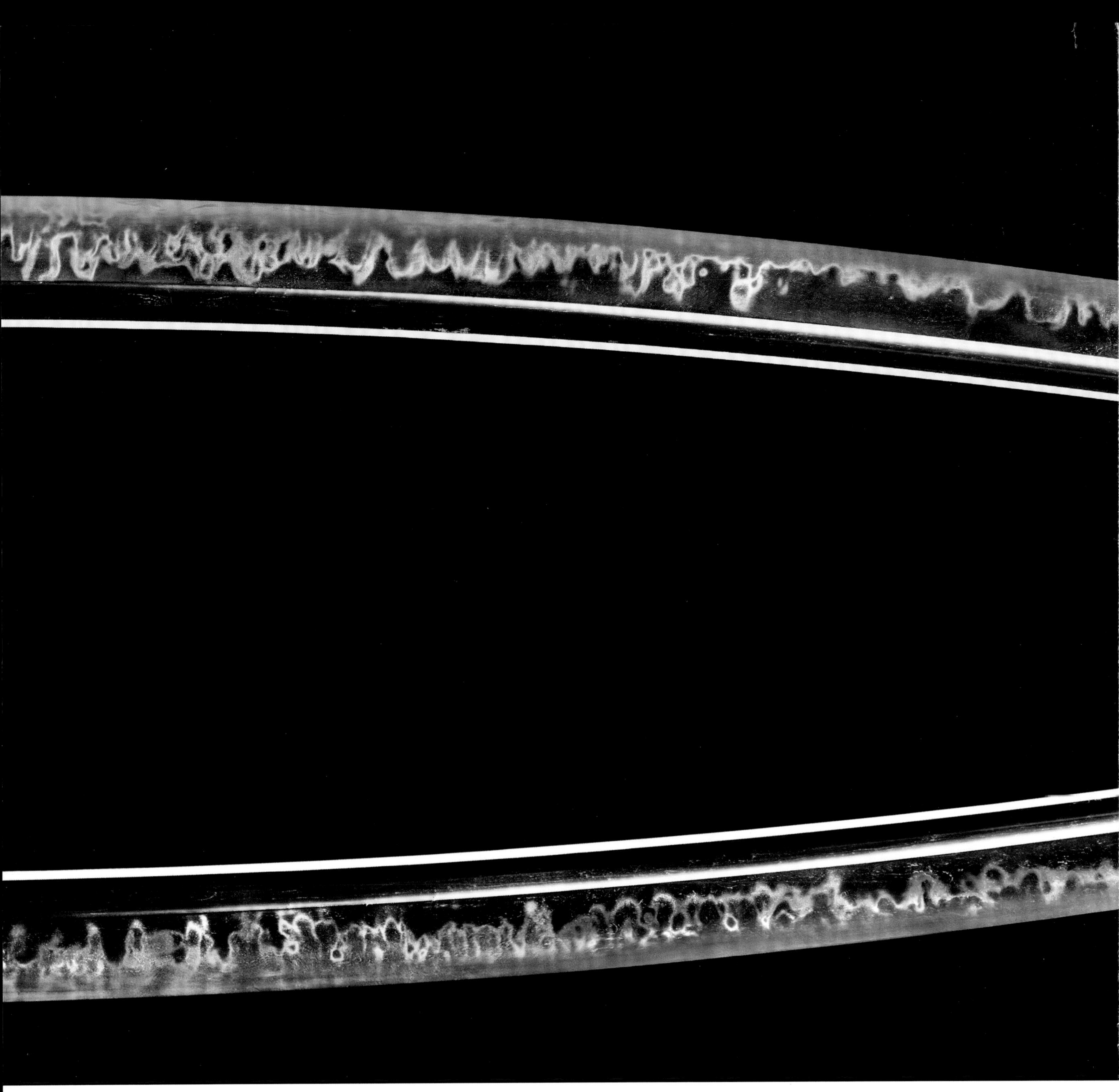

PERIOD **KAMAKURA, 13TH C.**
BIZEN OSAFUNE SWORD MUSEUM, OKAYAMA PREFECTURE
National Treasure

(Enlargement of pages 92–93)

TAIRA NO SADAMORI

平 貞盛

TACHI: IMPERIAL COLLECTION
● UNSIGNED
ATTRIBUTED TO AMAKUNI
OTHER NAME(S)
(MEIBUTSU) KOGARASU-MARU (THE LITTLE CROW)
CUTTING-EDGE LENGTH **62.7 CM (24⅝ IN)**
CURVATURE **1.2 CM (½ IN)**

PERIOD **NARA TO HEIAN PERIODS 8–10TH C.**
IMPERIAL HOUSEHOLD AGENCY
Imperial Collection

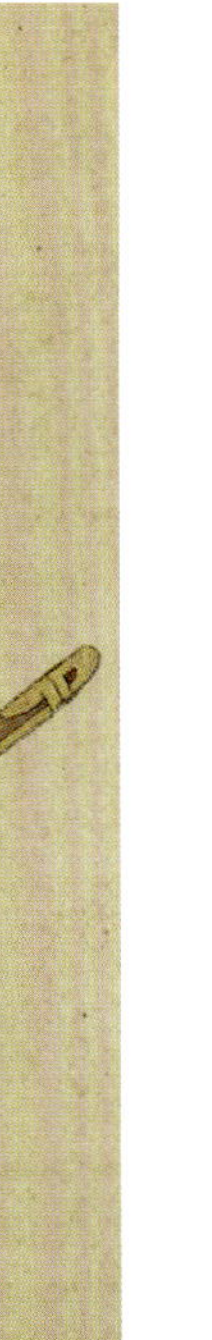

平貞盛

Left
Anonymous, *Taira no Sadamori*, color and gold on paper, 18th–19th c.

TACHI

The technical definition of this construction of *tachi* is, *kissaki moroha-zukuri*, as the top section of the blade has an edge on both sides. It is also commonly referred to as *kogarasu-maru-zukuri*. It has an *iori-mune* and deep curvature. The well-forged *hada* is *ko-itame* that flows in places, and is covered with a fine *ji-nie*. The *hamon* is *hoso-suguha*. However, there is a break in the *hamon* on both sides around the mid-section. It has a *shinogi-hi* on both sides with a deeply cut *naginata-hi* that ends in *kaki-nagashi*. The *ubu-nakago* is deeply curved and has no discernable signature. It is said to have been made by the legendary master smith Amakuni.

Amakuni is recorded to have worked in the Taihō era (701–703). However, there are no extant signed works by Amakuni. One of the legends associated with the sword is that it was presented to Taira no Sadamori after killing Taira no Masakado. It was then passed down within the Taira clan for many generations. The shape is considered a transitionary shape between the early straight swords and the perfected curved Japanese sword of the mid 10th century. There are several other examples of this type of construction in the Shōsō-in Imperial repository in Nara. However, all the other examples lack the deep curvature in the *tang* area. It is theorized that the curvature in the *tang* was added at a later time when curved swords became popular.

TAIRA NO SADAMORI (10TH C.)

Due to the lack of documents in early Japanese history, Taira no Sadamori's birth is not known. Sadamori's father, Kunika, was killed in 935 during a skirmish between other members of his family and his uncle, Taira no Masakado. At first, although distressed at the death of his father, he did not take sides as he viewed it as a family affair. However, fighting continued, and eventually Masakado led an uprising while claiming to be the new emperor. The Imperial court sent Sadamori, who was assisted by Fujiwara no Hidesato, to stop him. They pursued Masakado, and finally killed him at the Battle of Kojima in 940.

TACHI
太刀

SIGNED **YASUTSUNA**
MEIBUTSU **DŌJI-GIRI YASUTSUNA**
CUTTING-EDGE LENGTH **80.3 CM (31⅝ IN)**

CURVATURE **2.7 CM (1 IN)**
MOTO-HABA **2.9 CM (1⅛ IN)**
SAKI-HABA **1.9 CM (¾ IN)**

PERIOD **HEIAN PERIOD 11TH C.**
TOKYO NATIONAL MUSEUM
National Treasure

源 頼光

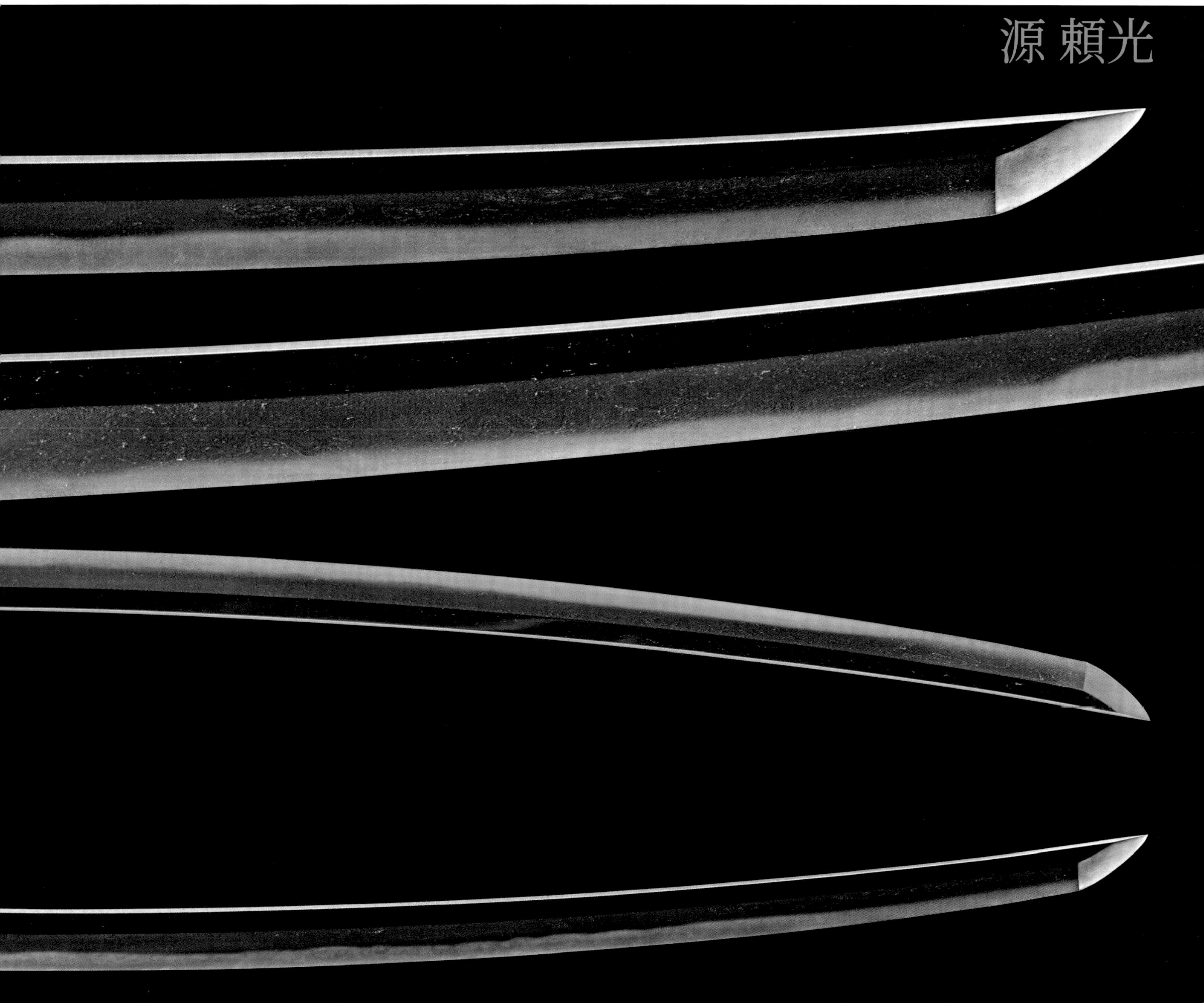

Right
Shibata Zeshin (1807–1891), *The Warrior Minamoto no Yorimitsu*, ink and color on paper, c. 1880-1891.

Opposite
Yashima Gakutei (1786–1868), *Minamoto no Yorimitsu*, from the series *Six Immortal Samurai Poets*, c. 1827.

TACHI

This *tachi* is *shinogi-zukuri* in construction with *iori-mune*, a deep *koshi-zori*, *funbari* and a *ko-kissaki*. It has a rather prominent flowing *itame-hada* that is covered with thick *ji-nie*, fine *chikei*, and a prominent *midare*, *nie-utsuri*. The *hamon* is a *nie* laced *ko-midare* with *chōji* that begins with *yaki-otoshi*. There are also *ashi*, and *kinsuji*. The *bōshi* is *midare-komi*, *ko-maru* with strong *hakikake* and a *kaeri*. The *ubu-nakago* has *kiri-yasurime*, one *mekugi-ana*, and ends in *kuri-jiri*. Above the *mekugi-ana*, close to the *mune*, it is inscribed with the two-character signature of Yasutsuna. The sword is accompanied by a Momoyama period *ito-maki tachi-koshirae*. The *saya* is plain gold lacquer. The fittings are *shakudō-nanako* ground, with gold colored *kiri-mon* carved in high-relief. The *tsuka* and *saya* have been wrapped in brown *ito*.

MINAMOTO NO YORIMITSU (944–1021)

Minamoto no Yorimitsu, also known as Raikō, is something of a folk hero in Japanese history. He also appears in several Japanese supernatural tales along with his four retainers, Wanatabe no Tsuna, Sakata no Kintoku, Urabe no Suetake and Usui Sadamitsu, collectively known as the Shitennō (the four heavenly kings). He is featured in the stories of Kintarō (Golden Boy), as the slayer of the giant demon spider, Tsuchigumo, and is said to have slayed the demon, Shuten-Dōji on Mt. Oe with the sword that became known as Dōji-Giri. It was known as one of the Five Great Swords Under Heaven since the Muromachi period, and has been owned by many famous warriors including, Toyotomi Hideyoshi, Tokugawa Ieyasu, Tokugawa Hidetada, (Echigo) Matsudaira Tadanao, until it was finally passed to the Matsudaira line of the Tsuyama domain.

武家六歌仙
源頼光
五柳園
岳亭

Left
Utagawa Kuniyoshi (1797–1861), *Minamoto no Yorimitsu (Raikō)*, c. 1820.

Right
Utagawa Kuniyoshi (1798–1861), central part of a triptych, *Minamoto Yorimitsu and the Earth Spider*, c. 1820–1824.

源頼光
一勇斎國芳画

TACHI

● SIGNED **YASUTSUNA**
OTHER NAME(S) (MEIBUTSU) **HIGEKIRI, ONIKIRI-MARU**
CUTTING-EDGE LENGTH **84.6 CM (33 5⁄16 IN)**
CURVATURE **3.6 CM (1 7⁄16 IN)**

PERIOD **HEIAN PERIOD, 10–12TH C.**
KITANO TENMANGŪ SHRINE, KYŌTO
Important Cultural property

Far left and left bottom
Artist unknown, *Sculpture Traditionally Identified as the Seated Portrait of Minamoto no Yoritomo*, wood with pigment and inlaid crystal eyes, Kamakura period, 13th–14th c., Tokyo National Museum, Important Cultural Property.

Right
Attributed to Fujiwara no Takanobu (1142–1205), *Portrait of Minamoto no Yoritomo*, hanging scroll, ink and color on silk, Kamakura period, 13th c., Jingo-ji, Kyōto.

Opposite
Torii Kiyonaga (1752–1815), *Yoritomo's Hunt at the Foot of Mount Fuji*, c. 1785.

TACHI

Along with the Hizamaru, the Higekiri *tachi* was passed down within the Minamoto clan for many generations. According to the *Taiheiki*, this sword was worn by Minamoto Yoritomo. It is also known as the Onikiri-maru, from an episode when Watanabe no Tsuna came across an ogre disguised as a beautiful woman at Ichijō-Modori Bridge in Kyōto. The ogre snatched Watanabe and took flight. However, while flying over Kitano Tenmangū Shrine, Watanabe used the sword to cut off the ogre's arm, thus saving his life.

This elegant shaped *tachi* is *shinogi-zukuri* in construction with an *iori-mune* and a *ko-kissaki*. It has a well forged *ko-itame hada*. The *hamon* is *notare* mixed with *ko-midare*. It has a *bō-hi* on both sides that end in *kaki-nagashi*. It has two *mekugi-ana*, and is signed with the two-character signature of Yasutsuna of Hoki province (Tottori pref.).

MINAMOTO NO YORITOMO (1147–1199)

Minamoto no Yoritomo was the first *shōgun* of the Kamakura period (1185–1336). He is famous for being the leader of the Minamoto clan in their victory of the Taira clan during the Genpei wars (1180–1185). Their victory over the Taira also avenged the death of his father, Minamoto no Yoshitomo, who had been vanquished from Kyoto by the Taira during the Heiji Rebellion (1160). While being hunted, Yoshitomo was assassinated by one of his own men while bathing in a hot spring. It is said that his last words were, "If I had even had a *bokutō* (wooden sword)…".

After Yoshitomo's death, Yoritomo and his brothers were also due to be executed, but due to the intervention of Kiyomori's stepmother, Yoritomo and his brothers' lives were spared and they were exiled. Around 1177, Yoritomo married Hōjō Masako, the daughter of Tokimasa. Yoritomo and the Hōjō family became great allies.

In 1180, Taira no Kiyomori took control of the Imperial succession by placing his grandson, Antoku, on the throne. In response, the son of Emperor Goshirakawa, and rightful heir, Mochihito, made a call to arms to the Minamoto clan. A war then escalated between the Taira and Minamoto clans. After five years of war, the Minamoto clan finally defeated the Taira in a naval battle at Dannoura in the Shimonoseki straights.

Yoritomo was officially appointed the first Seitai'i Shōgun (Generalissimo) of the Kamakura period in 1192. After his death in 1199, his wife Hōjō Masako became a nun, but continued to conduct military government affairs, along with the other Hōjō Regents, in the name of her young Shogun sons. She became known as the nun-*shōgun*.

清長画

● **Ō-YOROI TYPE ARMOR**
WITH PURPLE LACING
WEIGHT **23.4 KGS (51½ LBS)**

PERIOD **KAMAKURA PERIOD, 12TH C.**
ŌYAMAZUMI SHRINE, EHIME PREF.
National Treasure

Right
Yashima Gakutei (1786–1868), *The Warrior Ōkura Ubain Yorifusa, Imperial Secretary and Head of the Imperial Stables, Kneeling at the Feet of Minamoto no Yoritomo* (scene from the *Taiheiki*), from the series *Twenty-Four Japanese Examples of Filial Piety for the Honchōren*, c. 1821.

This *ō-yoroi* (old style armor) is made from both iron and leather small plates laced together with purple cord. It has large should guards (*ō-sode*). It is a very elegant and rare example of armor from the early Kamakura period. The leather covering the front of the cuirass is in an excellent condition of preservation. It has a lion-dog (*shishi*) and peony design. According to shrine records, it was a votive offering of Minamoto no Yoritomo.

NAGINATA

薙刀

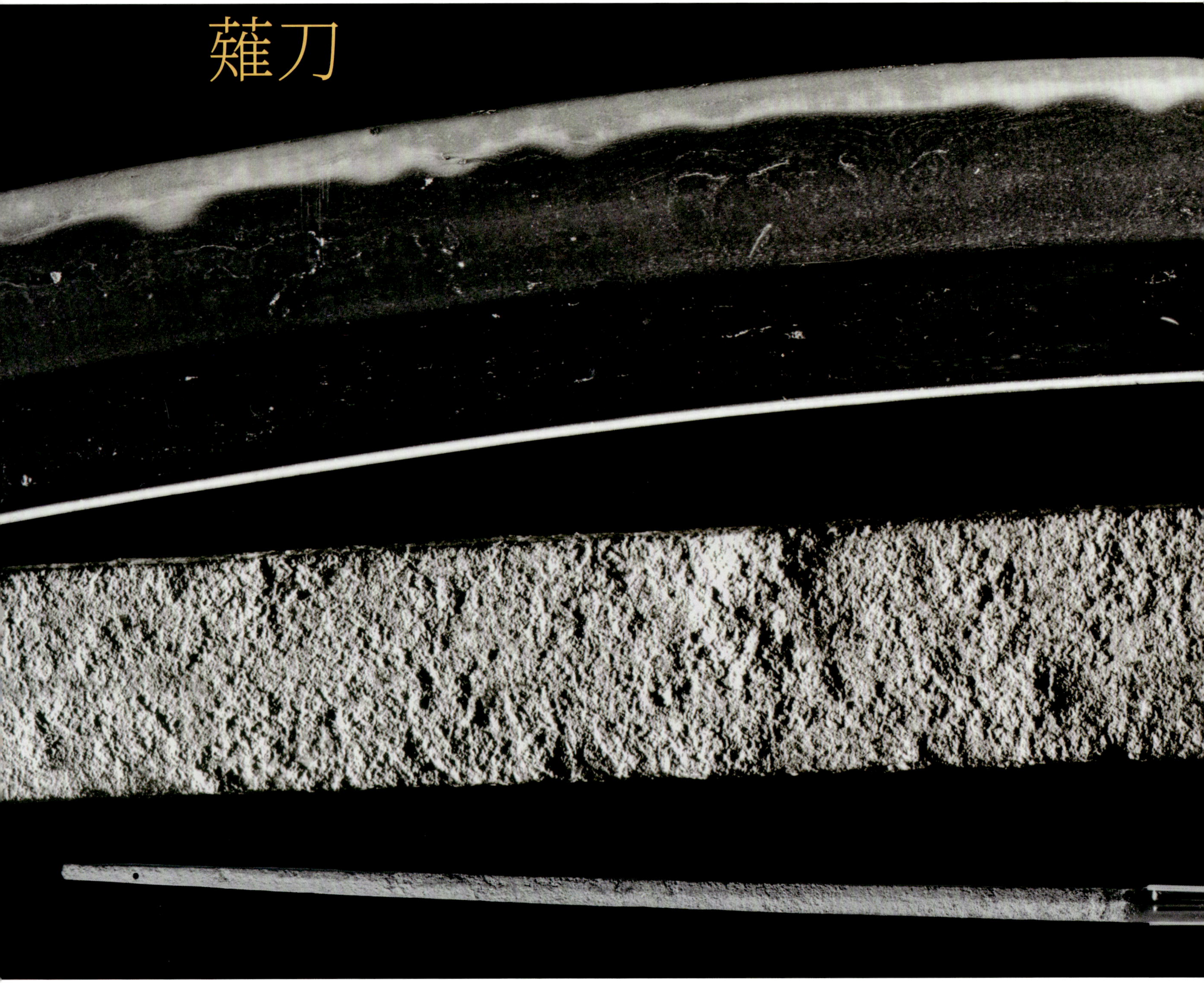

● UNSIGNED
CUTTING EDGE LENGTH **101.4 CM (39 15/16 IN)**
CURVATURE **4.5 CM (1¾ IN)**
TANG LENGTH **98.9 CM (38 15/16 IN)**

PERIOD **KAMAKURA-NANBOKUCHŌ PERIOD, 14TH C.**
ŌYAMAZUMI SHRINE, EHIME PREF.
Important Cultural Property

BENKEI
弁慶

Right and opposite
Toyohara Chikanobu (1838–1912), *Benkei and the Giant Bell*, c. 1897, triptych and detail.

NAGINATA

According to the shrine records at Ōyamazumi Shrine, this naginata was a votive offering of Benkei. This over-sized *naginata* has *iori-mune* and a deep curvature. It has a *naginata-hi* that ends in *kaku-dome* with *soe-bi* on both sides. The *hamon* is *ko-chōji* and *gunome*, and a rather tight *nioi-guchi*. The *bōshi* is *midare* and ends in *yakizume*. It is well forged with a *ko-itame-hada* and a prominent *utsuri*. It is speculated to possibly be the work of a smith of the Osafune school from the late Kamakura-Nanbokuchō period. It is thought that it became part of the shrine's legend as a votive offering of Benkei due to its extra-large size.

BENKEI (1155–1189)

Although technically not a samurai, warrior monk Benkei fulfills all of the requirements to be included in this compilation. Benkei is a benchmark in devotion and loyalty to one's master. He is recorded as being a very large man of over 2 meters tall. We are introduced to Benkei when he comes across the young warrior, Ushiwaka (Minamoto no Yoshitsune). A fight ensues between the two on Gojō bridge in Kyōto. Benkei lost the fight, but impressed by Ushiwaka, he pledged his undying loyalty to him. Following Yoshitsune's fued and subsequent pursuit by his brother Yoritomo, Benkei made his last stand defending Yoshitsune at the Battle of Koromo River, in Hiraizumi, Mutsu Province. The Minamoto warriors, who were too scared to face him in man-to-man combat, shot him repeatedly from a distance with arrows. However, Benkei refused to fall and died riddled with arrows while holding himself up with his *naginata*. Thus, allowing Yoshitsune enough time to commit *seppuku* (ritual suicide) rather than fall into the hands of his enemies.

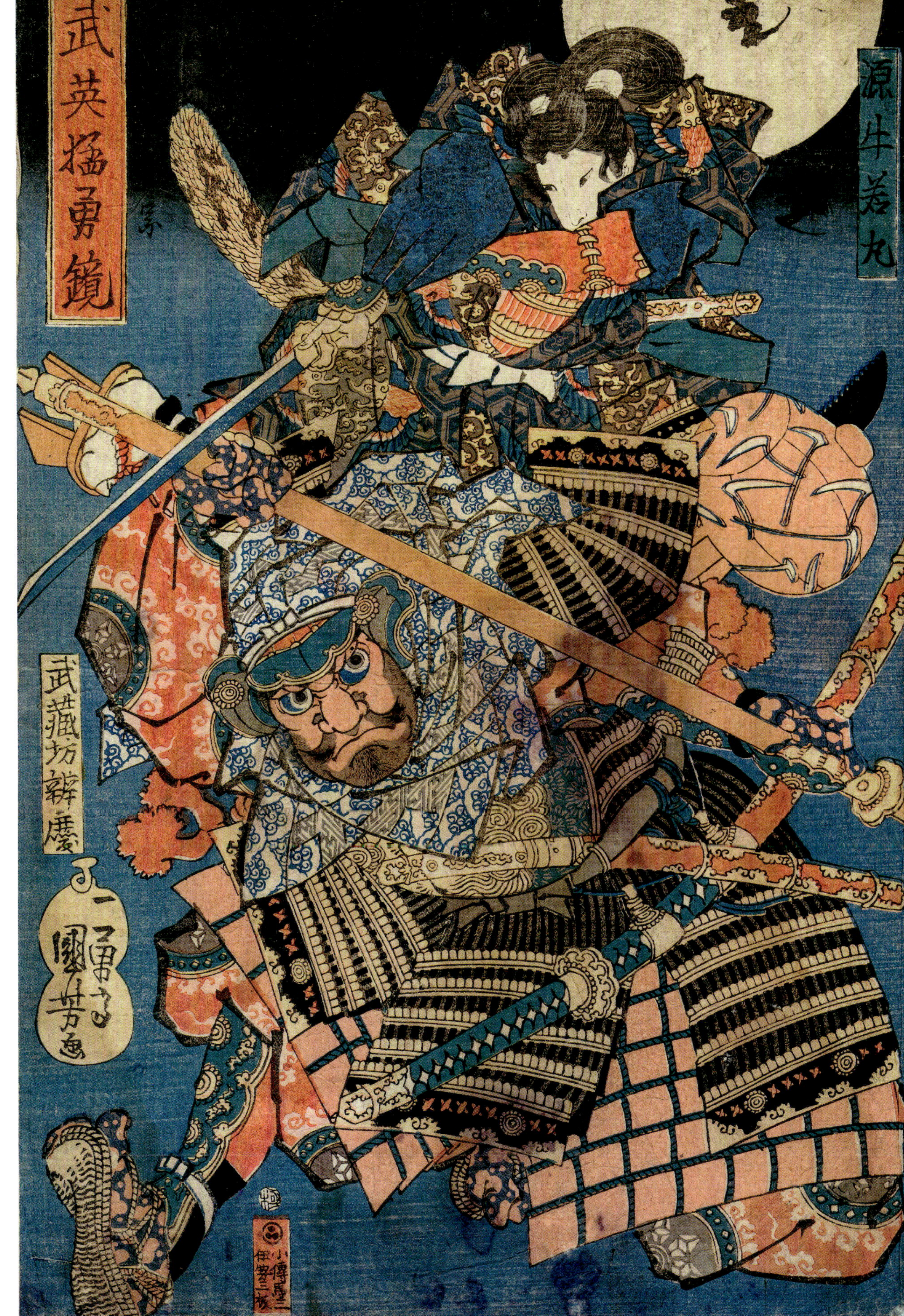

Left
Utagawa Hiroshige (1797–1858), *Ushiwakamaru Defeats Musashibō Benkei at Gojō Bridge*, from the series *The Life of Yoshitsune*, early-mid 19th c.

Right
Utagawa Kuniyoshi (1797–1861), *Minamoto Ushiwakamaru and Musashibō Benkei*, from the series *Mirror of Military Excellence and Fierce Courage*, c. 1836.

NAGINATA

薙刀

● UNSIGNED
CUTTING EDGE LENGTH **80.1 CM (31½ IN)**
CURVATURE **1.1 CM (7/16 IN)**
TANG LENGTH **76.4 CM (30 1/16 IN)**

PERIOD **NANBOKUCHŌ PERIOD 14TH C.**
ŌYAMAZUMI SHRINE, EHIME PREF.
Important Cultural Property

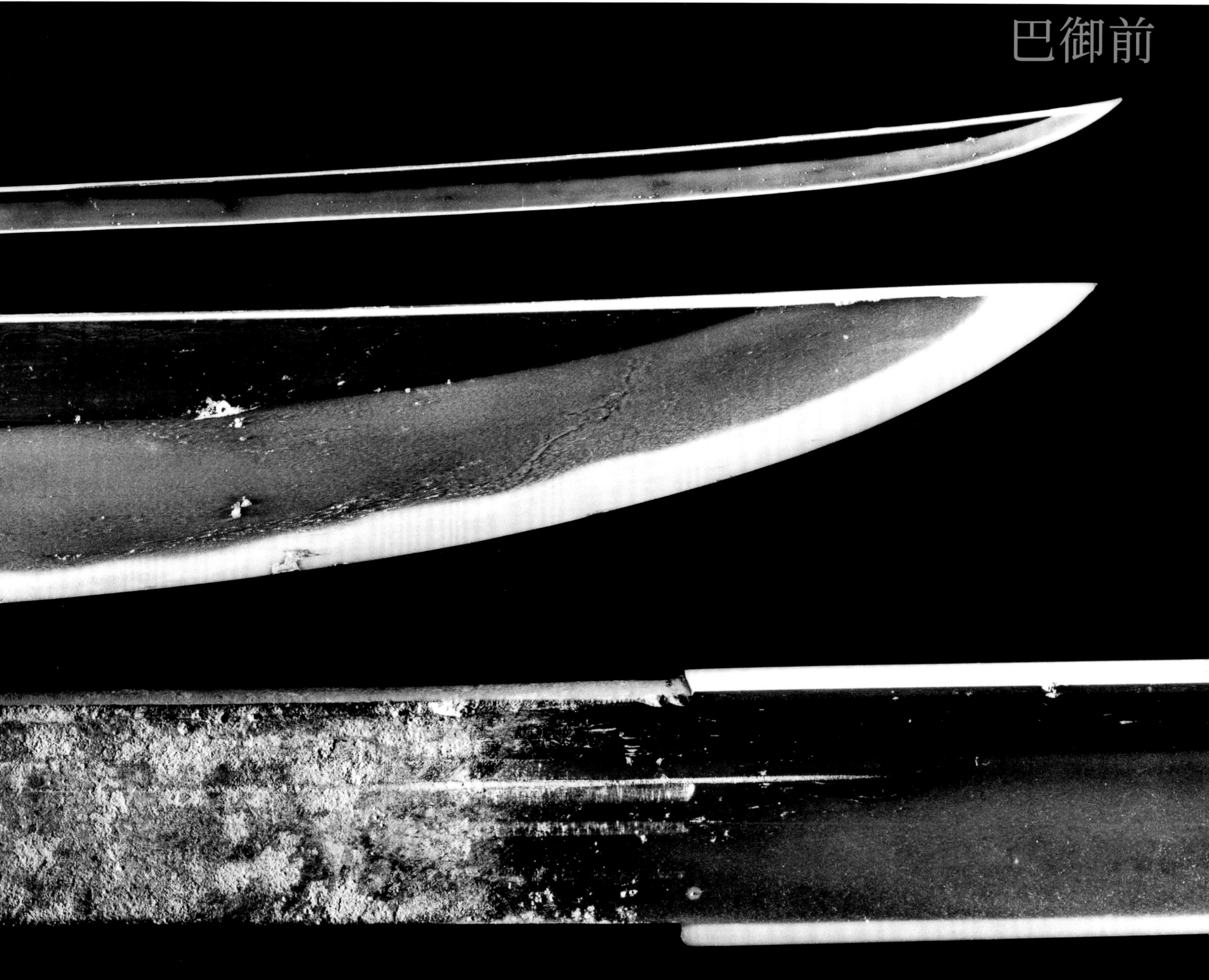
巴御前

Opposite left
Kitao Shigemasa, attr. (1739–1820), *Tomoe Gozen in Armor and with Sword on Horseback*, 1770–1780.

Opposite right
Utagawa Kunimasa (1773–1810), *Actor Iwai Kumesaburō as the Female Warrior Tomoe Gozen, in Armor, Holding a Spear behind his Back with Right Hand*, scene from the play *Hiragana seisuiki*, 1797.

NAGINATA

According to legend of Oyamazumi Shrine, this *naginata* (halberd) belonged to Tomoe Gozen, and has become part of the shrine's history. Furthermore, the *naginata* has also been designated an Important Cultural Property. However, scholars have appraised the blade to be from the 14th century. It is an over-sized *naginata* blade with a very shallow curvature. It has a *naginata-hi* (groove) that ends in *kaki-nagashi*, and the remains of a *soe-bi* on in the base of the blade on both sides. The hamon is *suguha* (straight) with a tight *nioi-guchi*. The *nakago* has been extended making it rather long with a single *mekugi-ana*. It has been appraised as the work of the Mihara school of Bitchū Province. Regardless of the provenance, this is a very rare *naginata* of the period and in remarkable condition.

TOMOE GOZEN (1157–1247)

Tomoe Gozen was a fearless female samurai who is said to have lived in the 12th century and fought in the Genpei wars under the leadership of Minamoto no Yoshinaka. Although there is no actual proof of her existence and exploits, she first appeared in the 14th century war tale *Heike Monogatari (The Tale of the Heike*) and its variant, the *Genpei Jōsuiki*. She is said to have fought bravely at the Battle of Awazu in 1184, and took the head of Honda no Morishige of Musashi Province. However, Yoshinaka was defeated at Awazu by his cousin Minamoto no Noriyori. In the final moments of the Battle, Tomoe Gozen offered to stay by his side, but Yoshinaka ordered her to flee, saying that he would be ashamed to be killed beside a woman. History records that Yoshinaka was killed alongside his foster brother, Imai Kanehira. There is a grave stone that is marked as Tomoe's at Gichoji (alternate reading of Yoshinaka) Temple in Ōtsu city, Shiga prefecture.

國政画

Kitao Masayoshi (1764–1824), *Tomoe Gozen*, c. 1787–1790.

Utagawa Yoshifuji (1828–1887), *Tomoe Gozen*, c. 1842.

TACHI
太刀

MINAMOTO NO YOSHITSUNE
源 義経

SIGNED [...] **TADA**
OTHER NAME(S) **USUMIDORI, HIZAMARU**
CUTTING-EDGE LENGTH **87.6 CM (31½ IN)**
CURVATURE **3.7 CM (1 7/16 IN)**
MOTO-HABA **3.4 CM (1 5/16 IN)**
SAKI-HABA **2.0 CM (13/16 IN)**

PERIOD **KAMAKURA PERIOD, 13TH C.**
THE FORMER SAGA IMPERIAL PALACE,
DAIKAKUJI, KYŌTO
Important Cultural Property

Left
Anonymous, *Portrait of Minamoto no Yoshitsune*, from the collection of the Chūson-ji (Hiraizumi, Iwate prefecture), color on paper.

TACHI

This blade was a treasure of the Minamoto family. It was owned by Minamoto no Mitsunaka along with another *tachi* known as Higegiri (see pages 36–37). It is said to have been passed down to and worn by Yoshitsune. The blade is *shinogi-zukuri* with *iori-mune* and *ko-kissaki*, and has a well-forged *ko-itame-hada* with a pale prominent *utsuri* and a *suguha* based *ko-chōji* and *ko-gunome hamon* with *ko-ashi*. It had a two-character signature, but one of the characters was damaged by the old iron *habaki*. The maker is unclear, but the workmanship appears to be that of the Ko-Bizen school. Therefore, it has been theorized that it could be the work of Mitsutada's father, Chikatada. However, as there are no extant works of Chikatada, this cannot be confirmed.

MINAMOTO NO YOSHITSUNE (1159–1189)

Minamoto no Yoshitsune was the younger half-brother of Minamoto no Yoritomo. Yoshitsune was called Ushiwaka (Ushiwakamaru) in his younger days and is a huge hero in Japan. He is defined by his bravery, swordsmanship skills, and agility. There are many stories about Yoshitsune and his exploits, and his most loyal servant, the warrior monk, Benkei. He first met Benkei when he was on the Gojō bridge in Kyōto. Benkei challenged the young Ushiwaka, but was defeated by him. However, Benkei was so impressed that he implored Ushiwaka to let him become his servant.

Tales about Yoshitsune are many, but ultimately, they are tinged with sadness as in the wake of the Minamoto victory over the Taira clan. Yoritomo is said to have become suspicious of Yoshitsune's popularity. Eventually, Yoshitsune and Benkei were hunted down and killed. The Noh play *Ataka*, written in 1465 by Kanze Nobumitsu, tells the story of Yoshitsune fleeing from Yoritomo disguised as a monk. The party have to pass through a Minamoto check-point at Ataka in Kaga province (Ishikawa prefecture), but the guard recognized Yoshitsune. Benkei refutes the guard's accusation telling him that Yoshitsune is merely a servant. Benkei then chastises Yoshitsune in front of everyone for a fictitious reason, and in order to convince the guards, he beats Yoshitsune to within an inch of his life. The guards moved by Benkei's loyalty cry tears of admiration, and allow them to pass. This story was adapted into one of Japan's most popular Kabuki plays: *Kanjichō*. It was made into a movie just after the second world war called, *Those Who Tread on the Tiger's Tail (Tora no o wo fumu otokotachi)*, by the Japanese director, Akira Kurosawa. However, the themes of loyalty and duty were considered too powerful and moving by the allied occupational forces, so the movie was banned until the forces withdrew in 1952.

KATCHŪ
甲冑

MINAMOTO NO YOSHITSUNE
源 義経

Left
Ichiyōsai Nobuaki (?-?), hanging scroll, *Minamoto no Yoshitsune*, ink and color on paper, 19th c.

This armor was given as a votive offering to Kasuga Shrine by Minamoto no Yoshitsune. It is thought that it was made specifically as a votive offering. It has large sized shoulder guards (*ō-sode*) that are rather luxuriously decorated with tiger and bamboo themed gilt fittings, with further decorations of sparrows, wisteria, chrysanthemums and butterflies. The armor is laced together with red dyed cords that still retain a very vibrant color. The helmet has a large wide gilt *maedate* (helmet front decoration) in the shape of the mandibles of a stag beetle.

● RED LACED *ŌYOROI* TYPE ARMOR

PERIOD **KAMAKURA PERIOD 14TH C.**
KASUGA TAISHA TREASURE MUSEUM, NARA
National Treasure

Kuwagata Keisai (1764–1824), *Minamoto no Yoshitsune and His Retainer, the Monk Benkei, Putting to Flight the Ghost of Taira no Tomomori*, late 18th c.

Utagawa Kuniyoshi (1797–1861), In the *Mountains of Yoshino, Yoshitsune Shows His Valor and Attacks Kakuhan*, from the series *Mirror of the Life of Minamoto no Yoshitsune, the Wellspring of Romance*, 1853.

Next spread
Utagawa Yoshitsuya (1822–1866), triptych, *The White Dragon Ascends to Heaven at the Koromo River during the Battle of Takadachi in the Third Year of the Bunji Era (1187)*, 1857.

武藏坊辨慶
駿河次郎
龜井六郎
伊勢三郎

文治三年
奥州高舘
合戦
白衣川
白滝昇天
伊豫守源義經
常陸房海尊
片岡八郎
御厩喜三
江田源
一英齋芳艷画

TACHI

太刀

● SIGNED **TOMONARI SAKU**
CUTTING-EDGE LENGTH **96.3 CM (37 15/16 IN)**
CURVATURE **3.1 CM (3 7/32 IN)**

PERIOD **LATE HEIAN-EARLY KAMAKURA PERIOD, 12TH–13TH C.**
THE JAPANESE SWORD MUSEUM, TŌKYŌ
Important Art Object

平 教経

Right
Kanō Motonobu, attr. (1476–1559), hanging scroll, *Taira no Noritsune*, from the collection of Akama Shrine (Shimonoseki, Yamaguchi Prefecture), color on paper, 15th–16th c.

Opposite
Katsukawa Shuntei (1770–1820), *Samurai Ichijō Jirō Tadanori and Noritsune During a Fight*, c. 1818–1820.

TACHI

This *tachi* is said to have belonged to Taira no Noritsune. It is a *shinogi-zukuri* construction large-sized *tachi*, with *iori-mune*, a deep *koshi-zori* and a medium sized point section. It has a an *itame-hada* with some *mokume* that is covered in *ji-nie*, and fine *chikei*, with a prominent *ji-fu utsuri*. The *nioi* rich *hamon* is a rather narrow *suguha* (straight) base, with *ko-midare*, *ko-chōji*, and *ko-gunome*. It is also rich in activity with abundant *ashi*, *yo*, *kinsuji*, and *sunagashi*. The *hamon* in the point section (*bōshi*) is straight and narrow, and appears to have little to no turn-back (*yakizume*). The original *nakago* has *katte-sagari* filemarks, one peg hole, and ends in *kuri-jiri*.

TAIRA NO NORITSUNE (1160–1185)

Taira no Noritsune was the son of Taira no Norimori. Noritsune was a commander of the Taira clan, and fought in many battles of the Genpei wars. He was not just a great commander, he was also a great rival of Minamoto no Yoshitsune. In one of their clashes at the Battle of Yashima, Noritsune got close enough to fire off an arrow at Yoshitsune. However, one of Yoshitsune's faithful warriors, Satō Tsugunobu, sacrificed himself for his lord by riding between Yoshitsune and the arrow.

There also is the famous story of Yoshitsune at the Battle of Dan-no-Ura where he nimbly leapt across eight boats one at a time, while being pursued by Taira no Noritsune. It is said that, once realizing that all was lost at the Battle of Dan-no-ura, Noritsune took a Minamoto warrior under each arm before plunging into the sea, never to be seen again.

一條治郎忠頼
能登守教經

Toyohara (Yōshū) Chikanobu (1838–1912), triptych, *The Death of Satō Tsugunobu: Protecting his Master, Tsugunobu is Felled by Noritsune's Arrow. Taira no Noritsune Aiming his Bow at Minamoto no Yoshitsune, but Hitting Satō Tsugunobu, who Rode between to Protect Yoshitsune, while Noritsune's servant Kikuo is running forward to behead Tsugunobu*, 1898.

TACHI
太刀

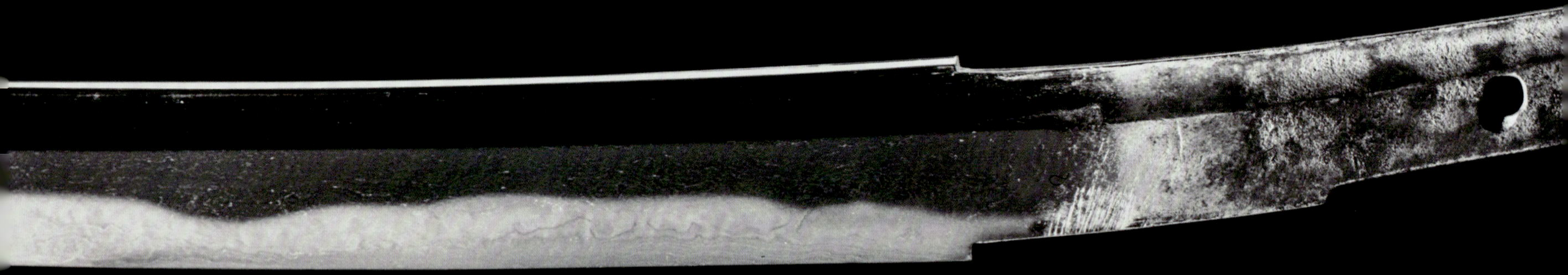

● UNSIGNED **ATTRIBUTED TO THE ICHIMONJI SCHOOL**
OTHER NAME(S) **HŌJŌ TACHI**
CUTTING-EDGE LENGTH **77.3 CM (30 7/16 IN)**
LENGTH **104.1 CM (41 IN)**
CURVATURE **3.0 CM (1 3/16 IN)**

PERIOD **KAMAKURA PERIOD, 13TH C.**
TOKYO NATIONAL MUSEUM
Important Cultural Property

HYŌGO-GUSARI TACHI KOSHIRAE
WITH HŌJŌ MITSU-URUKO CREST
TOKYO NATIONAL MUSEUM
Important Cultural Property

Opposite
Utagawa Kuniyoshi (1797–1861), right-hand part of a triptych, *Asahina Saburō Yoshihide Takes down the Great Gate during the Wada Revolt against the Hōjō in 1213*, 1852 (detail depicting Hōjō Yasutoki).

北条泰時

TACHI and **KOSHIRAE**

This is a rare *hyōgo-gusari tachi koshirae* with the original blade. *Hyōgo-gusari tachi koshirae* have belt hangers (*ashi*) that are made of chain. They were commonly used in the late Heian and early Kamakura periods (12th–13th c.). The scabbard is covered in metal plates that is secured with decorative metal bands (*sekigane*), belt hanger fittings, and a chape (*ishit-suke*). This *tachi* was originally devoted by the Hōjō clan to Mishimata Shrine in Izu province (Shizuoka pref.). It was later given to Emperor Meiji.

The blade is unsigned, but has been attributed to the Ichimonji school of Bizen province. It has a graceful *koshi-zori* shape, and is *shinogi-zukuri* in construction, with a *maru-mune* and a slightly extended medium sized *kissaki* that has a rather shallow *fukura* that almost appears to be *kamasu* shaped. It has a *bō-hi* on both sides that end in the *nakago* in *kaki-nagashi*. It has a wide, flamboyant *chōji-midare hamon*, with abundant *ashi* and *yo*. The *hada* pattern is a well-forged *itame* with a prominent *midare-utsuri*. The unsigned *nakago* is *kijimomo* shaped.

HŌJŌ YASUTOKI (1183–1242)

Hōjō Yasutoki was the eldest son of Yoshitoki. Yasutoki led one of the forces that ousted Emperor Gotoba from Kyōto in the Jōkyū Rebellion of 1221. After Emperor Gotoba's exile to the Oki Islands, Yasutoki remained in Kyōto and set up the Rokuhara Tandai which acted as a negotiating body with the court while also maintaining security in western Japan. In 1224, after the death of his father, he was appointed as the third regent of the Hōjō clan. His policies and diplomacy helped to solidify the Hōjō Shogunate right through until their demise at the end of the Kamakura period.

ト山口

TACHI

● INSCRIBED **HAIRLINE ENGRAVING OF A CHRYSANTHEMUM**
OTHER NAME(S) **KIKU-GO-SAKU, GOSHO-YAKI**
CUTTING EDGE LENGTH **78.1 CM (30¾ IN)**
CURVATURE **2.2 CM (⅞ IN)**

PERIOD **EARLY KAMAKURA PERIOD, 13TH C.**
KYOTO NATIONAL MUSEUM, KYŌTO
Important Cultural Object

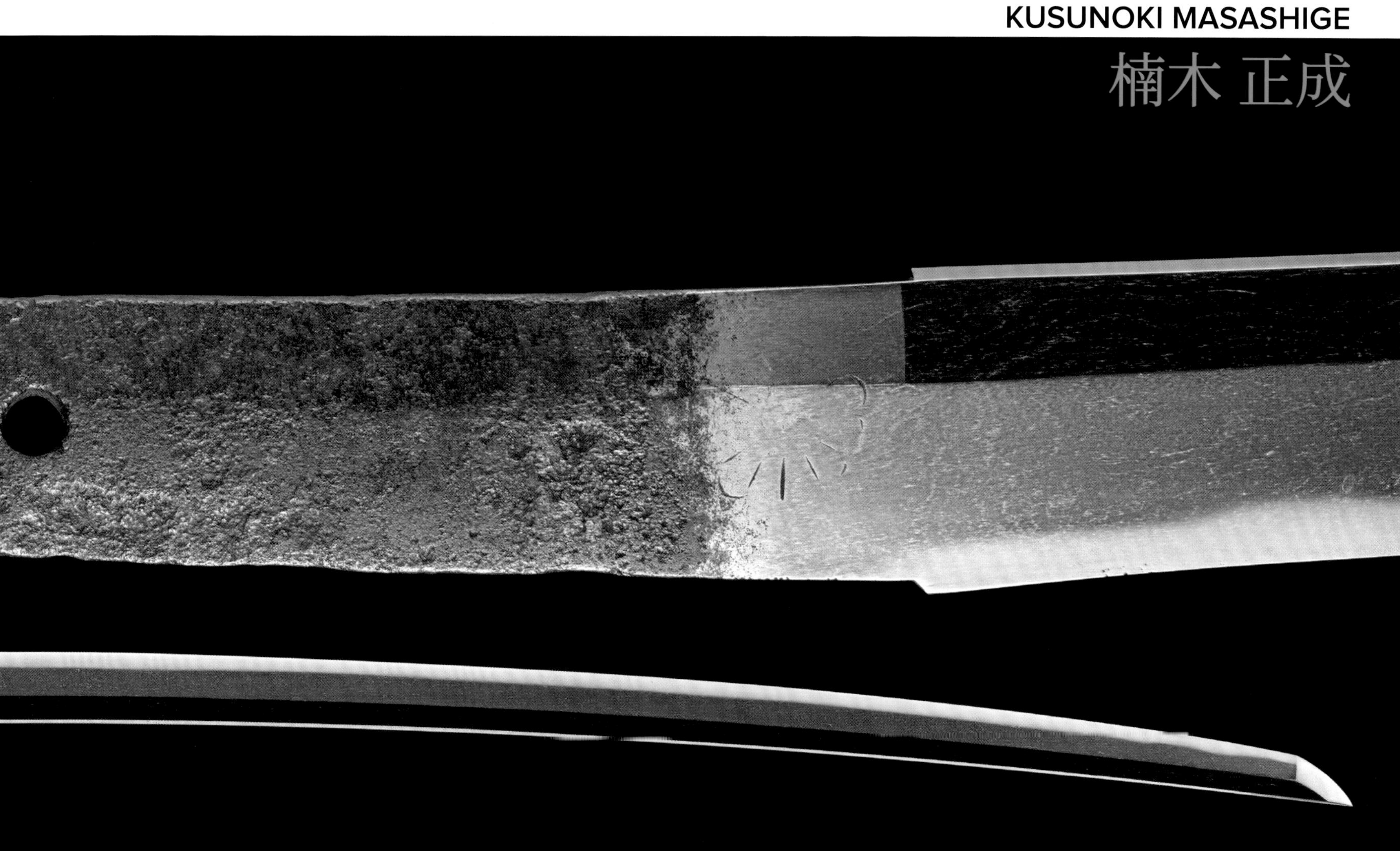
楠木 正成

Right
Kanō Sanraku (1559–1635), hanging scroll, *Kusunoki Masashige*, ink on paper, 16th–17th c.

Opposite
Hishikawa Morofusa (att. c. 1685–1703), hanging scroll, *Kusunoki Masashige Taking Leave of His Son at Sakurai*, ink and color on silk, c. 1688–1704 (detail).

楠木正成

TACHI

This *tachi* is *shinogi-zukuri* in construction with a very deep *koshi-zori* in the base of the blade. The upper part of the blade is straight and slender, ending with a *ko-kissaki*. This blade is considered to have characteristics of the Yamashiro tradition (Kyōto). Therefore, it is considered to have been made in collaboration with one of the Kyōto smiths. Hideyoshi, Tokugawa Ieyasu, Tokugawa Hidetada, (Echigo) Matsudaira Tadanao, until it was finally passed to the Matsudaira line of the Tsuyama domain.

KUSUNOKI MASASHIGE (1294–1336)

Kusunoki Masashige is regarded in Japan as the epitome of samurai loyalty. A loyalist to the Emperor Godaigo, he gained fame in the Kenmu restoration of 1333. Kusunoki was a brilliant tactician. However, in 1336, the Emperor ignored Kusunoki's advice and ordered him to attack Ashikaga Takauji in Settsu (Ōsaka). Despite Kusunoki knowing that the operation would end in certain defeat, he carried out the task with unwavering loyalty to the Emperor. They were surrounded by the Ashikaga at the Battle of Minatogawa and annihilated.

He is associated with the phrase, *Shichishō Hōkoku* (allegedly said by his brother, Masasue, in the final moments of the Battle of Minatogawa). The phrase means, *If I had seven lives, I would give them all for my country*. The phrase became popular again during the Second World War, and can be seen inscribed on sword tangs and other wartime paraphernalia. Masashige is also popularly known in Japan by the name, Dai Nanko, and his spirit is enshrined in Minatogawa Shrine, Kōbe City.

The night before the Battle of Minatogawa, Masashige met with his son, Masayuki, at Sakurai and passed him some of his personal belongings. According to one version of the *Taiheiki*, one of these items was a *Kiku-Go-Saku tachi*, said to have been made by Emperor Gotoba: "As Masashige wiped his tears, he handed his son the sword that had been made by the Emperor Gotoba, and bestowed upon him by the Emperor Godaigo. They then parted in opposite directions. All of the warriors that had witnessed the exchange were moved to tears."

There are approximately fifteen *Kiku-Go-Saku* blades in existence today, one of which is housed in the National Museum in Kyōto. It is unknown if one of those was owned by Masashige. There is an armor at Kasuga Shrine, Nara, that is said to have been a votive offering of Masashige.

菱川師房圖

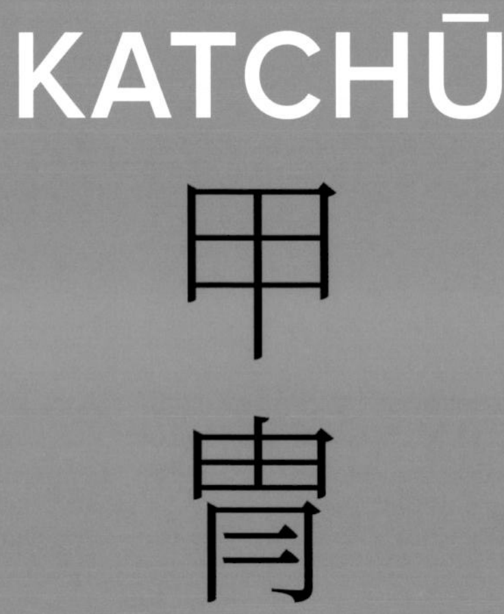

According to shrine records, this armor is said to have been a votive offering of Kusunoki Masashige. It is of the *dō-maru* type with large shoulder guards (*ō-sode*). The small fork type platelets (*iyozane*) of the cuirass are laced using dark indigo dyed deer skin and black tanned leather. The *suji-kabuto* type helmet bowl is made of 32 plates. The entire armor has matching chrysanthemum design fittings.

DŌ-MARU ARMOR
BLACK LACQUERED WITH DARK INDIGO LACING

PERIOD **NANBOKUCHŌ PERIOD, 14TH C.**
KASUGA TAISHA TREASURE MUSEUM, NARA
National Treasure

TACHI

太刀

● SIGNED [... ...] **KUNI NORIMUNE**
OTHER NAME(S) **SASA-MARU**
CUTTING-EDGE LENGTH **80.1 CM (31½ IN)**
CURVATURE **2.7 CM (1 IN)**
PERIOD **KAMAKURA PERIOD, 13TH C.**

(Enlargement on pages 187–188–189–190)

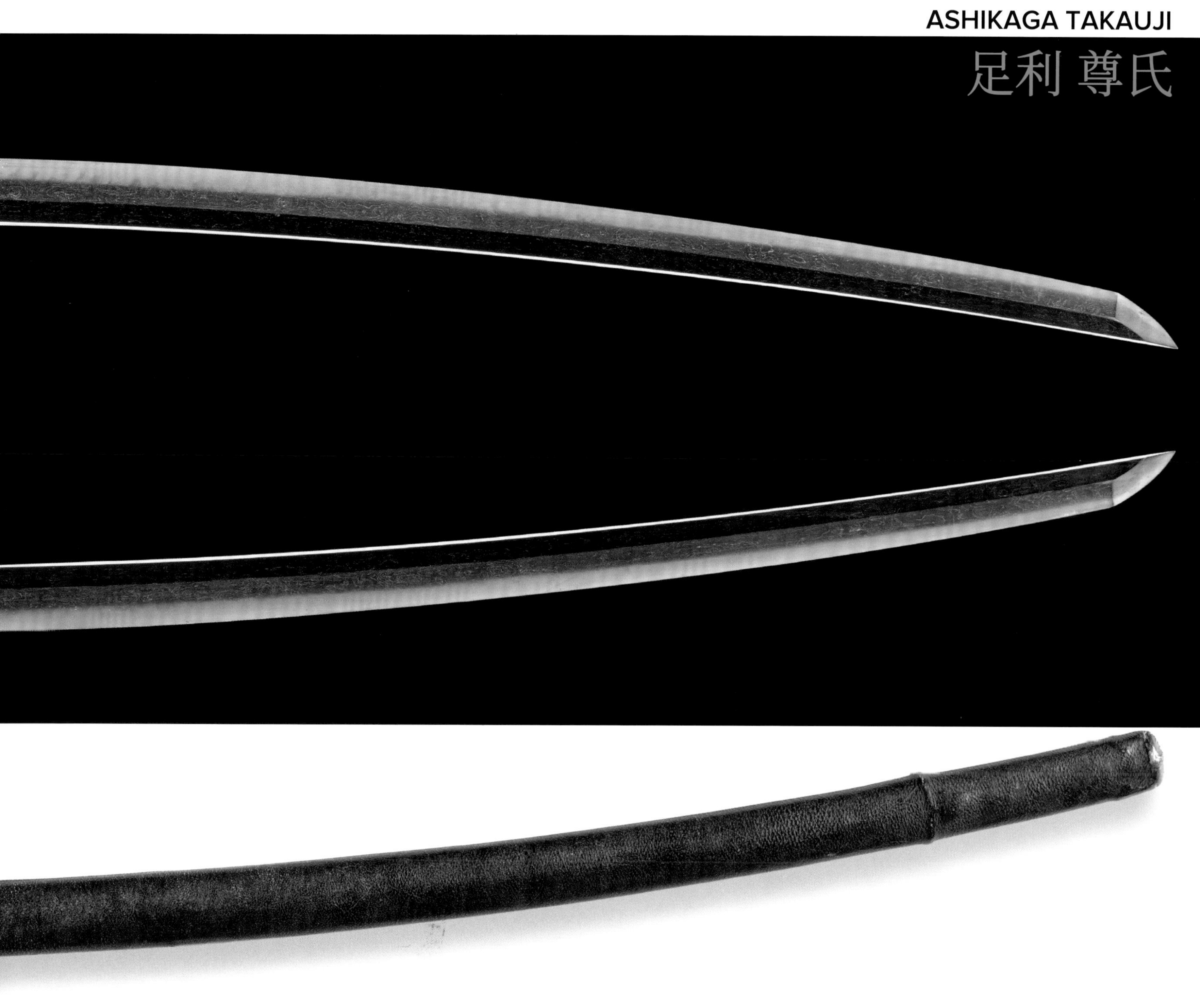

● **TACHI KOSHIRAE**
PERIOD **NANBOKUCHŌ PERIOD, 14TH C.**
ATAGO SHRINE, KYŌTO
Important Cultural Property

Right
Anonymous, hanging scroll, portrait of seated samurai (probably Ashikaga Takauji), color on silk, from the collection of Jōdo Temple (Onomichi, Hiroshima Prefecture), 14th–15th c.

Opposite
Anonymous (Ukiyoe school), *The* shōgun *Ashikaga Takauji in Armor,* ink and color on paper, 17th–19th c.

TACHI AND **KOSHIRAE**

This blade is made by Ichimonji Norimune and belonged to Ashikaga Takauji. It was passed down within the family for 15 generations until Ashikaga Yoshiaki gave it to Toyotomi Hideyoshi, who dedicated it to Atago Shrine in Kyōto. It is recorded in the Meibutsu-chō as Futatsu-mei Norimune (Two Inscriptions Norimune). As the top two characters of the inscription have been somewhat erased, and the bottom half of the character for (Bi)zen resembles the character for Nori, it is theorized that someone mistakenly assumed it was of joint manufacture by Norikuni and Norimune. However, it most likely originally inscribed Bizen (no) Kuni Norimune.

This *tachi* is *shinogi-zukuri* in construction, with *iori-mune*, and a deep curvature centered in the base of the blade that tapers towards the small point section. The *hada* is a flowing large *itame-hada* missed with *masame-hada*. The complex *hamon* begins as *ko-midare* in the base of the blade, becoming *chōji-midare* around the center and a wide *suguha* in the upper part of the blade, gently undulating in the *bōshi* before turning back at the tip. The *ubu-nakago* has a five-character signature of Norimune just above the rather worn single *mekugi-ana*. The filemarks are *katte-sagari*, and the *nakago* ends in *kuri-jiri*. The sturdy and practical leather wrapped *tachi-koshirae* acquired the name *Sasa-maru* as it has hairline engravings of bamboo in the fittings.

ASHIKAGA TAKAUJI (1305–1358)

Ashikaga Takauji was the first *shōgun* of the Ashikaga line. He had sided with Emperor Godaigo in the Kenmu Restoration and helped to overthrow the Kamakura Shogunate. However, it appears that Emperor Godaigo was an increasingly difficult man to please and due to his policies after restoration, he became increasingly unpopular. This led to Takauji eventually being ostracized by Godaigo. After several battles, Takauji finally emerged victorious against Nitta Yoshisada and Kusunoki Masashige at the Battle at Minatogawa. Takauji installed the Emperor Kōmyō as the sovereign of the Northern court ushering in the Nanbokuchō Period. However, the situation had left the Ashikaga Shogunate in a weak position. Various clans began fighting among themselves to claim lands and enhance their chances of claiming power. This was the seeds of destruction that eventually led to the Ōnin War and the start of the Warring States era.

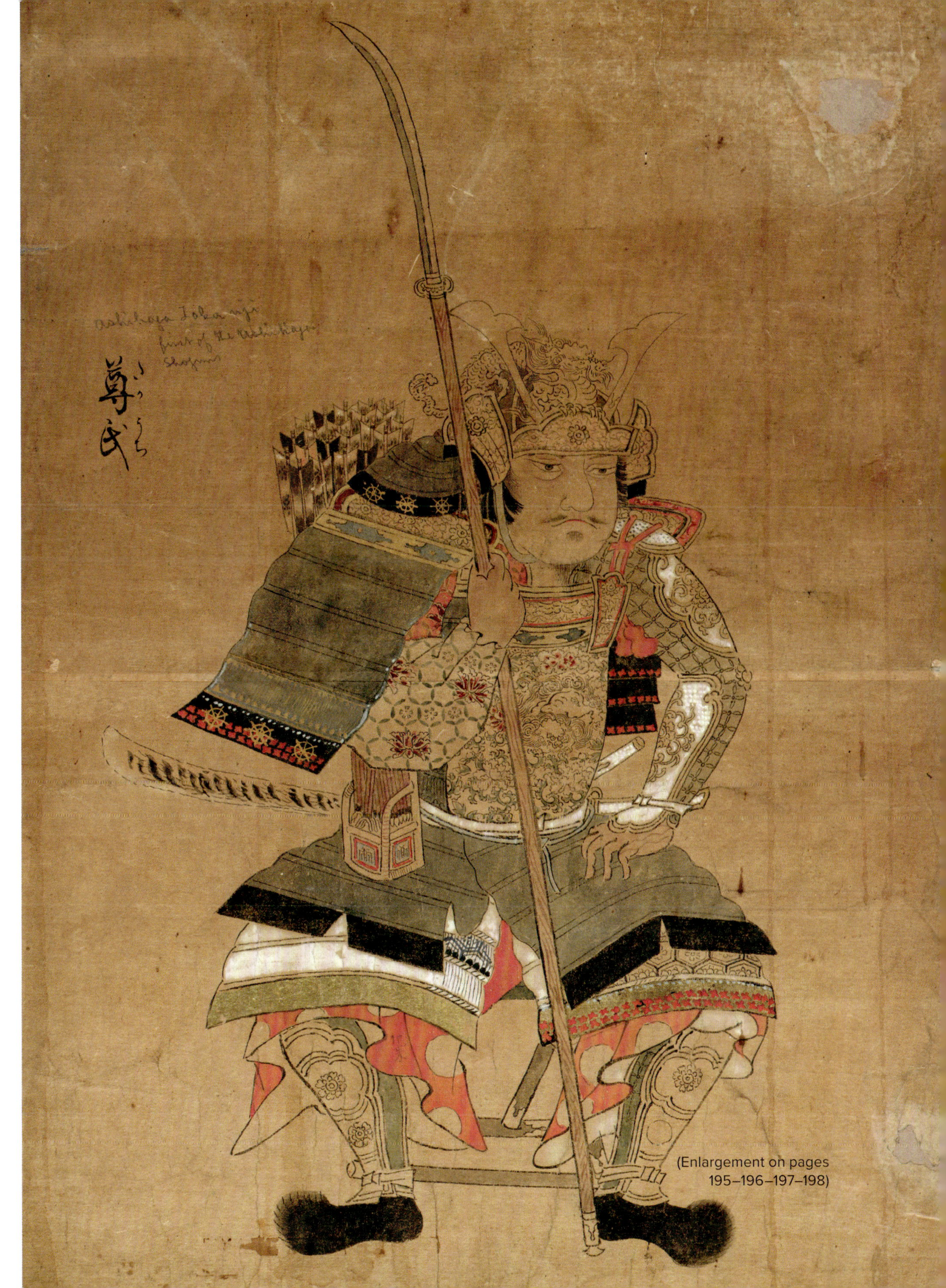

(Enlargement on pages
195–196–197–198)

KATCHŪ

This *ō-yoroi* type armor is said to have been given as a votive gift to Shinomura Hachimangū Shrine (Kyōto) by Ashikaga Takauji. The front of the cuirass is covered in a leather panel that is decorated with an image of the deity, Fudō Myō-ō, the immovable. The helmet has large *fukigaeshi* (turn-backs), and the *shikoro* (neck-guard) is rather wide and shallow. These attributes are indicative of this kind of armor that was used by samurai of the 10th to 14th centuries.

LEATHER ARMOR OF THE Ō-YOROI TYPE

PERIOD
KAMAKURA-NANBOKUCHŌ PERIOD, EARLY TO MID 14TH C.
METROPOLITAN MUSEUM OF ART, NEW YORK

KABUTO
兜

Left
On the leather panel covering the front of the breastplate of this armor is depicted Fudō Myo-o, a powerful Buddhist deity whose fierce attitude was appreciated by the samurai, yet accompanied by calmness and inner strength.

Above
The helmet, long associated with this rare specimen of medieval armor, dates to the mid-14th century and features large *fukigaeshi* (protective face flaps).

TACHI
太刀

● SIGNED **RAI KUNINAGA**
CUTTING-EDGE LENGTH **79.3 CM (31 7/32 IN)**
CURVATURE **2.5 CM (1 IN)**

PERIOD
KAMAKURA-NANBOKUCHŌ PERIODS, 14TH C

ITO-MAKI TACHI-KOSHIRAE
PERIOD **16TH C.**
LORD SHINGEN TREASURE HOUSE, KŌSHŪ, YAMANASHI PREFECTURE
Important Cultural Property

Opposite
Utagawa Kuniyoshi (1797–1861), *Shingen of Kai*, from the series *A Suikoden of Japanese Heroes*, c. 1843.

TACHI and **KOSHIRAE**

Rai Kuninaga was a smith of the Rai School of smiths from Kyōto, and was active between the Kamakura and Nanbokuchō periods. He was a student of Rai Kunitoshi. As he moved to Nakajima in Settsu Province (Ōsaka), he is also known as Nakajima Rai. This blade is *shinogi-zukuri* in construction, with *mitsu-mune*, and a slightly extended point section. It has been slightly shortened (*suriage*), but retains some of its *koshi-zori*. It has a well-forged *itame-hada* with *ji-nie*. The *hamon* is *suguha* (straight) but widens in the *monouchi* and *kissaki* before turning back. The *nakago* has three *mekugi-ana*, and it is signed with a three-character signature of Rai Kuninaga between the second and third holes. The *nakago-jiri* is *kiri*.

The *tachi* was devoted to the Erinji Temple in 1705 by the Lord of Kofu Castle, Yanagisawa Yoshiyasu. The gold *nashi-ji*-ground lacquer *koshirae* is decorated with the crest of the Yanagisawa clan. It is thought that it was repaired before being given as a votive offering to the temple.

TAKEDA SHINGEN (1521–1573)

Takeda Shingen is one of Japan's most acclaimed warlords of the Sengoku Period. He fought in many battles, but is most notably remembered for his several encounters at Kawanakajima with neighboring warlord, Uesugi Kenshin. During one encounter it is said that Uesugi Kenshin rode through the battle lines right up to Shingen and slashed at him with his sword from atop of his horse. However, Shingen just parried it away with his war fan. It is thought that despite their commitment to battle each other several times, that they actually had great mutual respect for one another. When Shingen died in 1573 aged 51, it is said that Uesugi Kenshin wept on hearing the news. His death is something of a mystery as he died while encamped outside Noda Castle. One theory is that he was killed by a sniper. This theory formed the basis of the Akira Kurosawa fictional movie, *Kagemusha* (Shadow Warrior).

He is also famous for his samurai banner that had the words *Furin-kazan*—"wind, forest, fire, mountain"—emblazoned upon it. They were taken from the Chinese classic on strategy, *The Art of War* by Sun Tzu. It means, *Be swift like the wind, gentle like a forest, fierce like fire, and unmovable like a mountain.*

水滸傳
裴信玄
一勇斎國芳画

Utagawa Kuniyoshi (1791–1861), left and middle parts of a triptych, *Takeda and Uesugi at the Battle of Kawanakajima*, c. 1845.

今井伊勢守
左馬助信繁
武田晴信入道信玄
一勇齋國芳画

TACHI

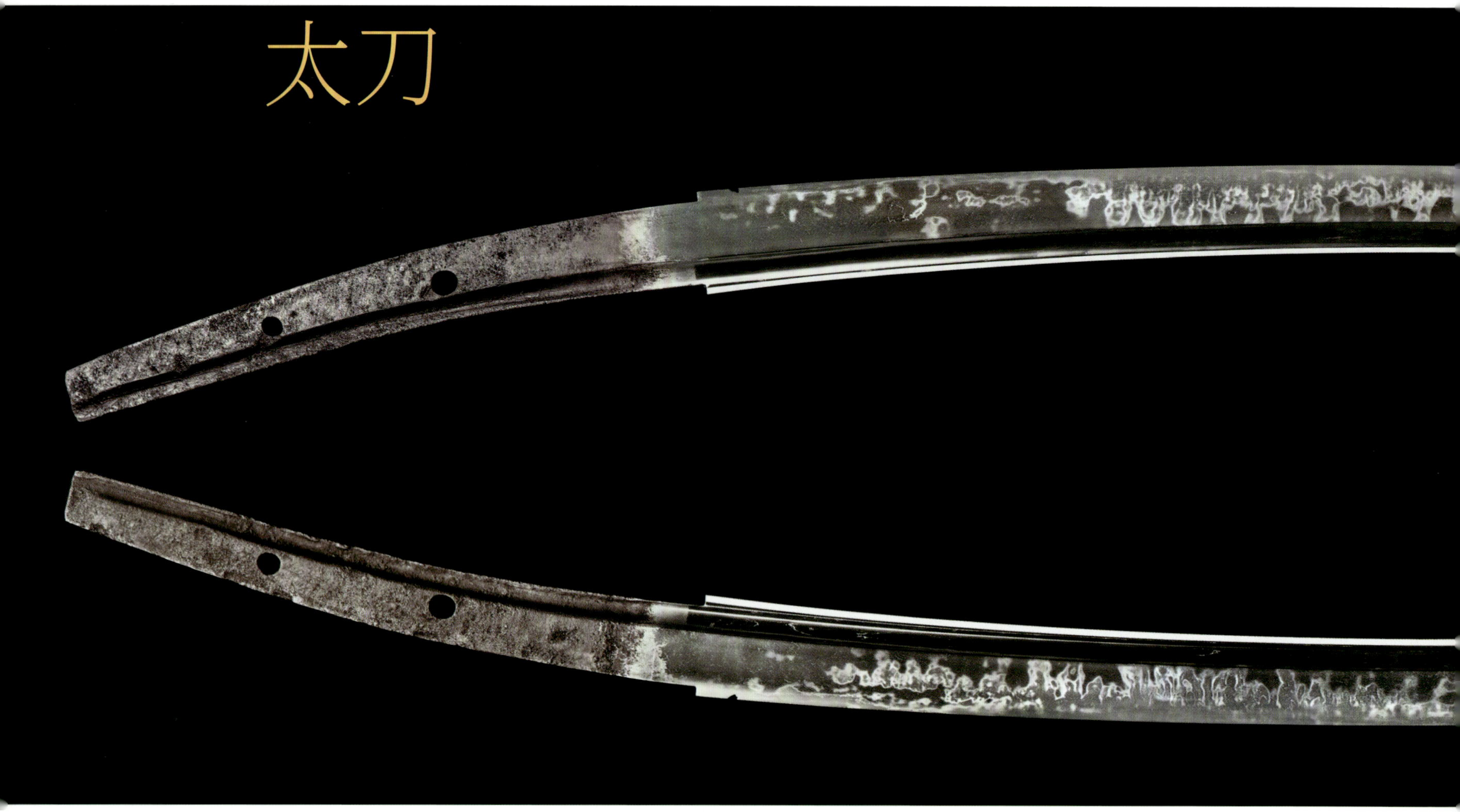

● UNSIGNED
ATTRIBUTED TO THE ICHIMONJI SCHOOL
OTHER NAME(S) **YAMATORIGE, SANCHŌMŌ**

CUTTING-EDGE LENGTH **79.5 CM ($31\frac{7}{32}$ IN)**
CURVATURE **3.4 CM ($1\frac{5}{16}$ IN)**
PERIOD **KAMAKURA PERIOD, 13TH C.**

● **UCHI-GATANA KOSHIRAE**
PERIOD **MOMOYAMA PERIOD, 16TH C.**

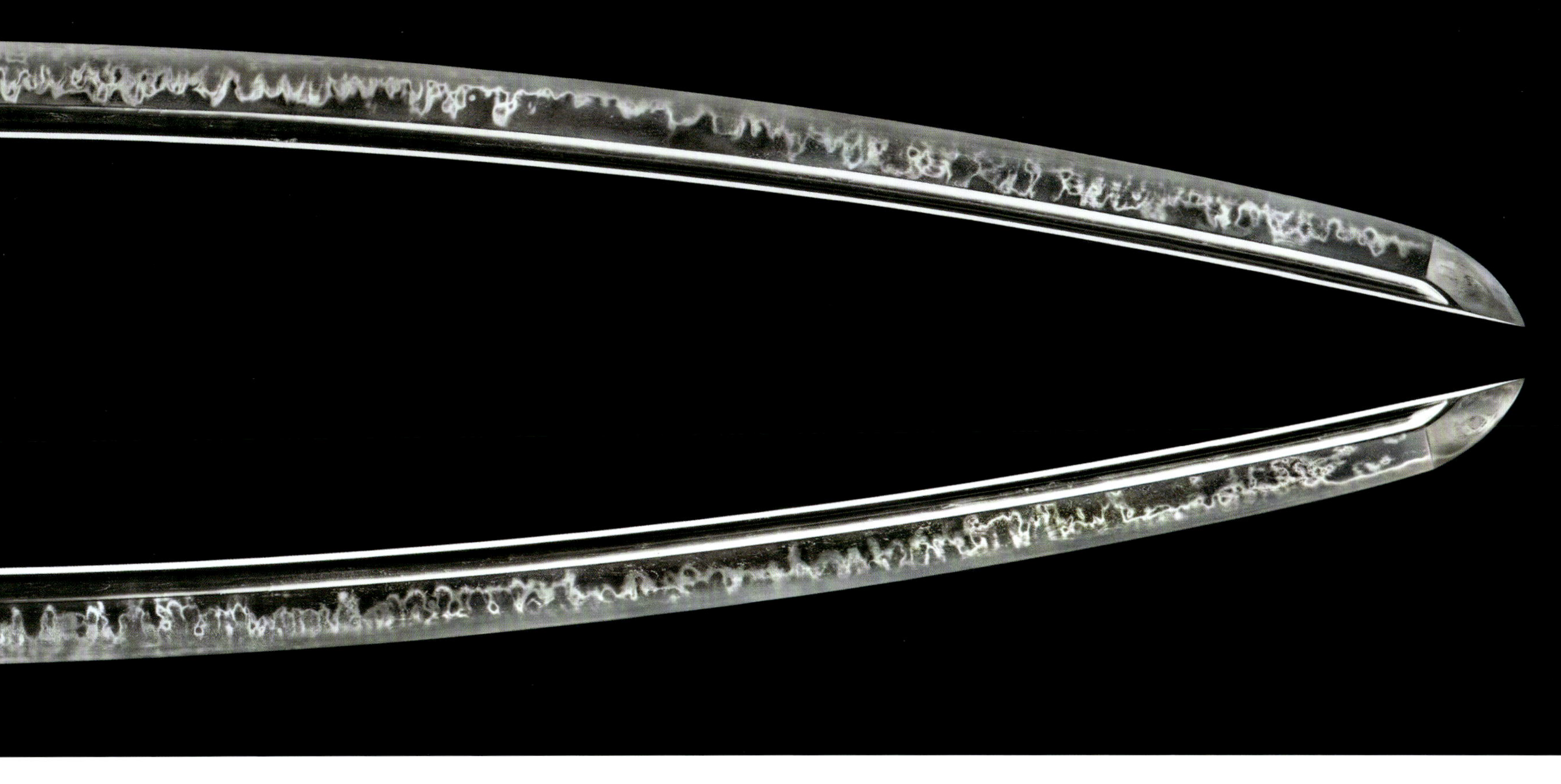

(Enlargement on pages 23–24–25–26)

BIZEN OSAFUNE SWORD MUSEUM,
OKAYAMA PREFECTURE
National Treasure

Right
Anonymous, hanging scroll, *Portrait of Uesugi Kenshin*, from the collection of the Taigan Historical Museum (Tōkyō), originally in Rinsen Temple (Nakamonzen, Jōetsu, Niigata Prefecture), ink and color on paper, c. 1570.

Opposite
Tsukioka Yoshitoshi (1839–1892), *Uesugi Kenshin*, from the series *Selection of One Hundred Warriors*, 1868.

TACHI and KOSHIRAE

This *tachi* is *shinogi-zukuri* in construction with *iori-mune*, a deep *koshi-zori*, *funbari*, and a *chu-kissaki*. The *hada* is a rather prominent *itame*, with *ji-nie* and a prominent *midare-utsuri*. The *hamon* is a complex mix of *juka-chōji* and *ō-chōji midare* that rise up towards the *shinogi*. There are abundant *ashi* and *yo*, with *kinsuji*. The *bōshi* is *notare-komi* on the *omote* with *hakikake*, and *notare-komi*, *ko-maru* with a turnback on the *ura*. There is a *bō-hi* on both sides of the blade that ends in *kaki-toshi*. The unsigned *nakago* has *katte-sagari* filemarks, two *mekugi-ana*, and ends with *kiri-jiri*. The *nakago* retains some curvature, but has been adjusted at some time to repurpose as a *katana*.

The blade is accompanied by an a*ikuchi uchi-gatana koshirae* (*katana koshirae* without a *tsuba*). The *tsuka* has a large horn *kashira*, with *shakudō* ground tiger *menuki*, and is wrapped in indigo leather. The *saya* is plain black lacquer. The *kozuka* and *kōgai* are *shakudō-nanako* ground with matching tigers carved in high relief with gold inlay.

UESUGI KENSHIN (1530–1578)

Uesugi Kenshin is one of the more internationally famous Sengoku period warriors. He is well known for his rivalry and admiration of Takeda Shingen. They fought many times at Kawanakajima. During the time Takeda was fighting with the Mōri clan, they blocked shipments of salt to his domain. On hearing this, Kenshin sent salt to Shingen along with a note saying, "Warriors fight with swords, not salt."

Kenshin and his son Kagekatsu had a famous collection of 35 masterpiece swords. The crowning blade of the collection was the current National Treasure sword, Yamatorige (also known as Sanchōmō). Even today, it is called a National Treasure among National Treasures. It is believed that Kenshin inherited it when he changed his name from Nagao Kagetora upon his adoption by the Kantō Kanrei. The name originates from its recording in Kagekatsu's list of thirty-five great swords. The names are interpreted in two ways. Yamatorige as the feathers of mountain pheasant, and Sanchōmō as a burning mountain. There is a large chip missing near the base from its actual use in battle. Many modern smiths aspire to recreate this kind of *tachi*.

題百撰相
一魁斎芳年筆
上杉輝虎入道謙信

Utagawa Kuniyoshi (1791–1861), left and middle parts of a triptych, *The Battle of Kawanakajima, Showing the Fight between Uesugi Kenshin (left) and Takeda Shingen (right)*, 1855.

一勇齋
國芳画
武田大膳太夫晴信入道信玄

KATANA
刀

● **CONVERTED TACHI** GOLD INLAID INSCRIPTION
EIROKU SANNEN GO-GATSU JŪ-KU NICHI *(the 19th day in the fifth month in the 3rd year of the Eiroku era, 1560)*
YOSHIMOTO UCHITORAERU TOKIHI NO SHŌJI NO KATANA *(Sword taken from Yoshimoto upon capture)*
ODA OWARI NO KAMI NOBUNAGA (ODA NOBUNAGA LORD OF OWARI PROVINCE)
NAME (MEIBUTSU) **SOZA SAMONJI** - OTHER NAME **YOSHIMOTO SAMONJI**

ODA NOBUNAGA
織田 信長

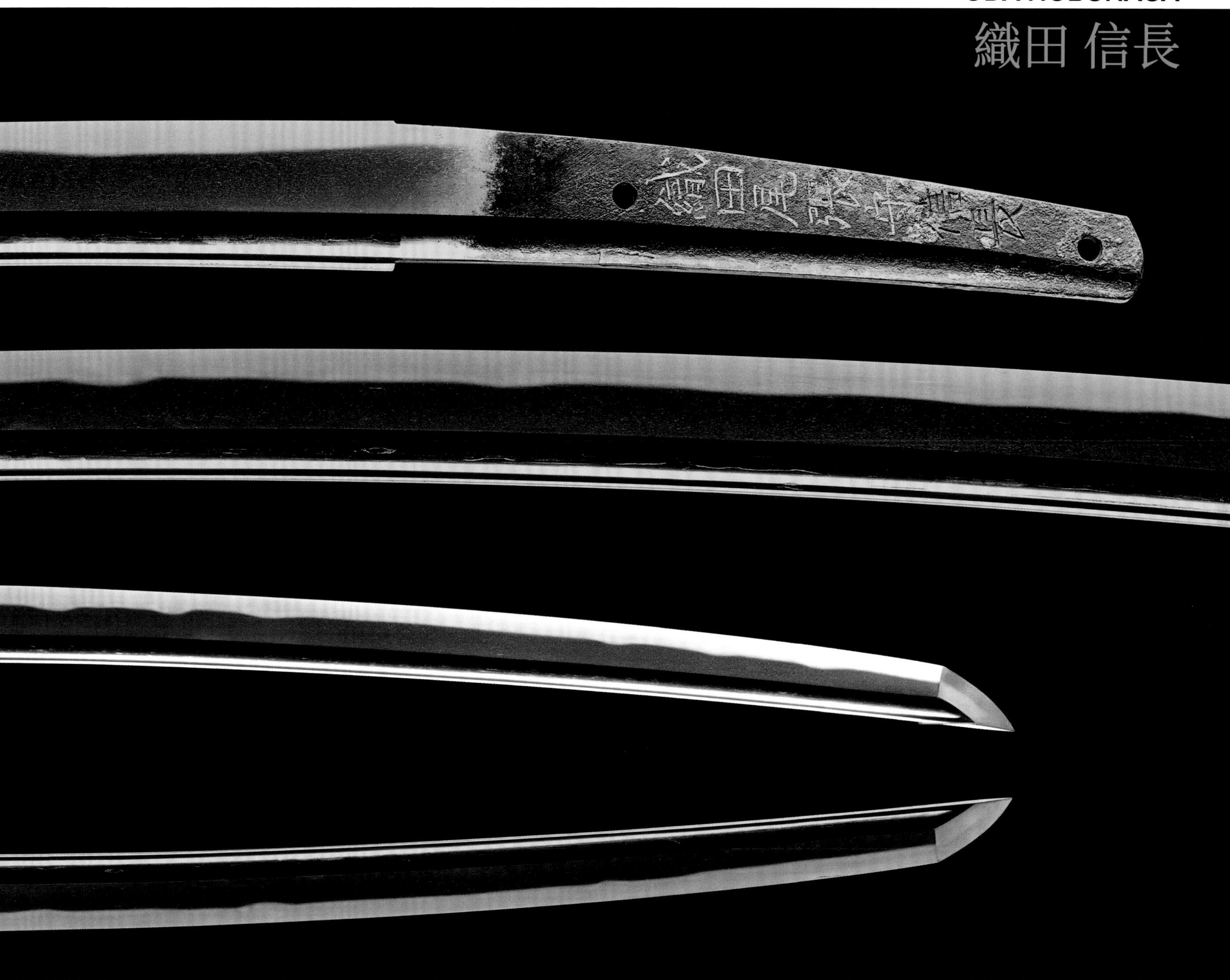

CUTTING-EDGE LENGTH **67 CM (26⅜ IN)**
CURVATURE **1.6 CM (⅝ IN)**
PERIOD **NANBOKUCHŌ PERIOD, 14TH C.**
KENKUN (OR TAKEISAO) SHRINE, KYŌTO
Important Cultural Property

(Enlargement on pages 191–192–193–194)

Right
Kanō Sōshū (1551–1601), hanging scroll, *Portrait of Oda Nobunaga*, from the collection of Chōkō Temple (Toyota, Aichi Prefecture), color on paper, 1583, Important Cultural Property (detail).

Opposite
Tsukioka Yoshitoshi (1839–1892), *Oda Udaijin Taira no Nobunaga Fights in the Burning Honnō-ji*, from the series *Mirror of Famous Generals of Japan*, c. 1878-1879.

Next spread
Kiyū Kaedegawa (?-?), triptych, *Night Attack at Honnō-ji: on the right, Mori Ranmaru Holds at Bay Yasuda Sakubei, an Akechi Mitsuhide warrior, while Oda Nobunaga Escapes Jumping into the Flames*, 19th c.

KATANA (Converted Tachi)

This *katana* is inscribed with the statement that it was taken from Imagawa Yoshimoto by Nobunaga (at the battle of Okehazama). The blade was previously owned by Miyoshi Masanaga, who was also known as Soza, so it was called Soza Samonji. It is recorded as originally being a signed work by Samonji with a cutting edge length of 78.7 cm (31 in). It is said that after obtaining the sword, Nobunaga had it shortened to the current length, and the gold inlaid inscription added. The sword was later passed to Toyotomi Hideyoshi, and then Tokugawa Ieyasu.

ODA NOBUNAGA (1534–1582)

The three *daimyō* who are considered the three unifiers of Japan are Oda Nobunaga, Toyotomi Hideyoshi and Tokugawa Ieyasu. The first of the three unifiers, Nobunaga was a complex character with many stories of both his fairness, and his ruthlessness that included attacking rude servants to killing the whole population of Eiraku-ji temple on Mt. Hiei in his quest to unify Japan under his sole control.

He is also known for his use of guns, which had only been introduced to Japan in 1543. He won the decisive battle of Nagashino with his masterly use of his troops trained in their use.

Nobunaga died, or was killed, at Honnō-ji Temple in Kyōto, 1582. He was betrayed and attacked by his vassal, Akechi Mitsuhide, who sieged and burnt down the temple. It is said that Nobunaga committed *seppuku* (ritual suicide) in the flames of the burning temple. Akechi's troops then trapped Nobunaga's son, Nobutada, who committed *seppuku* to avoid capture. Nobunaga's death was avenged within two weeks by his retainer, Toyotomi Hideyoshi, who became the second of the three unifiers.

将鑑
長

織田信長
楓川亀遊画
楓川亀遊画

本能寺夜軍
森蘭丸
安田作兵衛

KATANA

刀

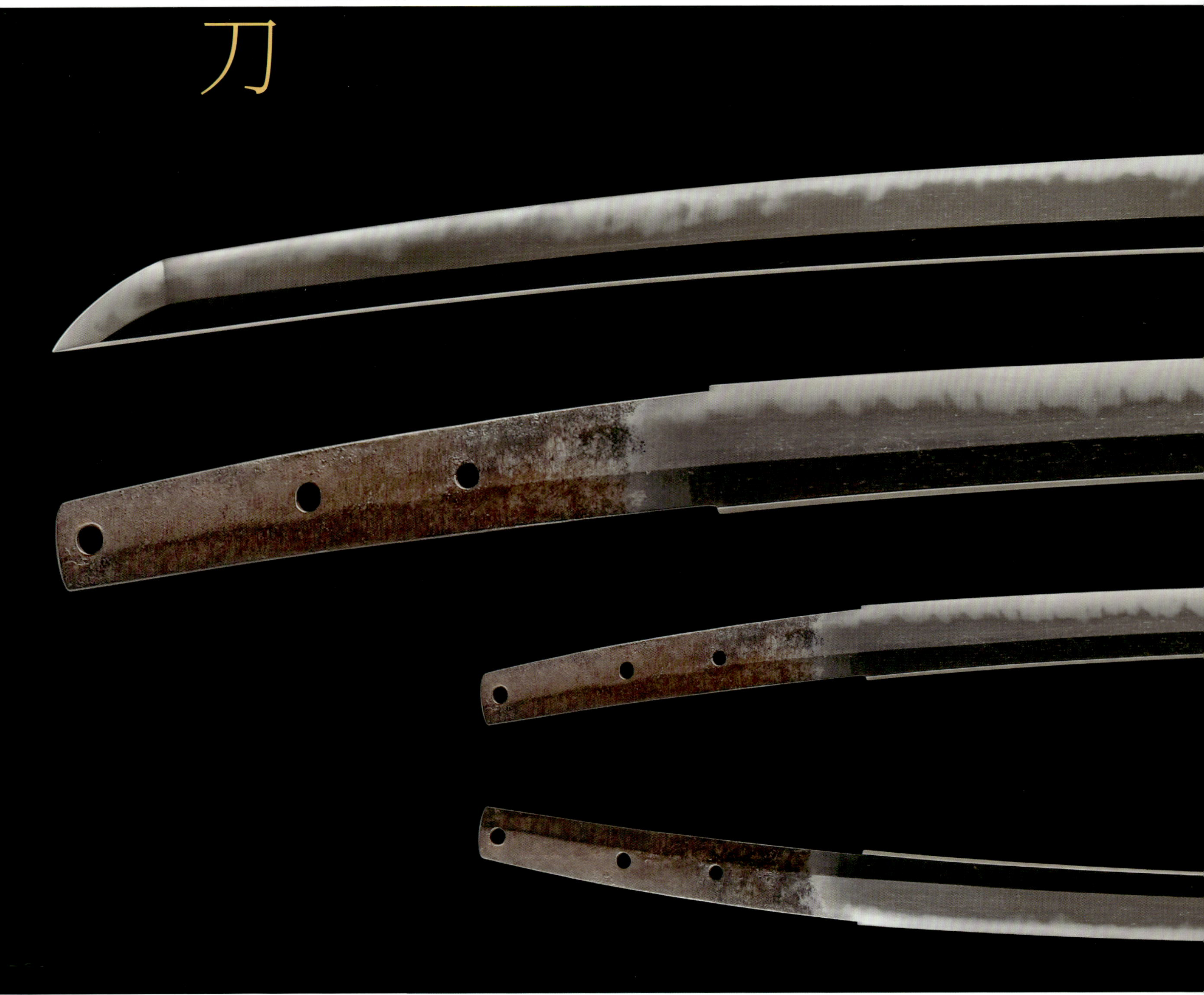

CONVERTED TACHI
UNSIGNED
OTHER NAME(S) (MEIBUTSU) **NANSEN ICHIMONJI**
CUTTING-EDGE LENGTH **61.6 CM (24¼ IN)** - CURVATURE **1.8 CM (23/32 IN)**

PERIOD **KAMAKURA PERIOD, 13TH C.**
TOKUGAWA ART MUSEUM,
AICHI PREFECTURE
Important Cultural Property

TOYOTOMI HIDEYOSHI
豊臣 秀吉

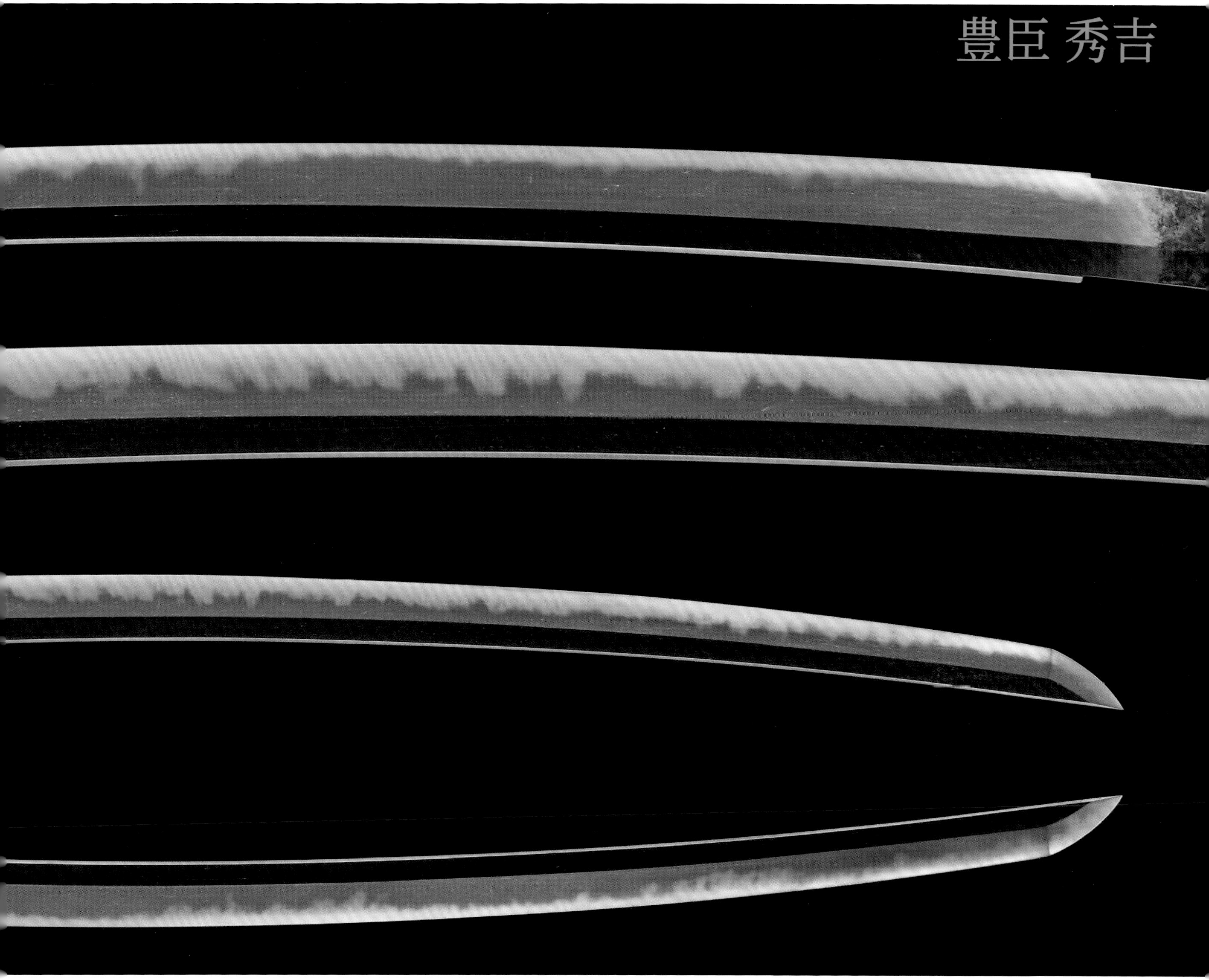

Opposite
Matsudaira Sadanobu (1759–1829), handscroll, *Portrait of Toyotomi Hideyoshi*, color on paper, 1795.

KATANA (Converted Tachi)

This magnificent flamboyant work of the Kamakura period Fukuoka Ichimonji school is one of the 31 masterpiece swords of the Toyotomi family. Its name comes from the combination of two stories. The first is that while it was in the possession of a Muromachi period shogunal family, a cat that came into contact with the blade was instantly cut in two. The other story is that a Chinese priest called, Nansen, enlightened all his students when he cut a cat in two.

The blade is *shinogi-zukuri*, *iori-mune*, with an *ikubi* style *ko-kissaki*. It has been greatly shortened (*ō-suriage*) probably significantly reducing the original curvature. It has a *ko-itame-hada* with a prominent *midare-utsuri*. The *hamon* is a very active *juka-chōji*, with abundant *ashi*. The *bōshi* is *midare-komi* with a small turnback (*kaeri*).

The sword is said to have previously been owned by the Ashikaga family. Hideyoshi's son, Hideyori, gave the sword to Tokugawa Ieyasu in 1611. It was later given to Ieyasu's ninth son, the first lord of the Tokugawa Owari domain, Yoshinao.

TOYOTOMI HIDEYOSHI (1536–1598)

Toyotomi Hideyoshi is the second of the three great unifiers of Japan. Little is known about Hideyoshi's early life. There are many stories about how Hideyoshi and Nobunaga's relationship developed, but it is thought that Hideyoshi made the transition to one of Oda Nobunaga's must trusted retainers from lowly beginnings as a peasant farmer (*ashigaru*). During the Sengoku era farmers were frequently called to arms as *ashigaru* when required to fight on the lord's behalf, and it was not unusual for peasants to become warriors.

Hideyoshi was also a shrewd negotiator. While in conflict with the Mōri clan, on hearing of the death of his lord, Nobunaga, he quickly negotiated a peace treaty and immediately sought revenge by chasing down the culprit, Akechi Mitsuhide, and engaging him in battle at Yamazaki, where Mitsuhide was eventually killed.

Although Hideyoshi assumed control after Nobunaga's death, he also did not attain the title of *shōgun*. However, he did continue Oda's legacy of unifying Japan making many societal reforms. He abolished the system that made it possible to transition from peasant farmer to warrior, creating a clear separation between the two classes. Furthermore, in 1588 he ordered a sword hunt to completely disarm the peasant population. He is also accredited with the rebuilding of Kyōto, which had fallen mostly into ruins following over a century of civil war. However, Hideyoshi was also behind two unsuccessful invasions of Korea, and the creation of the twenty-six martyrs of Japan. Worried about the influence of Christianity, he forbade his *daimyō* from becoming Christian, and as an example to the rest of the population, had a mixed group of Japanese and European Christians, tortured and eventually crucified. Another example of Hideyoshi's wrath was the ordered ritual suicide of the tea master, Sen no Rikyū. It is something that Hideyoshi is said to have later regretted.

同像
秀吉公像

DAISHŌ KOSHIRAE
大小拵

Right
Ogata Gekkō (1859–1920), *Toyotomi Hideyoshi and Akechi Mitsuhide (Killer of Nobunaga) before a Cherry Screen*, 1892.

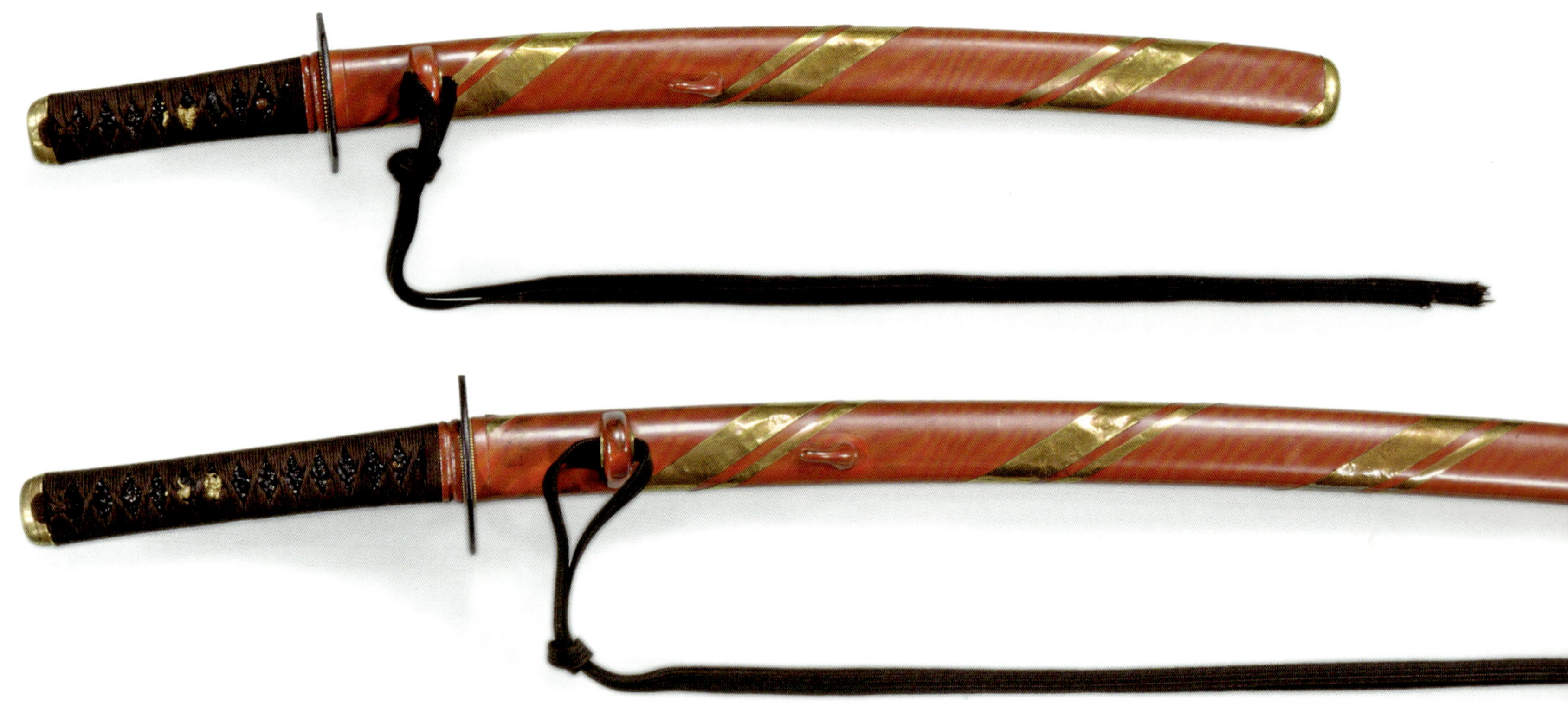

Although the wearing of a pair of long and short swords originated in the late Muromachi period, this is a very early example of a formalized matching set of *koshirae*. This set was given to Hideyoshi by Oda Nobunaga. The *daishō koshirae* originally had a matching pair of gold *kiri-mon sukashi* (pierced) *tsuba* said to have been made by Gotō Tokujō (1550–1631). However, at the time of Hideyoshi's death, the *tsuba* were given to the Asano clan. The blades (*dai*: Magoroku Kanemoto—*shō*: Mumei Naoe Shizu) and the rest of the mountings were given to the Mizoguchi clan.

This *daishō koshirae* illustrates the typical extravagance of the Momoyama period with its richly decorated vermilion lacquered scabbards with gold *hirumaki*, and solid gold fittings. The long sword currently has a round iron *tsuba* and the *wakizashi* has an octagonal shaped iron *tsuba*.

DAISHŌ KOSHIRAE
VERMILION LACQUERED WITH GOLD FOIL HIRUMAKI SPIRAL WRAP UNSIGNED
KATANA KOSHIRAE LENGTH
95 CM (37 13/32 IN)
WAKIZASHI KOSHIRAE LENGTH
70.2 CM (27 10/16 IN)
PERIOD **AZUCHI-MOMOYAMA PERIOD, 16TH C.**
TOKYO NATIONAL MUSEUM

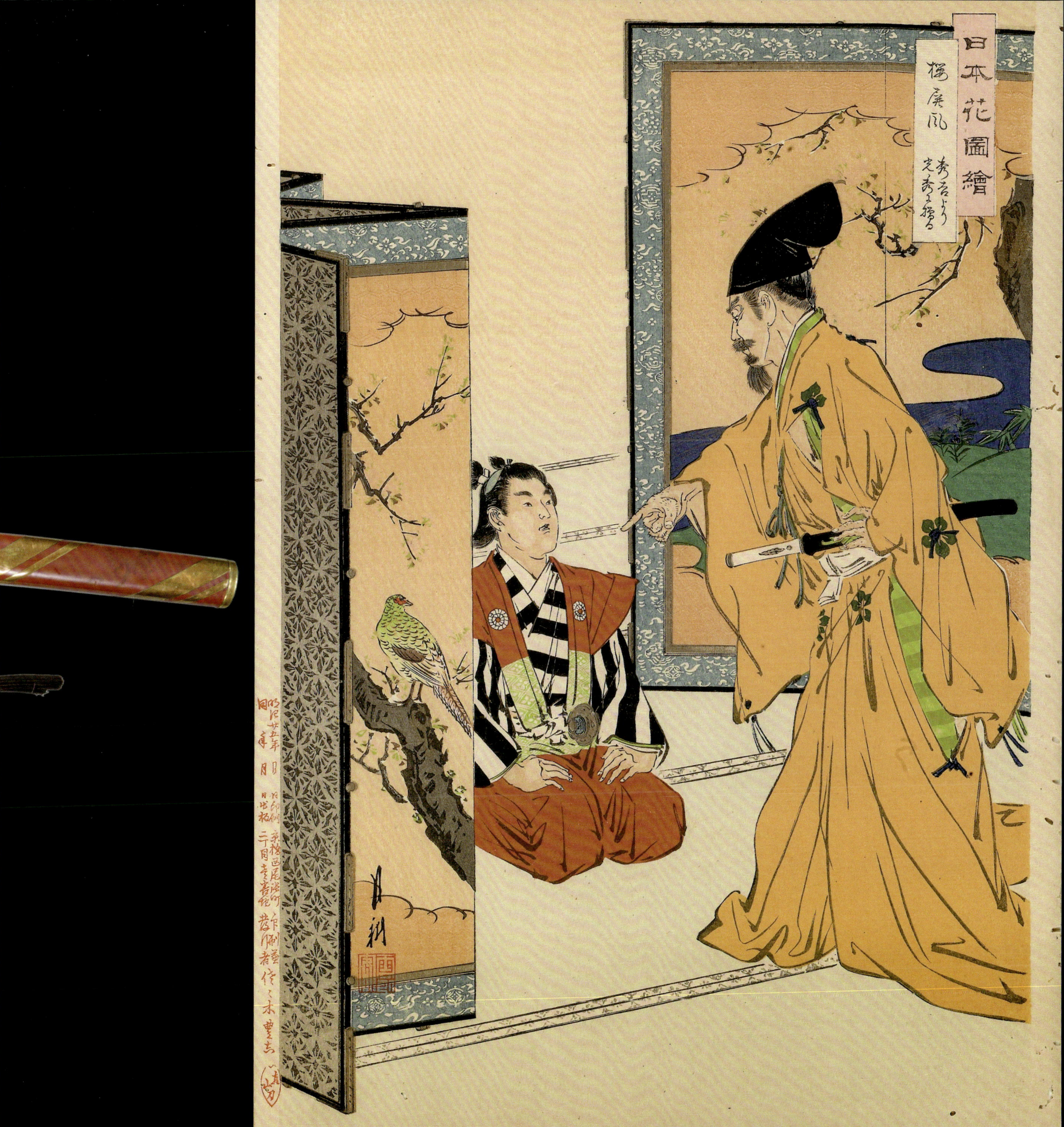
日本花圖繪
桜屏風
秀吉より光秀を辱る
月耕
明治廿五年 月 日印刷 同年 月 日出版
京橋区尾張町二丁目壹番地 印刷兼発行者 佐々木豊吉

TACHI

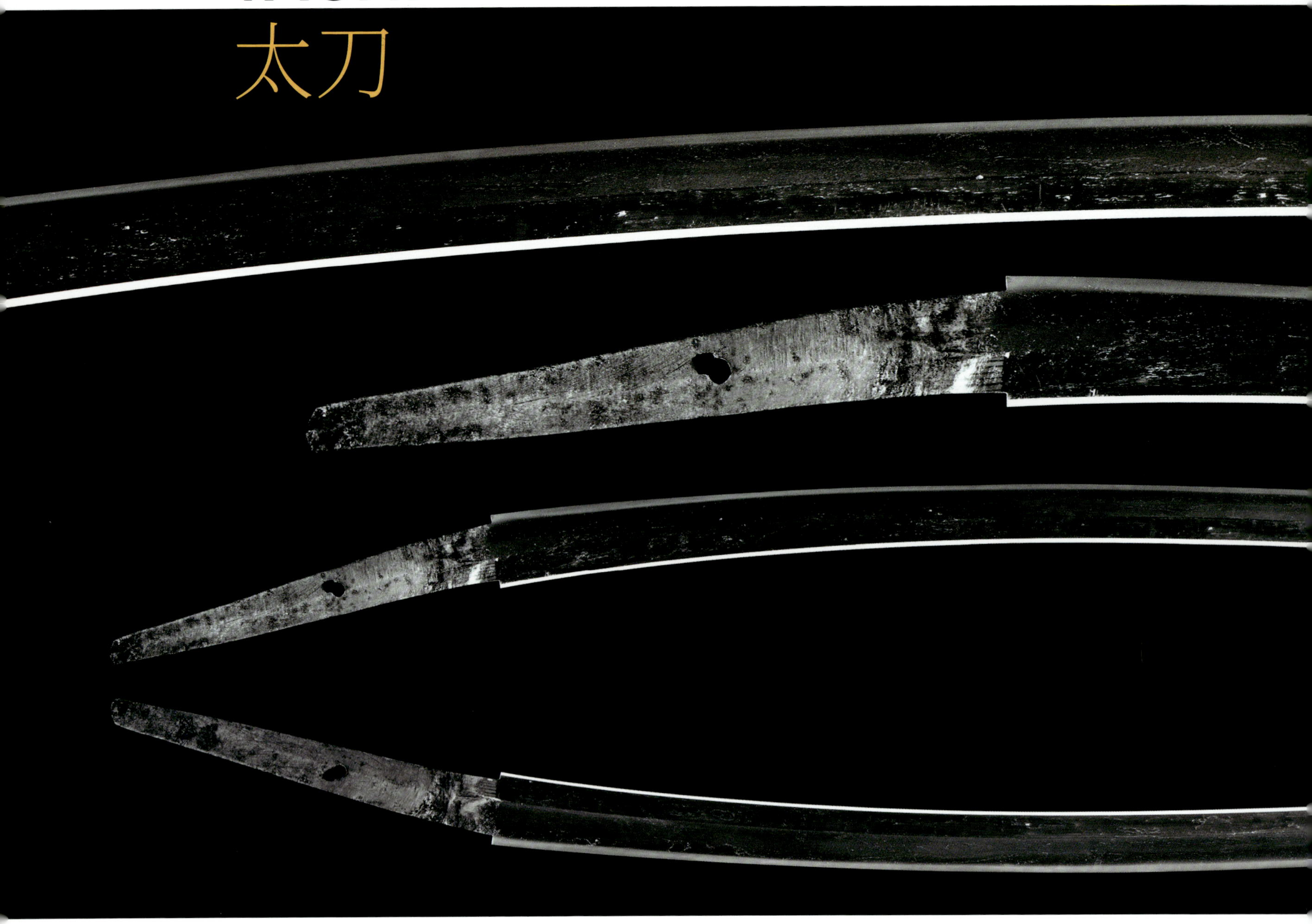

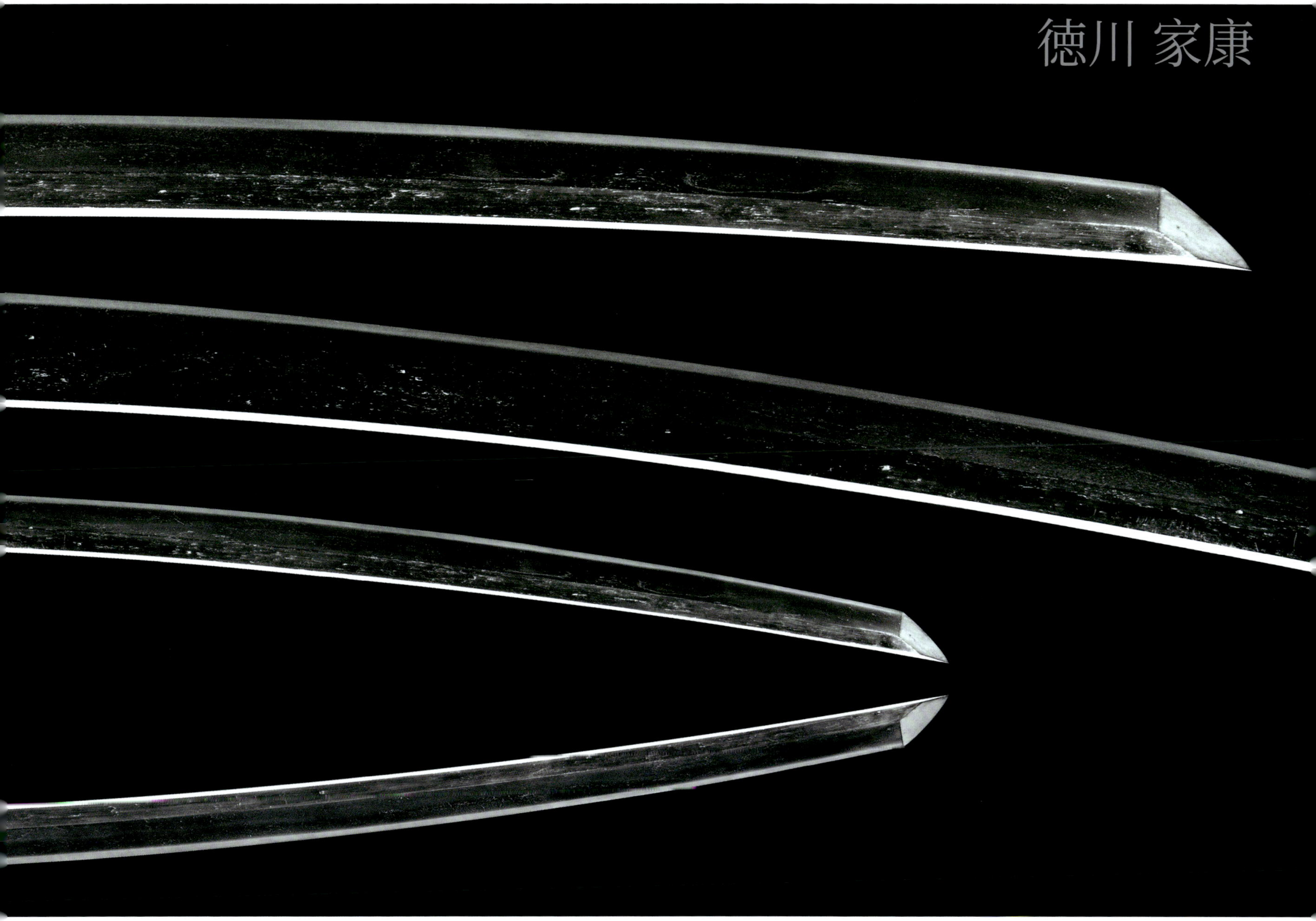

TOKUGAWA IEYASU
徳川 家康

● UNSIGNED
OTHER NAME(S): (MEI-BUTSU) **SHISHI-Ō** (THE LION DOG KING)
CUTTING-EDGE LENGTH **77.3 CM (37 7/16 IN)** - CURVATURE **2.7 CM (1 IN)**
PERIOD **LATE HEIAN PERIOD, 12TH C.**

● **TACHI KOSHIRAE** WITH BLACK LACQUERED SCABBARD
PERIOD **KAMAKURA PERIOD, 13TH–14TH C.**
TOKYO NATIONAL MUSEUM
Important Cultural Property

Right
Kanō Tan'yū (1602–1674), hanging scroll, *Portrait of Tokugawa Ieyasu, from the Main Tower of Ōsaka Castle*, color on silk, 17th c.

Opposite
Tsukioka Yoshitoshi (1839–1892), right-hand part of a triptych, *Tokugawa Ieyasu Rewarding the Brave Generals of the Battle of Sekigahara*, 1873.

TACHI and KOSHIRAE

This blade is attributed to the workmanship of the Yamato tradition. The blade is *shinogi-zukuri* in construction with a deep *koshi-zori*, *iori-mune*, and *kamasu* (barracuda) shaped point section. The blade is accompanied by this exquisite black lacquered *ito-maki tachi koshirae* that is from the Kamakura period. It is said to bestowed upon Minamoto no Yorimasa by Emperor Konoe when he was requested to slay the mythical Nue beast. The sword later came into the possession of Ieyasu, and he returned it to the Toki family who were the descendants of Yorimasa. The family later presented it to Emperor Meiji.

TOKUGAWA IEYASU (1543–1616)

Tokugawa Ieyasu is the third of the three unifiers of Japan. There is a story used to describe the main attributes of the three unifiers. They are asked how to make a nightingale sing. Oda Nobunaga responds that he would kill the bird if it did not sing. Toyotomi Hideyoshi said that he would force it to sing. Tokugawa Ieyasu said that he would just wait, and the nightingale would eventually sing. This story is a good summary of the way in which they individually rose to power. Tokugawa waited until the death of Toyotomi Hideyoshi, then sprang into action, taking control of Japan by winning the Battle of Sekigahara in 1600, and affirming his position by sieging Ōsaka castle in 1615. He established the Tokugawa Shogunate that remained in power for over 260 years until the Meiji restoration in 1868.

Tokugawa Ieyasu's success in retaining power for so long was due to the strategic positioning of *daimyō* (warlords) across the country who were loyal to him prior to Sekigahara. These are called *fudai daimyō* as opposed to the *tozama daimyō* who came under Tokugawa rule after Sekigahara. The strategic positioning meant that *tozama daimyō* were kept a careful watch of by *fudai daimyō*.

Tokugawa Ieyasu died in 1616 aged 73 years old. Mausoleums were established in his honor at Kunōzan Tōshōgū in Shizuoka Prefecture, and Nikkō Tōshōgū in Tochigi prefecture.

勇士軍賞之圖
臣源家康公

Ō-NAGINATA
大長刀

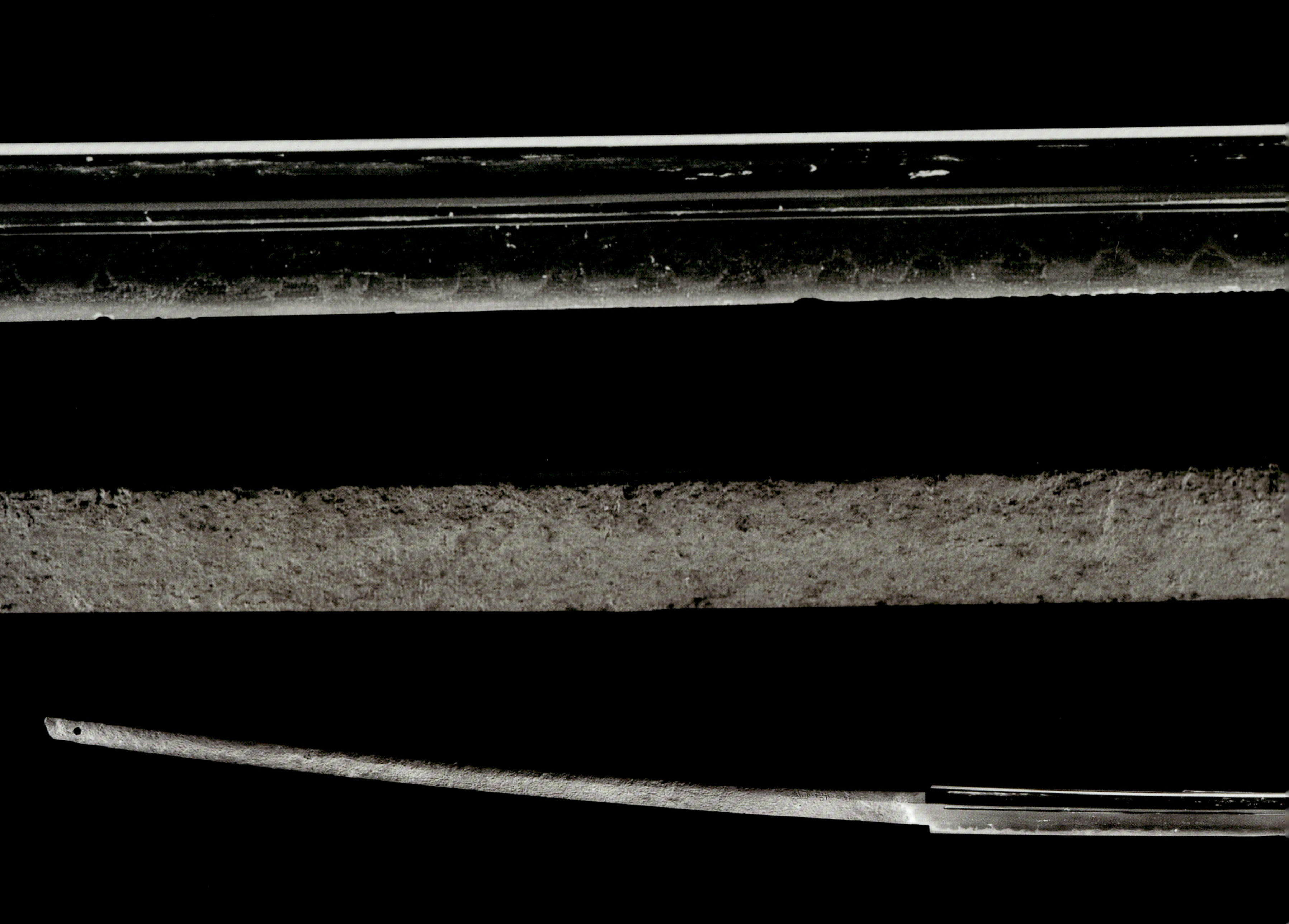

● SIGNED **SEKISHU KAZUSADA SAKU**
CUTTING-EDGE LENGTH **172 CM (67²³⁄₃₂ IN)**
CURVATURE **3 CM (1³⁄₁₆ IN)**

PERIOD **MUROMACHI PERIOD, 15TH C.**
ŌYAMAZUMI SHRINE, EHIME PREFECTURE
Important Art Object

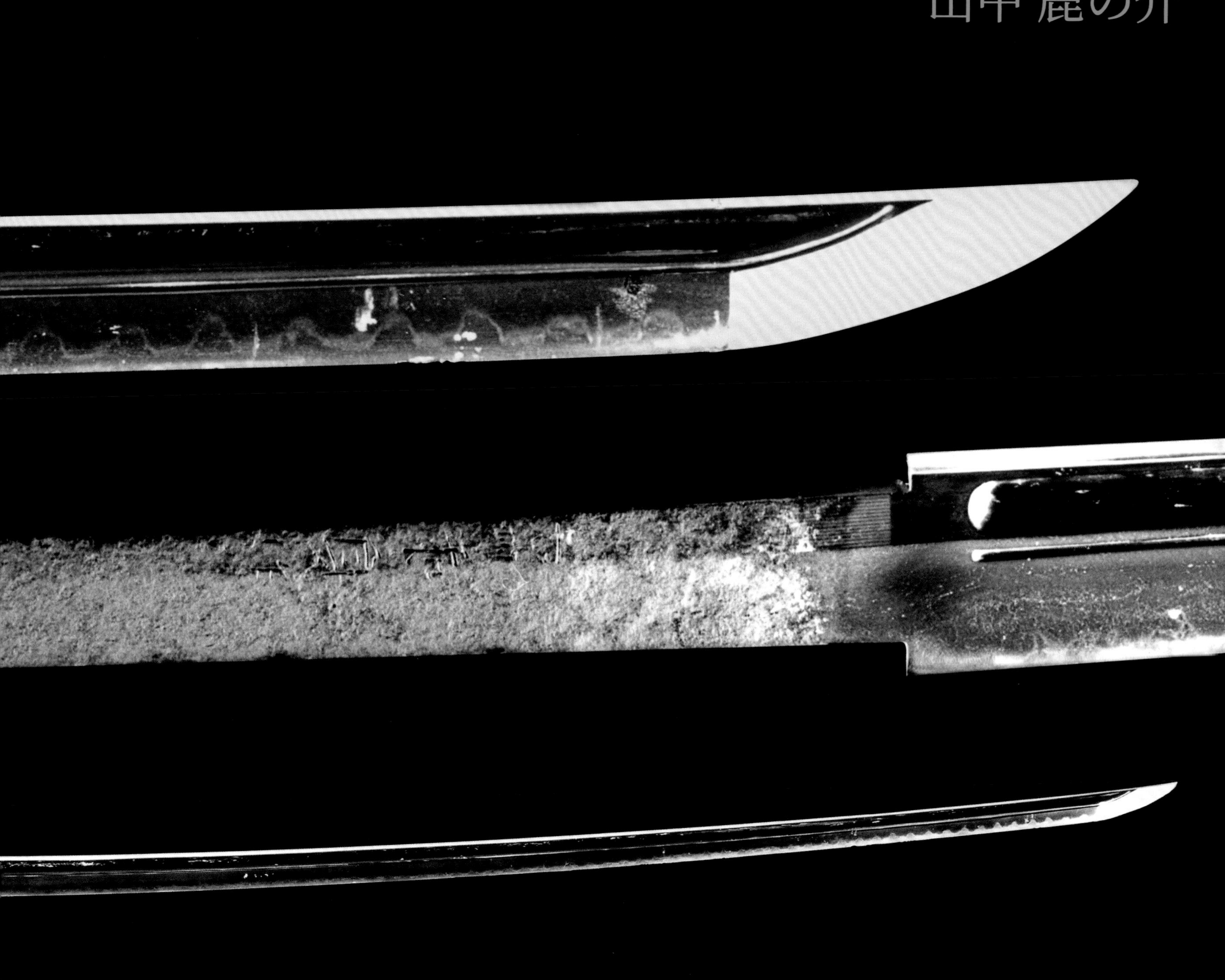
山中 鹿の介

Opposite
Tsukioka Yoshitoshi (1839–1892), *Fidelity: The Sixteenth-Century Vassal Yamanaka Shikanosuke Yukimori Praying under a Full Moon*, 1878.

Ō-NAGINATA

This blade is said to have been donated to Ōyamazumi shrine by Shikanosuke. It appears to be an *ō-dachi*, but due to the long *nakago* it is classified as a type of *ō-naginata*. It is *shinogi-zukuri* with *iori-mune*. It has a shallow curvature and is rather wide with a large sized point section. The *nakago* is in its original condition with one peg-hole, but the file marks are unclear. The *nakago-jiri* is a rather *iriyama-gata* shaped. The *hada* is *itame* with a pale *utsuri*. The *hamon* is a uniformly spaced *gunome* that continues into the point section before turning back. It has a *bō-hi* and *soe-bi* on both sides that end in *maru-dome*.

YAMANAKA SHIKANOSUKE (1545–1578)

Yamanaka Shikanosuke was a samurai general of the Amago clan in Izumo province (Yasugi, Shimane prefecture). An interesting local legend in Yasugi is that the lord of Amago owned one of the five famous swords under heaven, Mikazuki Munechika (National Treasure), and that the real reason behind the siege of Gassan Toda Castle and destruction of the Amago clan was to obtain that sword. There are lots of local stories concerning Shikanosuke. One of which is that he sharpened his *yari* on a large stone close to Kiyomizu Temple in Yasugi. Another is that following the fall of Gassan Toda Castle, he said the famous quote while praying under a crescent moon, "*Let me endure seven hardships (in order to revive the Amago clan)*". It is also said that Shikanosuke was the favorite historical samurai of Sakamoto Ryōma.

KABUTO
兜

● **TWELVE PLATE RUSSET HELMET (KABUTO)**
PERIOD **MUROMACHI PERIOD, 16TH C.**

KIKKAWA HISTORICAL MUSEUM,
YAMAGUCHI PREFECTURE

Right
Tsukioka Yoshitoshi (1839–1892), *The Warrior Yamanaka Shikanosuke Yukimori and the Crescent Moon of Faith,* from the series *One Hundred Aspects of the Moon*, 1886.

This helmet belonged to Yamanaka Shikanosuke. It has been in the Kikkawa family for many generations. In 1578, when Kozuki castle fell and Amago Katsuhisa committed *seppuku*, Shikanosuke surrendered to Kikkawa Motoharu. Motoharu then turned Shikanosuke over to the Mōri Terumoto. However, Shikanosuke was killed by one of Mōri's retainers while crossing the Bitchu-Kobe river. In recognition of being a great samurai, Kikkawa Motoharu ordered that Shikanosuke's helmet be kept in their family as a tribute to his memory.

TACHI
太刀

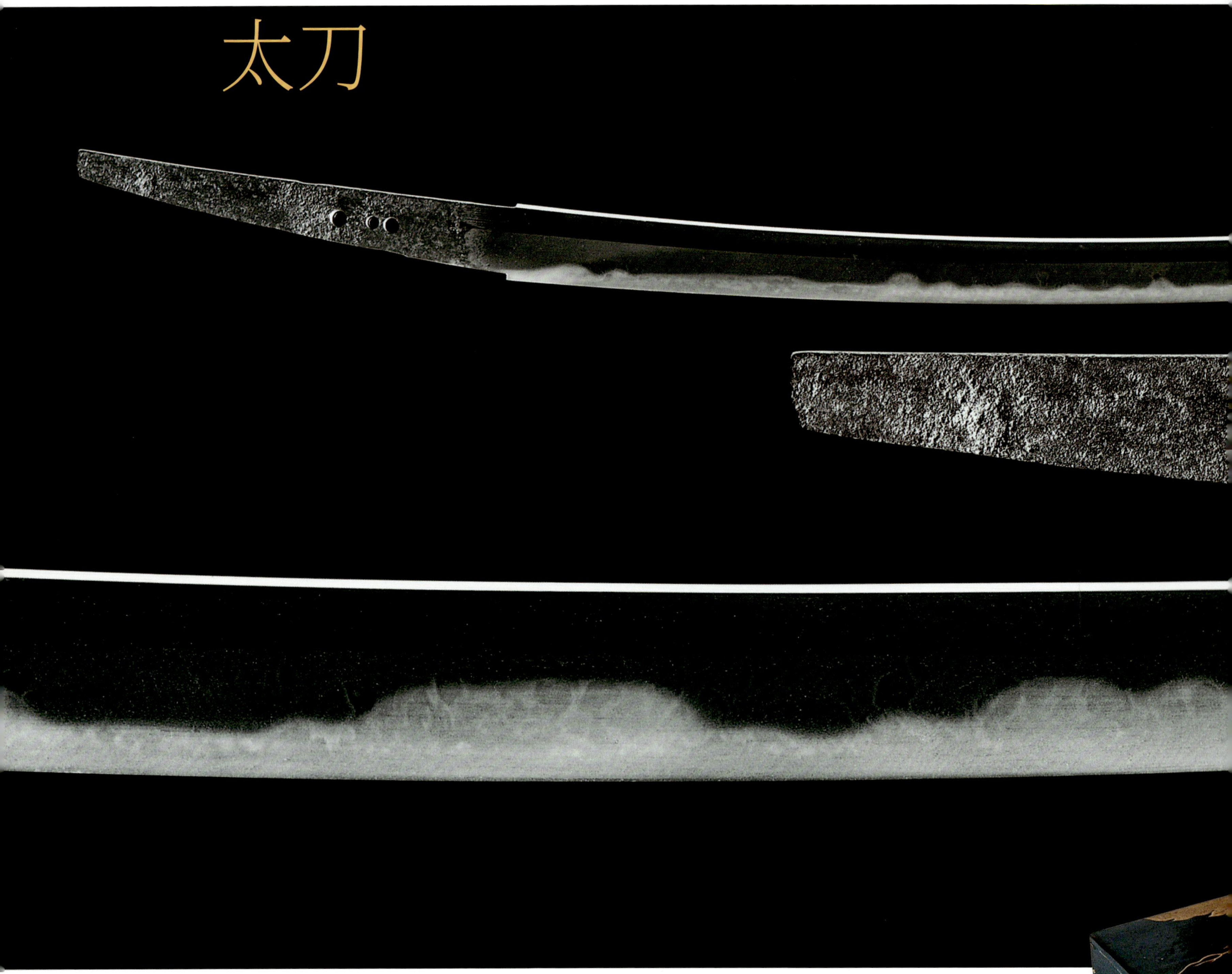

● UNSIGNED **ATTRIBUTED TO THE ICHIMONJI SCHOOL**
OTHER NAME(S) (MEIBUTSU) **NIKKŌ-ICHIMONJI**
CUTTING-EDGE LENGTH **67.8 CM (26¹¹⁄₁₆ IN)**
CURVATURE **2.3 CM (2⁹⁄₃₂ IN)**

PERIOD **KAMAKURA PERIOD, 13TH C.**
FUKUOKA CITY MUSEUM, KYŪSHŪ
National Treasure (both the sword alone and the set consisting of sword and box)

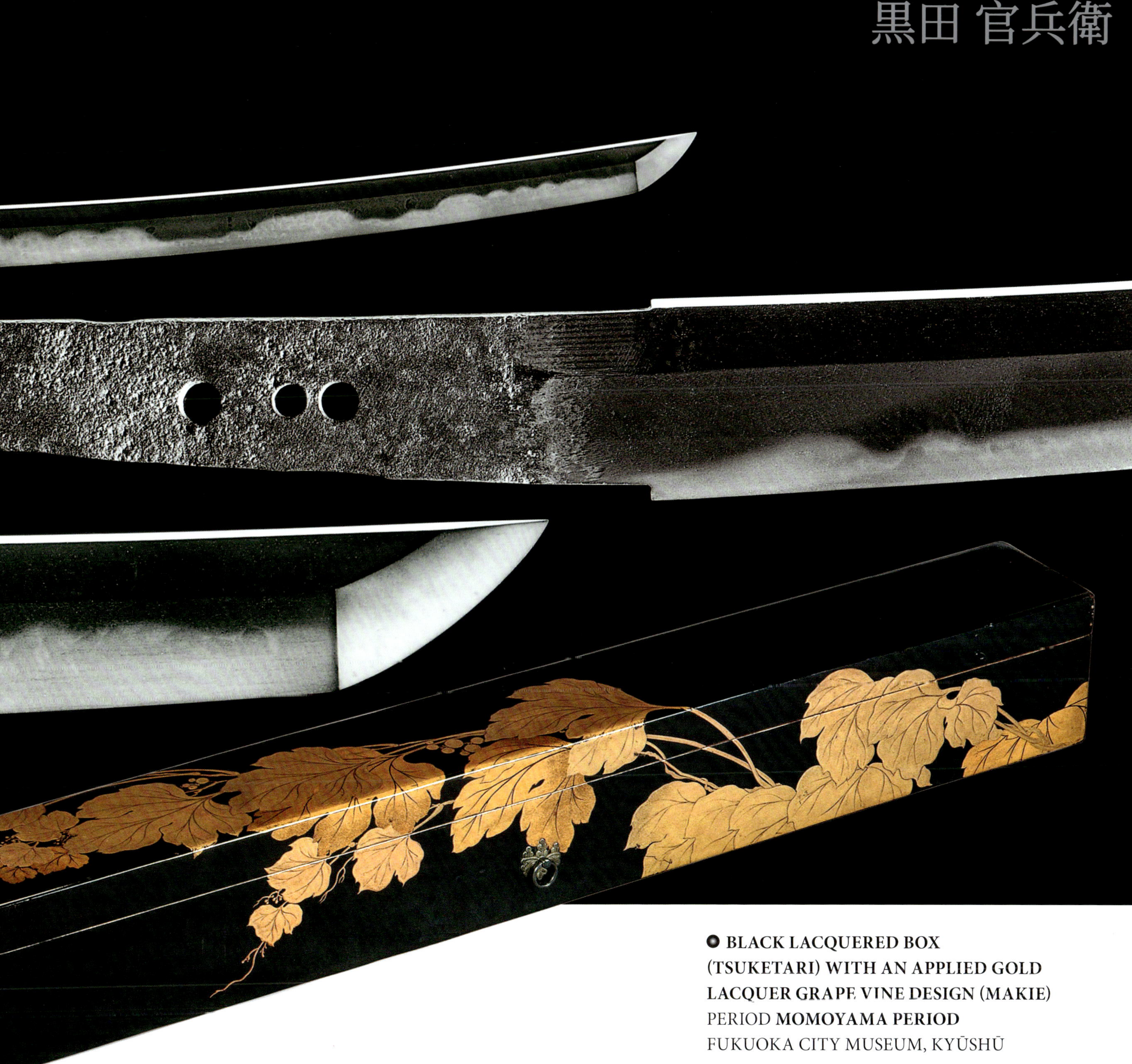

BLACK LACQUERED BOX (TSUKETARI) WITH AN APPLIED GOLD LACQUER GRAPE VINE DESIGN (MAKIE)
PERIOD **MOMOYAMA PERIOD**
FUKUOKA CITY MUSEUM, KYŪSHŪ

TACHI

This blade is *shinogi-zukuri* in construction with a rather thin *kasane*, *iori-mune* and an *ikubi-kissaki*. It retains a deep curvature in the base of the blade. It has a well-forged *itame-hada* with *mokume*, *ji-nie* and a prominent *midare-utsuri*. The *hamon* is a very active *juka-chōji-midare*.

This sword was originally dedicated to Nikkō-Gongen shrine. However, it was taken by the first-generation head of the Later Hōjō clan, Sōun, and passed down within the family. In 1590, when Toyotomi Hideyoshi laid siege to Odawara castle, Kuroda volunteered to enter the castle alone and negotiated a bloodless victory. In gratitude, the lord of the castle, Hōjō Ujinao presented this sword to Kanbei in a black lacquered box with an applied gold lacquer grape vine design. It was passed down within the Kuroda family for several generations.

KURODA KANBEI (1546–1604)

Kuroda Kanbei is a well-known strategist of the Sengoku Period. He is also famous for his unique armor that features a helmet in the form of an upturned bowl. His uncanny ability to foresee situations and make excellent strategies saw him pledge allegiance to Oda Nobunaga before he seized power. Kuroda then went on to serve Toyotomi Hideyoshi and assisted him in avenging Oda's death at the Battle of Yamazaki (1582).

Kanbei became a Christian and took the name, Don Simeon, but once Hideyoshi decreed that Christianity was to be banned, expelled the Jesuits and ordered all the *daimyō* to renounce their faith, Kuroda become a monk and took the Buddhist name of Jōsui.

After Hideyoshi's death, Kuroda foresaw the events leading up to the Battle of Sekigahara. Kuroda did not like Ishida Mitsunari. They had clashed during the Korea campaigns. Although, they had been allies under Hideyoshi, following his death, Kuroda no longer saw any reason to maintain a relationship with Ishida. At the battle of Sekigahara, Kuroda's son, Nagamasa, went to fight alongside Ieyasu while Kanbei gathered troops and fought on Ieyasu's behalf in Kyūshū.

KABUTO
兜

UPTURNED BOWL DESIGN HELMET
PERIOD **MOMOYAMA PERIOD, 16TH C.**

MORIOKA HISTORY AND CULTURE MUSEUM, IWATE PREFECTURE
Important Cultural Property of the Iwate Prefecture

KATCHŪ

甲冑

KURODA KANBEI

黒田官兵衛

According to Kuroda family records, this Momoyama period *gomai-dō* (five plate cuirass) laced with black cord is said to have been worn by Kuroda Kanbei. However, the accompanying helmet was re-commissioned in Kanbei's honor by his grandson, Mitsuyuki, in 1688. The original helmet is known as "Jōsui's *akagosu*" (Kuroda Kanbei's bowl helmet) and is said to have struck fear into his enemies when seen on the battlefield. Kanbei gave the helmet to Kuriyama Toshiyasu. It was later passed to the Nabu clan, and currently resides at the Morioka History and Culture Museum, Iwate prefecture.

● **GOMAI-DŌ GUSOKU TYPE ARMOR**
WITH BLACK LACING
PERIOD **MOMOYAMA PERIOD, 16TH C.**

● **UPTURNED BOWL DESIGN HELMET**
VERMILION LACQUERED
SIGNED **HARUTA JIBEI, IWAI KANNOJŌ,**
DATED 1688
FUKUOKA CITY MUSEUM, KYŪSHŪ

KATCHŪ

甲冑

SAKAKIBARA YASUMASA

Left
Seki Yasunosuke (1868–1945), hanging scroll, *Portrait of Sakakibara Yasumasa*, color on paper, 20th c., copy of an Edo-era (17th c.) original. Yasumasa wears the same armor as seen in the image on the left).

KATCHŪ

The helmet is a 62 plate *suji-kabuto* inscribed, Yoshimichi saku. The *suji* (ridges) are all finished in a rope pattern and it has a gilt *sankozuka-ken maedate* (front decoration). The *dō* (cuirass) is a two-piece construction (*nimai-dō*) of black lacquered iron plates with an exquisite *kanagai* (silver foil) and gold *maki-e* lacquer design of a dragon. The lower two plates of the *kusazuri* (skirt sections) also have *maki-e* designs of turbulent waves. The armor and helmet are decorated with the Sakakibara Genji-guruma family crests.

● **NIMAI-DŌ GUSOKU ARMOR**
WITH BLACK LACING
PERIOD **MOMOYAMA PERIOD, 17TH C.**
TOKYO NATIONAL MUSEUM
Important Cultural Property

SAKAKIBARA YASUMASA (1548–1606)

A long-time retainer of the Matsudaira and Tokugawa clan, Sakakibara Yasumasa went to become one of Ieyasu's most trusted military commanders. Yasumasa was one of Tokugawa's Shitennō (Guardians of the four directions: Sakakibara, Honda Tadakatsu, Ii Naomasa and Sakai Tadatsugu), included in his 36 famous generals, and one of his three great nobles (Sakakibara, Honda Tadakatsu, and Ii Naomasa) in the late Muromachi period.

He was given the *Yasu* character of his name by a young Tokugawa Ieyasu (Matsudaira Motoyasu at the time) after his success in the battle of Azukizaka in Mikawa (1564). He fought in many battles on behalf of the Tokugawa clan, eventually dying at the age of 59 in 1606 from complications stemming from folliculitis. His son, Yasukatsu, went on to take part in the siege of Ōsaka Castle in 1615.

MENPŌ

頬

Menpō (face guards) are commonly made from iron plate or leather and are often lacquered. They usually also have a throat guard (*yodare-kake*) attached. They usually have a fierce expression and often have facial hair. This *menpō* has gold colored teeth.

● Left **CORAZZA (DŌ)**

● Right **FACE GUARD (MENPŌ)**
PERIOD **MOMOYAMA PERIOD, 17TH C.**
TOKYO NATIONAL MUSEUM

KATANA

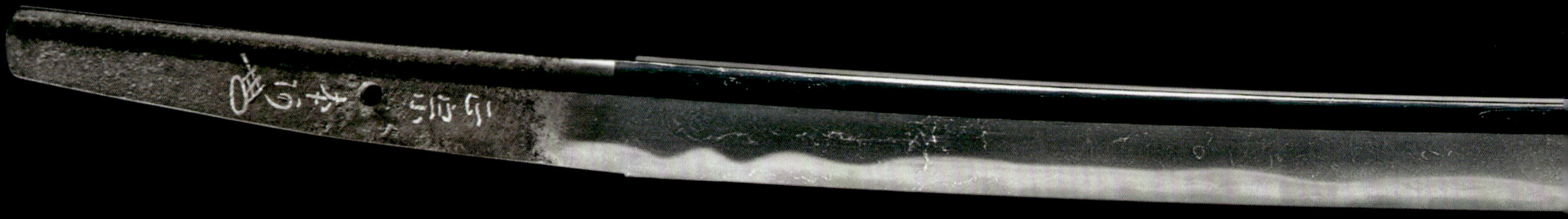

● **CONVERTED TACHI**

GOLD INLAID INSCRIPTION **HONDA NAKATSUKASA SHOJI / MASAMUNE HON'A (KAŌ)**

OTHER NAME(S) (MEIBUTSU) **NAKATSUKASA MASAMUNE, KUWANA MASAMUNE**

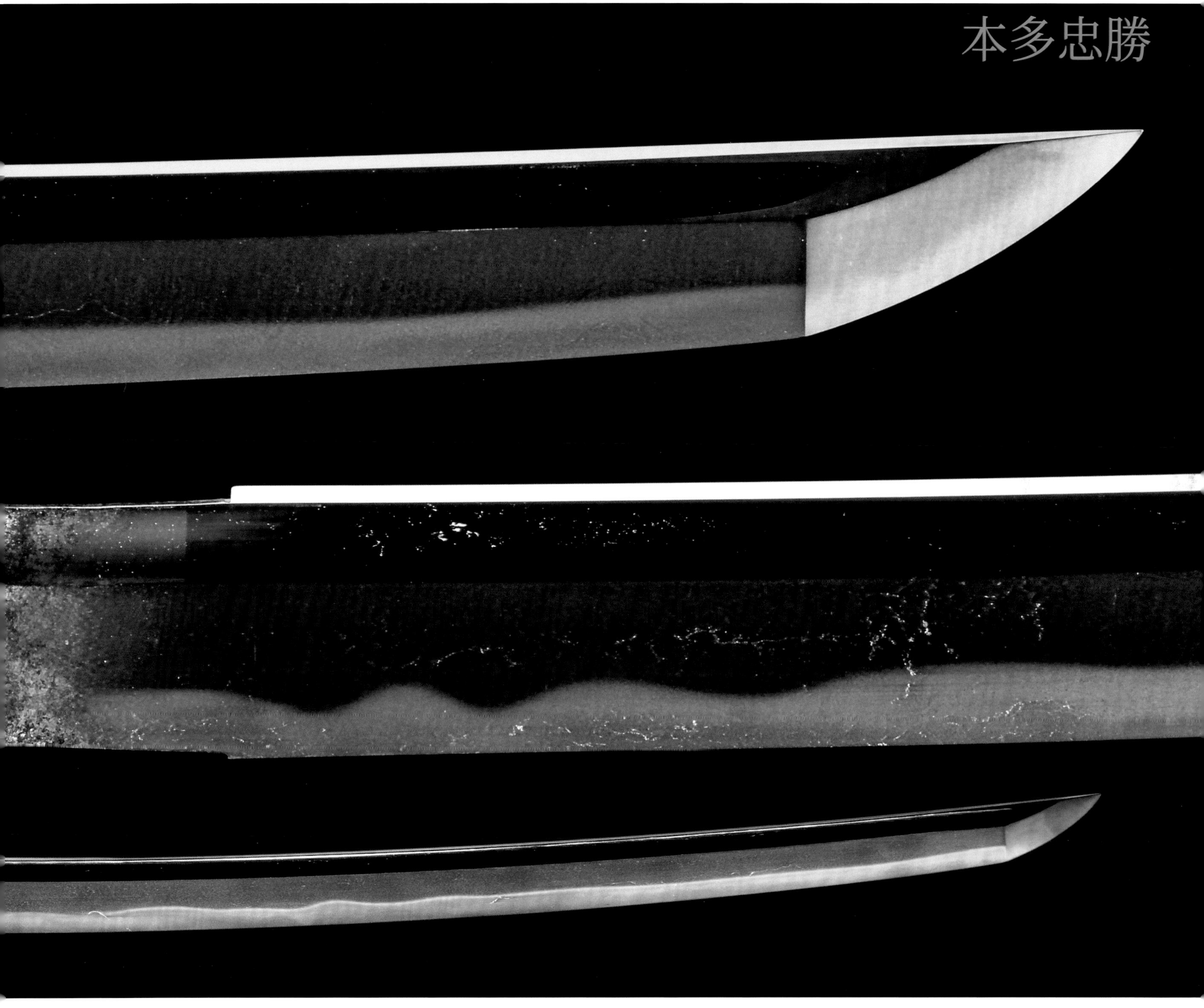

本多忠勝

CUTTING-EDGE LENGTH **67.0 CM (26⅜ IN)**
CURVATURE **1.7 CM (21/32 IN)**

PERIOD **NANBOKUCHŌ PERIOD, 14TH C.**
KYŪSHŪ PREFECTURAL MUSEUM
National Treasure

YARI

◉ SIGNED **FUJIWARA MASAZANE SAKU**
(MADE BY FUJIWARA MASAZANE)
OTHER NAME **TONBO-GIRI**
CUTTING-EDGE LENGTH **43.6 CM (17⁵⁄₃₂ IN)**
WIDTH AT BASE **2.4 CM (¹⁵⁄₁₆ IN)**

PERIOD **MUROMACHI PERIOD, 16TH C.**
SANO ART MUSEUM (YABE COLLECTION),
SHIZUOKA PREFECTURE
Important Cultural Property of Shizuoka Prefecture

KATANA (Converted Tachi)

Nakatsukasa Masamune was made by Sōshū Masamune and is recorded in the Kyōhō Meibutsuchō. Honda Tadakatsu purchased it through the intermediation of Hon'ami Kōtoku. Nakatsukasa was Tadakatsu's official name (Nakatsukasa Shōyu). The sword is also known as Kuwana Masamune as Tadakatsu was the first head of the Kuwana clan. As the sword had been shortened and lost its inscription, Tadakatsu requested Kōtoku for the inscription and attribution in gold inlay that was performed by Umetada Jusai.

YARI

This *ō-sasaho* (large sized bamboo leaf shaped) *yari* (spear) was made by Fujiwara Masazane, who is said to have been a student of Muramasa. It is triangular in cross-section. The base is rather narrow at 2.4 cm ($\frac{15}{16}$ in), and it fans out towards the top. On the largest flat section of the blade it has a shallow bamboo leaf shaped cartouche with several *bonji* (Sanskrit characters), a *sankozuka-ken* and a lotus flower shaped pedestal carved in excellent detail. The other two surfaces both have two narrow *bō-hi* cut into them. It has the name, Tonbo-giri, as it is said that when a dragonfly landed on the tip, that it was instantly cut in two.

HONDA TADAKATSU (1548–1610)

Honda Tadakatsu, also known as Heihachihiro, was one of Tokugawa Ieyasu's most loyal generals. Along with Sakai Tadatsugu, Ii Naomasa, and Sakakibara Yasumasa, he is one of Ieyasu's Shitennō (Guardians of the Four Horizons). He is also included in Tokugawa's 36 great generals and the three nobles along with fellow Shitennō, Sakakibara Yasumasa and Ii Naomasa. He gained distinction fighting in many battles in support of the Tokugawa clan. He was praised by many of his contemporaries as a fearless warrior, and was even praised by Oda Nobunaga as someone who lived up to his name as a samurai.

His famous deer antler armor depicted in his portraits is in the collection of the Ieyasu and Mikawa Bushi Museum in Okazaki, Aichi Prefecture. He is also famous for being owner of the spear, Tonbo-giri, or the Dragonfly Cutter. The Tonbo-giri has been recognized since the Muromachi period as one of the Three Great Spears of Japan.

Hashimoto Chikanobu (1838–1912), diptych, *The Battle of Komaki (1584)—Honda Tadakatsu (left) and Katō Kiyomasa (right)*, late 19th c.

KATANA

刀

● **CONVERTED TACHI**
UNSIGNED
OTHER NAME(S) (MEIBUTSU) **ISHIDA MASAMUNE / ISHIDA KIRIKOMI MASAMUNE**
CUTTING-EDGE LENGTH **68.8 CM (27³⁄₃₂ IN)** - CURVATURE **2.48 CM (³¹⁄₃₂ IN)**

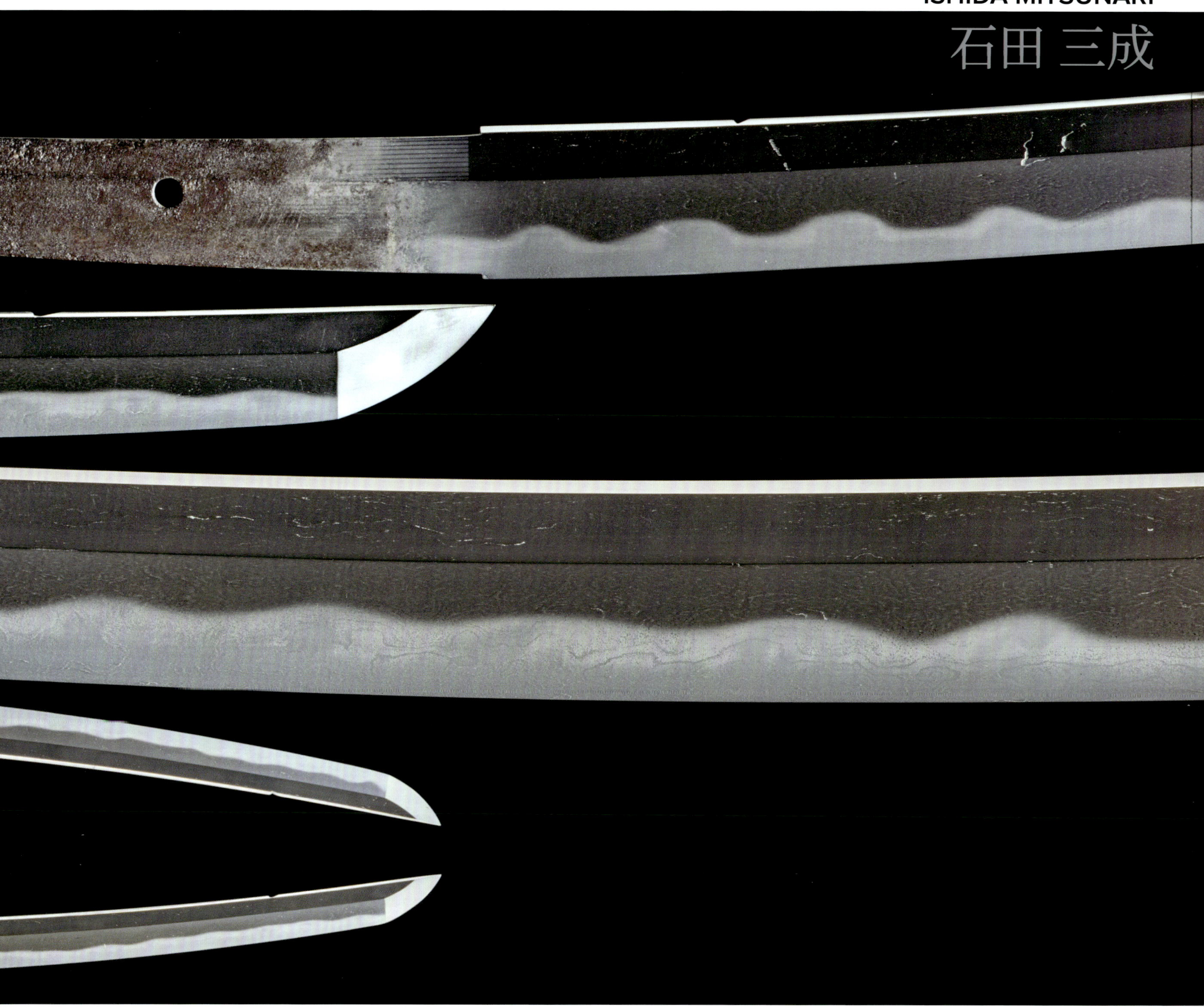

PERIOD **LATE KAMAKURA-NANBOKUCHŌ PERIODS, 14TH C.**
TOKYO NATIONAL MUSEUM
Important Cultural Property

Opposite
Anonymous, hanging scroll, *Ishida Mitsunari*, color on silk, 17th–18th c.

KATANA (Converted Tachi)

This blade is also known as Ishida Kirikomi Masamune as it is attributed to the work of Masamune of the Sōshū tradition, and has two cut marks from another sword remaining in the back of the blade. One is in the *mono-uchi* area and the other is close to the *nakago*. The blade is *shinogi-zukuri* in construction. Despite being classed as *ō-suriage* (greatly shortened), it still retains a rather deep curvature. It has a medium sized point section. Due to the shortening of the blade and refinishing of the *nakago*, any signature has been lost and the *nakago-jiri* has been fashioned into an *iriyama* shape. The *hada* is a well-forged *itame* with *ji-nie* and *chikei*. The very active *nie-deki hamon* is *notare* with *ko-gunome*, and has much *sunagashi* and *kinsuji*.

ISHIDA MITSUNARI (1560–1600)

Ishida Mitsunari was in the employ of Toyotomi Hideyoshi. Due to his talents not only on the battlefield, but also as a financial manager, he quickly rose in the ranks and was appointed as one of Hideyoshi's five Bugyō (Governors). After the death of Toyotomi Hideyoshi, Ishida Mitsunari was appointed as one of the regents to collectively govern in Hideyoshi's son, Hideyori's, name. However, divisions grew between Mitsunari and Tokugawa Ieyasu, eventually leading to the battle of Sekigahara in 1600 where Mitsunari was defeated, and then caught by villagers trying to escape.

Ishida Mitsunari's clan crest was the inscription, *Dai Ichi, Dai Man, Dai Kichi* (大一大万大吉). The characters mean "All for one, and one for all brings great prosperity". He seems to have been quite an optimist. There is a story that when he was taken to Kyōto to be executed, Mitsunari was offered a persimmon, but he refused it as they gave him heartburn. His companion said, *"What does it matter? You are going to be executed!"*, to which he replied that *"You never know how these things will turn out"*.

KATAKAMA-YARI
片鎌槍

KATŌ KIYOMASA
加藤 清正

VERMILION LACQUER INSCRIPTION **KATŌ KIYOMASA SOKUJO YŌRIN'IN SAMA OIRIKOSHI NO SETSU WO OMOCHIKOMU** (THIS WAS GIVEN TO KATŌ KIYOMASA'S DAUGHTER, YŌRIN'IN, ON THE OCCASION OF HER MARRIAGE)
CUTTING-EDGE LENGTH **32.7 CM (12⅞ IN)**

PERIOD **MUROMACHI PERIOD, 16TH C.**
TOKYO NATIONAL MUSEUM

加藤清正

Left
Mizuno Toshikata (1866–1908), center and right parts of a triptych, *Katō Kiyomasa, Standing on a Rock and Looking down at Orankai Fortress, while in the Background His Soldiers Roll a Large Boulder to the Edge of the Mountain to Destroy the Building*, 1895.

Next spread
Hashimoto Chikanobu (1838–1912), triptych, *Kiyomasa Attacking a Fierce Tiger while on Campaign in Korea*, 1899.

KATAKAMA-YARI

This is the spear that Kiyomasa used when hunting tigers in Korea. Legend says that it was originally a *jumonji-yari* with full blades protruding on both sides, but one side broke off. However, scholars believe that it was originally made in this construction. The inscription states that it was presented to Kiyomasa's daughter, Yōrin'in, on her marriage (to Tokugawa Yorinobu, of Kishū domain). Tokugawa Yorinobu was the 10th son of Ieyasu.

KATŌ KIYOMASA (1562–1611)

Katō Kiyomasa is known as one of Toyotomi Hideyoshi's 'Seven Spears of the Battle of Shizugatake.' The others included Fukushima Masanori, Hirano Nagayasu, Kasuya Takenori, Katagiri Katsumoto, Katō Yoshiaki and Wakizaka Yasuharu. For his service, Hideyoshi awarded him a 195,000 Koku stipend and half of Higo Province. Kiyomasa was also known for his castle building. After taking over Kumamoto castle in 1588, he went onto expand the castle into the size that it is in today.

Kiyomasa was also instrumental as one of Hideyoshi's generals in the Korean campaigns. It was during his time in Korea that he hunted tigers with his famous *katakama-yari*. However, as Kiyomasa disliked Ishida Mitsunari, after Hideyoshi's death he sided with Tokugawa Ieyasu at the Battle of Sekigahara (1600). Following Sekigahara, he was awarded the rest of Higo province as part of his domain by Ieyasu. Using his position as a known figure in both factions, he went on to act as a negotiator between Toyotomi Hideyori and Ieyasu. Unfortunately, while returning from one such mission, he became ill and passed away soon after returning home in 1611.

朝鮮之役ニ
清正撃レ
猛虎ヲ

NAGINATA AND KATANA

薙刀 刀

● **NAGINATA** – UNSIGNED
CUTTING-EDGE LENGTH **65.0 CM (25 19/32 IN)**
PERIOD **LATE MUROMACHI PERIOD, 16TH C.**
ECHIZEN MATSUDAIRA COLLECTION, FUKUI CITY HISTORY MUSEUM

● **KATANA** – INSCRIPTION **MORITAKA SAKU / EISHO GO NEN NI GATSU JITSU (1508)**
CUTTING-EDGE LENGTH **73.0 CM (28 3/4 IN)**
CURVATURE **1.4 CM (9/16 IN)**

SANADA YUKIMURA
真田 幸村

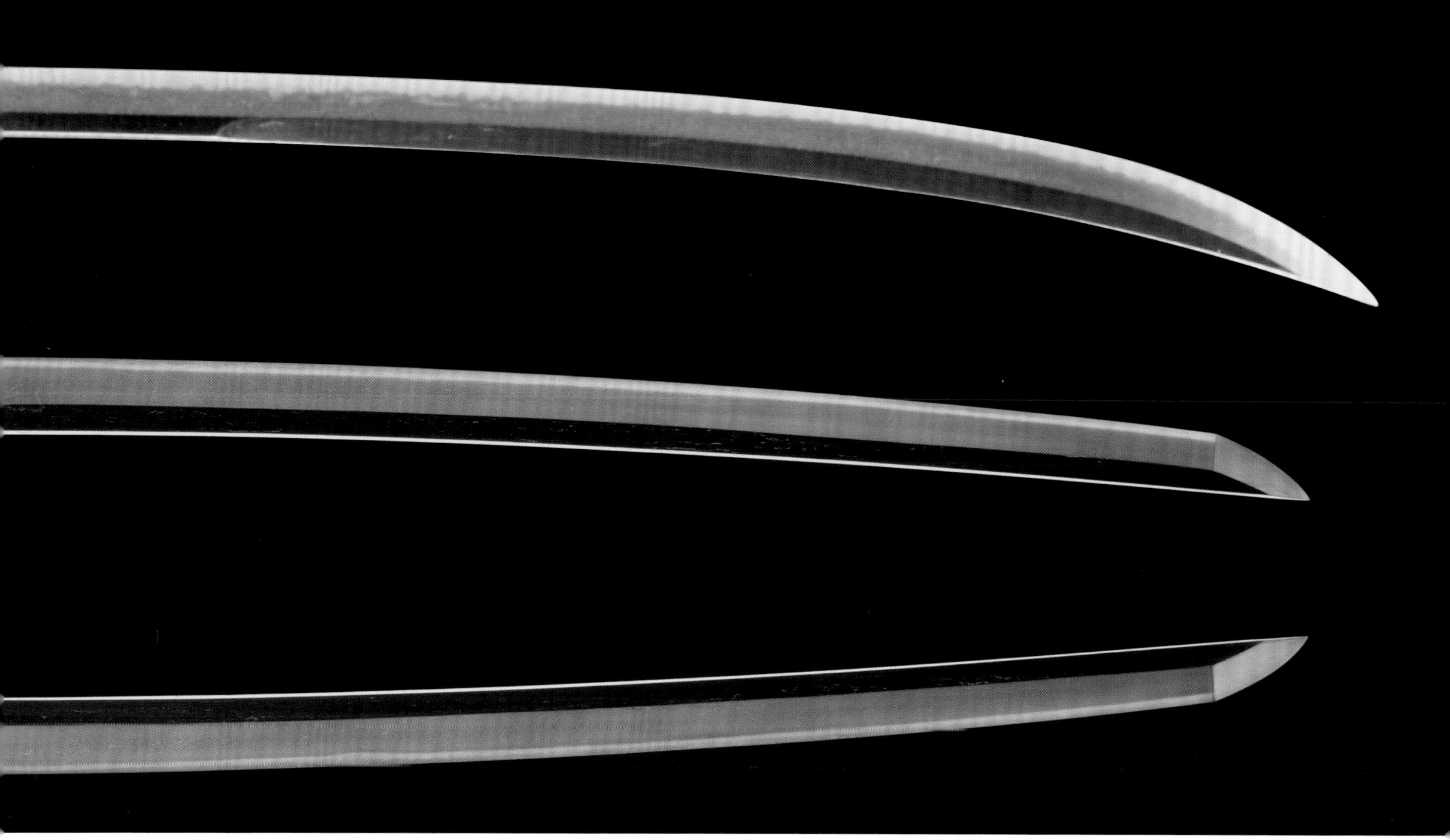

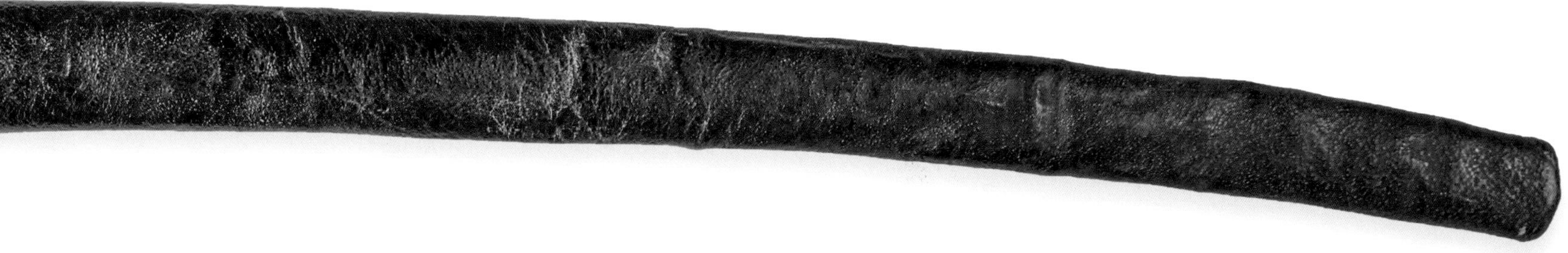

PERIOD **MUROMACHI PERIOD, 16TH C.**
ZAO BOARD OF EDUCATION, MIYAGI PREF.,
SANADA TETSU COLLECTION

● **HANDACHI KOSHIRAE**
PERIOD **PROBABLY LATE EDO PERIOD, 19TH C.**
ZAO BOARD OF EDUCATION, MIYAGI PREF.,
SANADA TETSU COLLECTION

Right
Anonymous, hanging scroll, *Portrait of Sanada Yukimura*, color on silk, Edo period

Opposite
Tsukioka Yoshitoshi (1839–1892), *The Exiled Retainer Sanada Saemon'nojō Yukimura Waiting in a Lotus Pond to Ambush His Enemy Tokugawa Ieyasu in 1615*, from the series *Essays*, 1872.

真田幸村

NAGINATA, KATANA and KOSHIRAE

This *naginata* is said to have been used by Yukimura at the Siege of Ōsaka castle. It was taken by Nishio Munetsugu (commonly known as Nizaemon) who was serving the Echizen Matsudaira clan at the summer campaign of the Siege of Ōsaka, 1615. It was then passed down in his family for several generations, before being gifted to the Lord of the Echizen Matsudaira clan of Fukui province in the late Edo period.

According to Sanada family records, this rather conservative and utilitarian katana is thought to have been passed down from Sanada Yukimori's grandfather, or father. It is signed, Moritaka saku, of the Kongōhyōe (Kongōbei) school of Chikuzen province (Fukuoka pref.) in Kyūshū. It has a *suguha-komidare hamon*, a *itame-mokume hada*, a *ko-maru bōshi* with *haki-kake* and a short *kaeri* (turnback). The overall shape is somewhat rustic. It has two *mekugi-ana* in the *nakago* as the cutting-edge length appears to have been shortened slightly, but retains its original shape.

The *han-dachi* style *koshirae* has matching fittings made from *suaca* (Japanese copper) engraved with tendrils. The iron *tsuba* is engraved with fans and Japanese characters. The black lacquered *saya* has a short leather cover.

SANADA YUKIMURA (1567–1615)

Sanada (Nobushige) Yukimura was the second son of Sanada Masayuki who had been a retainer of both Takeda Shingen and his son Katsuyori. Following the Katsuyori's defeat at Nagashino, Masayuki inherited the Sanada clan, along with Ueda Castle in Shinano province (Nagano Prefecture). He pledged his loyalty to Oda Nobunaga, but following Oda's demise at Honnō-ji, the clan became independent until they eventually pledged allegiance to Toyotomi Hideyoshi. Yukimura garnered fame as an exemplary warrior during Hideyoshi's Korean campaigns. His real name was Nobushige, but due to the popularity of Edo period fiction that used the name Yukimura, he has become more popularly known by that name.

Following Hideyoshi's death, in the lead up to Sekigahara, the Sanada clan had agreed to support Tokugawa Ieyasu. In a surprising move, Yukimura and his father, Masayuki, suddenly decided to side with Ishida Mitsunari, while Yukimura's older brother, Nobuyuki, remained with Tokugawa Ieyasu. It is theorized that this was a plan to guarantee the survival of the Sanada clan whatever the outcome of the power struggle.

In 1600, Tokugawa Ieyasu's son, Hidetada, laid siege to Ueda castle on his way to support his father in the Battle of Sekigahara. Heavily outnumbered, Yukimura managed to resist Hidetada's forces until they gave up and left. Hidetada's loss was two-fold as the unsuccessful siege also made him too late to participate in his father's victory. Later, Ueda castle was confiscated and given to Nobuyuki, while Yukimura and Masayuki were exiled to Mt. Kōya in Kii province (Wakayama Prefecture).

Yukimura continued to support the Toyotomi clan in the wake of Sekigahara, and etched his name in samurai history at the Siege of Ōsaka castle in 1615. He built a small earthwork fortress called 'Sanada-Maru,' where he successfully repelled Tokugawa forces during the winter campaign, but following concessions made during a truce, he and his troops were finally overwhelmed in the summer campaign, and he was finally killed by Nishio Munetsugu.

華
幸村
一魁斎芳年

TACHI
太刀

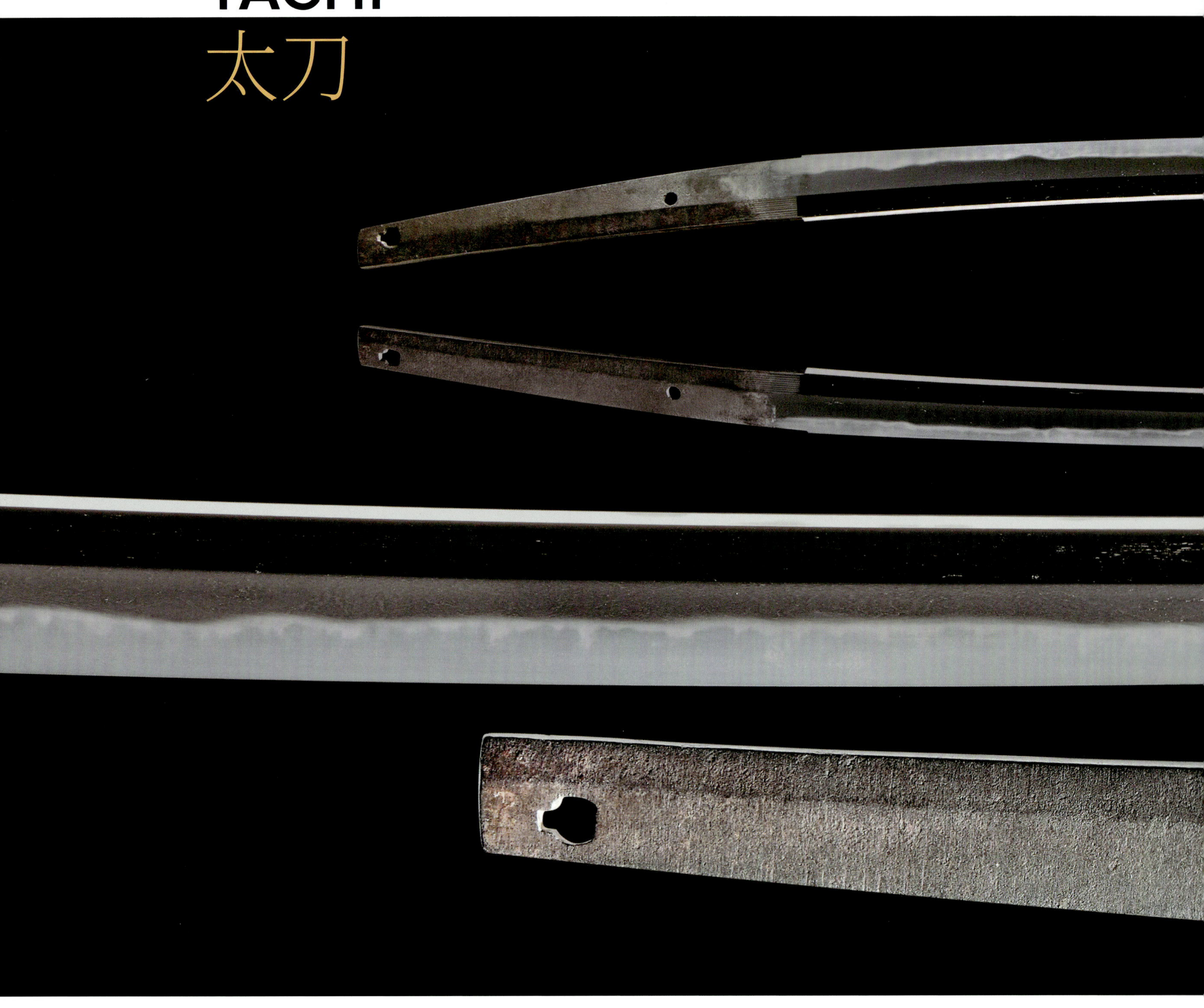

● UNSIGNED **ATTRIBUTED TO KUNIYUKI**
OTHER NAME(S) HABAKI-KUNIYUKI
CUTTING-EDGE LENGTH **72.1 CM (28⅜ IN)**
CURVATURE **2 CM (25/32 IN)**

PERIOD **KAMAKURA PERIOD, 13TH C.**
SENDAI CITY MUSEUM, MIYAGI PREFECTURE
Important Cultural Property

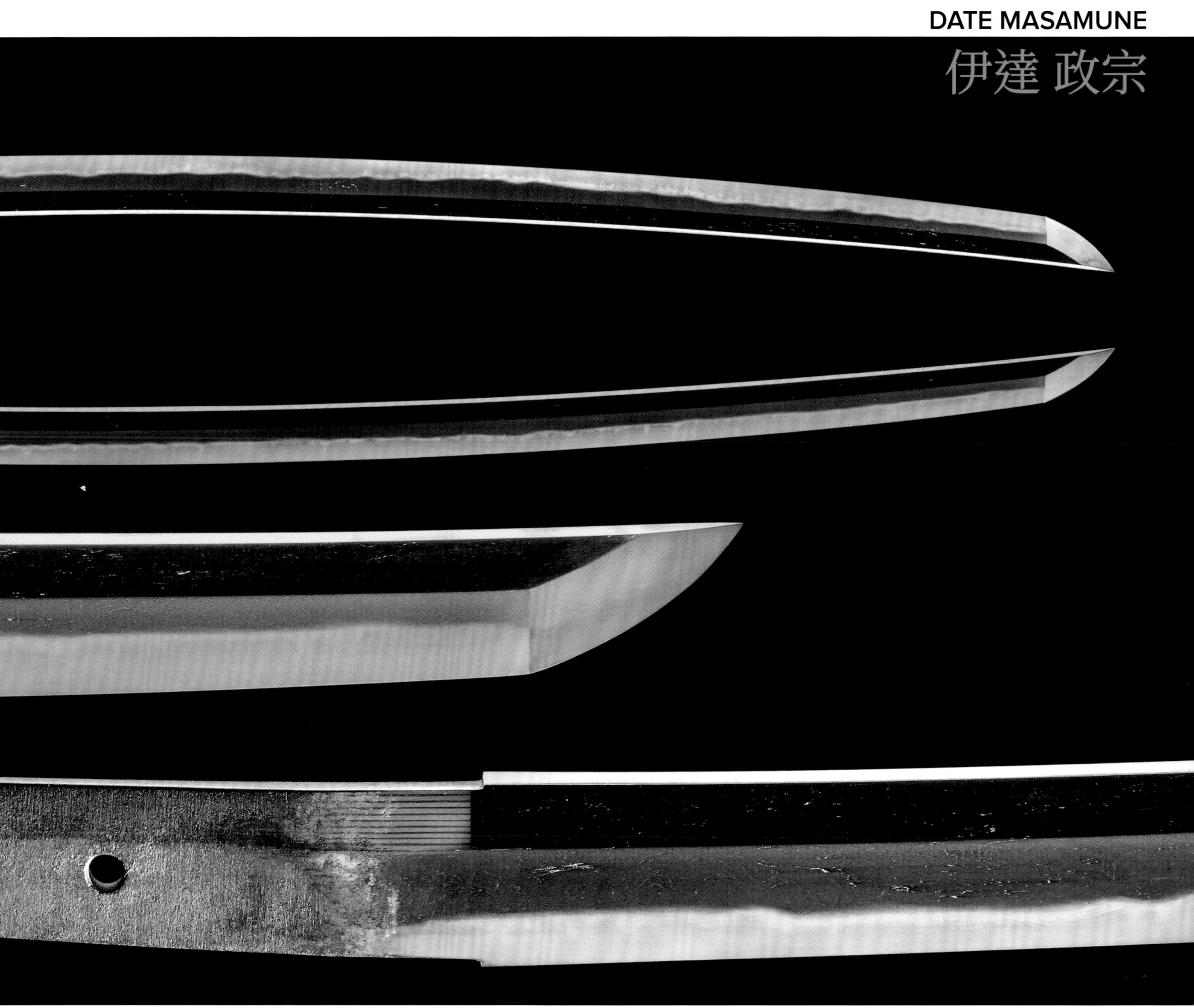
伊達 政宗

Tsukioka Yoshitoshi (1839–1892), *Date Shōshō Masamune in Armor Looking at Banner*, from the series *Selection of One Hundred Warriors*, 1868.

TACHI

The *tachi*, Habaki-Kuniyuki, was given to Date Masamune by Toyotomi Hideyoshi in 1589. It is called the Habaki-Kuniyuki as it is said to have been made by the founder of the Rai school, Kuniyuki, of Yamashiro province (Kyōto). However, it was greatly shortened at some point in its history, and lost the maker's signature. When a new gold-foil double *habaki* was made for it, the characters for Kuni and Yuki were carved into each side of the *habaki* giving rise to its name.

DATE MASAMUNE (1567–1636)

Date Masamune contracted small pox as a child, and as a result, lost the sight in his right eye. It is unclear how the situation progressed, but he eventually lost the eye completely. Due to this he was known as *the one-eyed dragon* (Dokuganryū). He is popularly portrayed in dramas and movies with a sword guard as an eye patch, but this seems to be a romantic addition.

In 1581, Masamune led his first battle aged 14, when his father was fighting the Sōma clan. His father, Terumune, retired as *daimyō* in 1584, and made seventeen-year-old Masamune the head of the clan. Later, Terumune was kidnapped by Nihonmatsu Yoshitsugu. However, both Terumune and Yoshitsugu were killed during a rescue attempt. The Date clan fought many battles with their neighbors with Masamune at the helm. He became a fearsome commander. However, he acquiesced to the power of Toyotomi Hideyoshi, but after Hideyoshi's death, Masamune supported Tokugawa Ieyasu, fighting for him in the Sekigahara campaigns and the following sieges of Ōsaka castle.

Tokugawa gave Masamune the Domain of Sendai, of which he turned a small fishing village into a thriving city, which is known today as Sendai City, Miyagi Prefecture.

大膳大夫政
大橋

HABAKI

KUNI

YUKI

At some point in its history, a new gold-foil double *habaki* was made for the Kuniyuki *tachi*. The characters for Kuni and Yuki were carved into each side of the *habaki* giving rise to its name.

This imposing *gomai-dō* (five plate construction cuirass) armor was worn by Date Masamune. It is mostly black lacquer on iron plates with gold colored trim, and has a large gold colored helmet decoration of a crescent moon. It is said that this armor was the inspiration for Darth Vader's costume in the *Star Wars* movie series.

KATCHŪ

甲冑

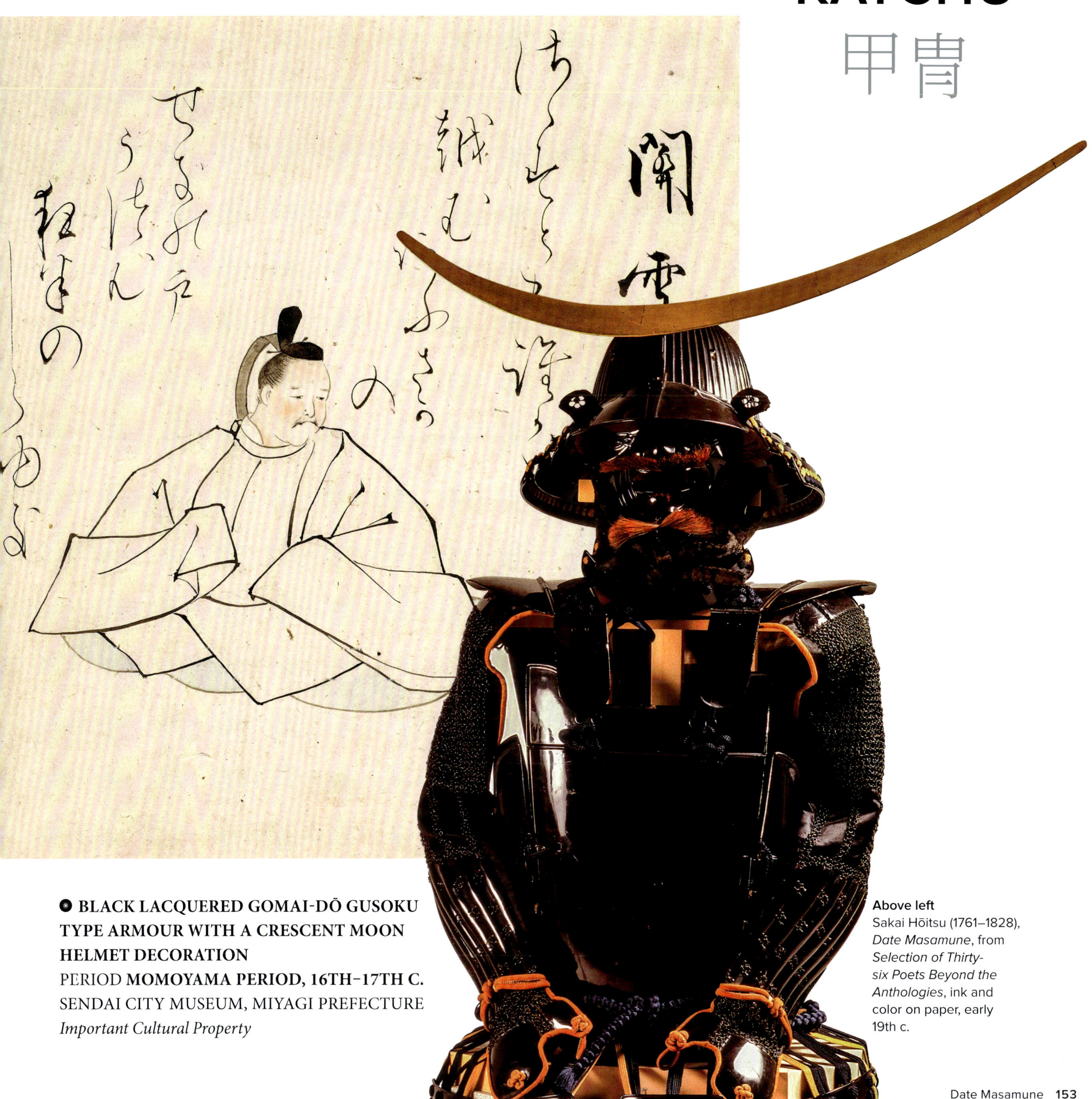

BLACK LACQUERED GOMAI-DŌ GUSOKU TYPE ARMOUR WITH A CRESCENT MOON HELMET DECORATION
PERIOD **MOMOYAMA PERIOD, 16TH–17TH C.**
SENDAI CITY MUSEUM, MIYAGI PREFECTURE
Important Cultural Property

Above left
Sakai Hōitsu (1761–1828), *Date Masamune*, from *Selection of Thirty-six Poets Beyond the Anthologies*, ink and color on paper, early 19th c.

TŌSŌGU
刀装具

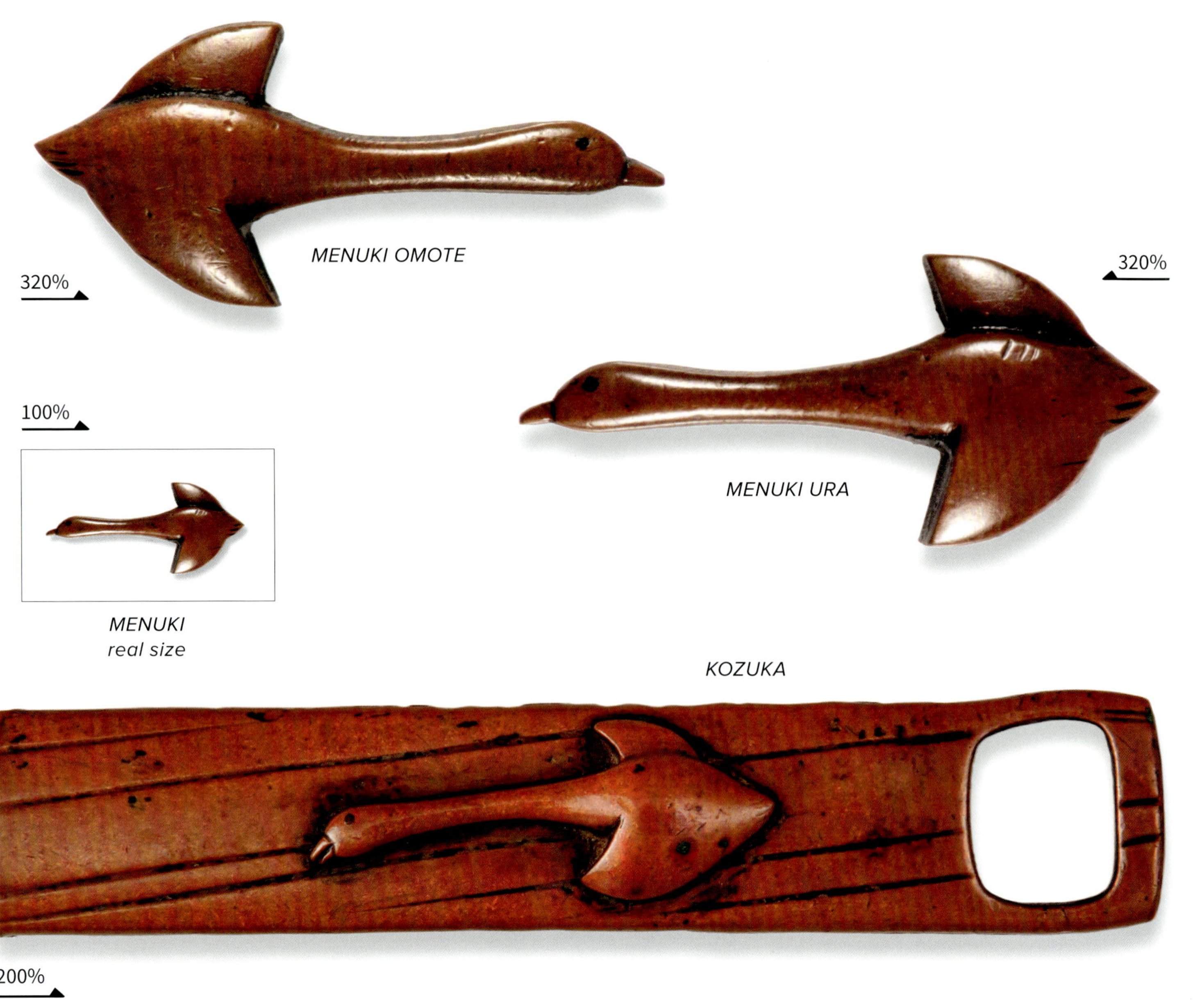

MENUKI OMOTE

MENUKI URA

MENUKI
real size

KOZUKA

● **MENUKI**
ATTRIBUTED TO MIYAMOTO MUSASHI
OMOTE LENGTH **3.3 CM (1 9/32 IN)**
WIDTH AT WINGS **1.4 CM (9/16 IN)**
WIDTH AT HEAD **3.8 MM (5/32 IN)**
URA LENGTH **3.3 CM (1 9/32 IN)**
WIDTH AT WINGS **1.5 CM (19/32 IN)**
WIDTH AT HEAD **3.8 MM (5/32 IN)**
PERIOD **EDO PERIOD, 17TH C.**
KAWABATA TERUTAKA COLLECTION

● **KOZUKA**
ATTRIBUTED TO MIYAMOTO MUSASHI
LENGTH **9.8 CM (3 27/32 IN)** - WIDTH **2.1 CM (13/16 IN)**
PERIOD **EDO PERIOD, 17TH C.**
EISEI BUNKO MUSEUM, TŌKYŌ

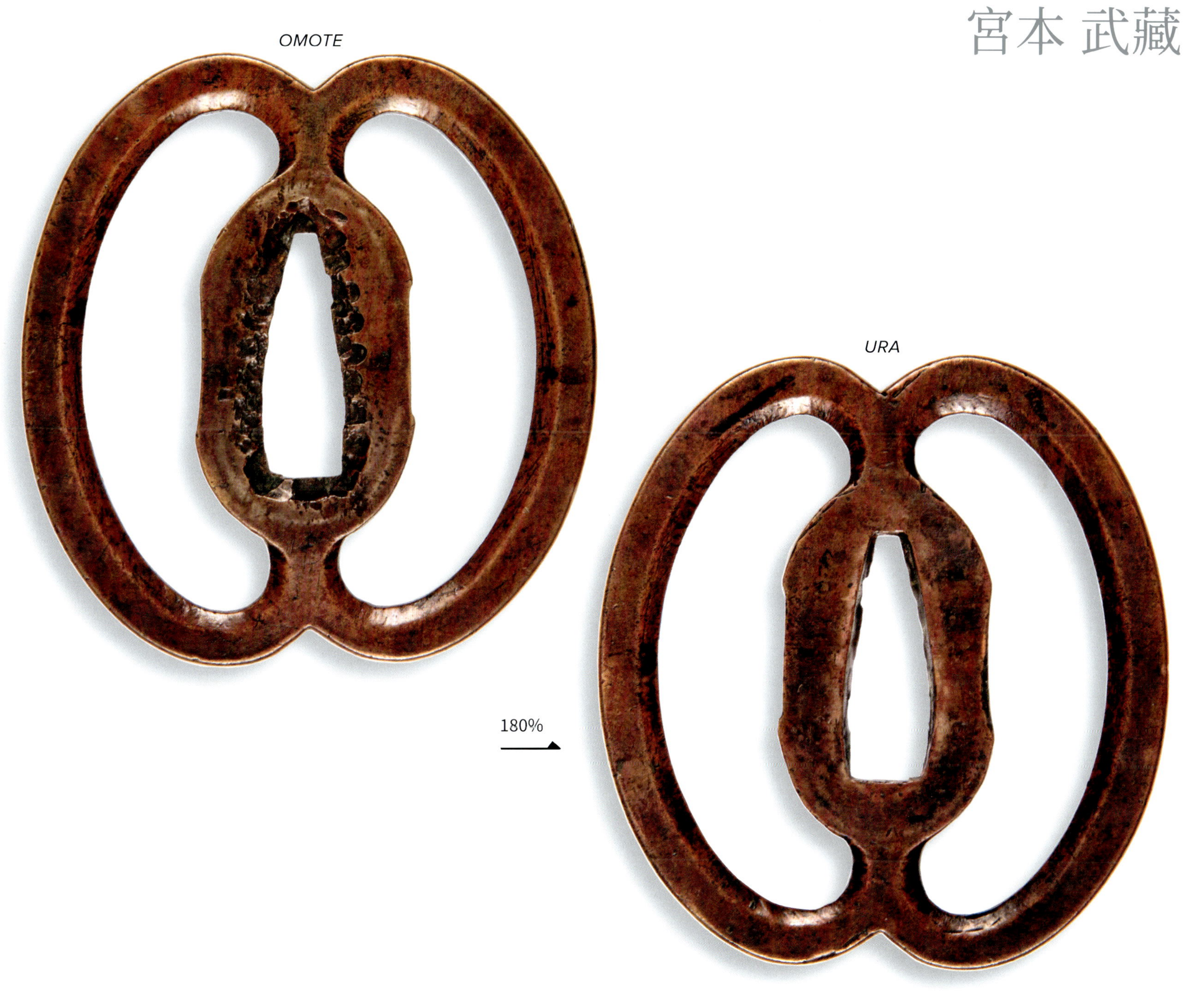

● **TSUBA**
ATTRIBUTED TO MIYAMOTO MUSASHI
OTHER NAME(S): **MUSASHI TSUBA, SAYŪ NAMAKO-SUKASHI TSUBA**
HEIGHT **7.2 CM (2 27/32 IN)** - WIDTH **6.9 CM (2 23/32 IN)** - DEPTH **3.9 MM (5/32 IN)**

PERIOD **EDO PERIOD, 17TH C.**
KAWABATA TERUTAKA COLLECTION

宮本武蔵

TŌSŌGU

These *menuki* (decorative hand grips) are made from Japanese copper (*suaca*) and feature geese in flight. The matching *kozuka* (decorative handle for a utility knife), is also made in *suaca* with a goose in flight design. The set was given to Musashi's student Terao and then passed down for many generations in the Hosokawa family. It is the only known *kozuka* in existence made by Musashi.

It is said that following Musashi's enlightenment he began to excel in many things, calligraphy, painting, sculpture, and making sword fittings. This *suaca tsuba* is one of several that have been attributed to the hand of Musashi. He also made other *tsuba* and *menuki*, but this design is his most famous and has been replicated many times by craftsman and on mass-production swords. It is a *tsuba* design called *sayū namako-sukashi* (pierced), as it is a symmetrical depiction of two sea cucumbers.

BOKUTŌ

This wooden sword was made by Miyamoto Musashi at the request of the lord of Matsui Castle, Matsui Yoriyuki. He asked Musashi to make a *bokutō* (wooden sword) to the same dimensions as he had used in his last duel on Ganryūjima. The *bokutō* is of fairly standard dimensions ensuring its ease of use, just in an extended length.

MIYAMOTO MUSASHI (ca. 1584–1645)

Miyamoto Musashi is engrained in the minds of most Japanese and non-Japanese alike as a most fearless and famous warrior. He was a master duelist killing his first opponent aged thirteen, and winning sixty duels. He formed the Ni-Ten Ichi Ryū school of swordsmanship and attained spiritual enlightenment before writing his treatise on sword combat, *The Book of Five Rings*, that has been translated many times and published all around the world. However, his history has become muddied with fiction from *kabuki* plays, the novel by Eiji Yoshikawa and various movies and manga.

His last duel on Ganryūjima (formerly Funajima), with a man said to be Sasaki Kojirō, has also been heavily embroidered and is beset by several theories. However, the oldest actual surviving record of Musashi's life is inscribed on a monument that stands in Kokura Park, Kyūshū, that was written and commissioned by his adopted son, Miyamoto Iori. It quite simply states that he had a duel on the island with a man known as Ganryū and that he beat him with a long wooden sword. In later years, the lord of Yatsushiro castle, Matsui Yoriyuki, asked Musashi to make him a replica of the wooden sword that he used in the duel. That wooden sword is in the collection of the Yatsushiro Municipal Museum in Kumamoto. It is a standard wooden sword but with an extended length of 126.7 cm ($49\frac{29}{32}$ in).

BOKUTŌ – ATTRIBUTED TO MIYAMOTO MUSASHI
LENGTH **126.7 CM ($49\frac{29}{32}$ IN)**

PERIOD **EDO PERIOD, 17TH C.**
YATSUSHIRO MUNICIPAL MUSEUM, KUMAMOTO PREF.

Utagawa Yoshifusa (act. c. 1840–1860), *The Famous Duel between the Sword Master Miyamoto Musashi (left) and Sasaki Kojirō (Ganryū) on the Island Later Named Ganryū-jima*, c. 1843–1847.

Left
Utagawa Kuniyoshi (1797–1861), central part of a triptych, *Miyamoto Musashi*, from the series *Selection of Eight Views [of Heroes]*, c. 1843–1847.

Right
Utagawa Yoshiiku (1833–1904, also known as Ochiai Yoshiiku), *Miyamoto Musashi Masana and the Old Man of Kasahara (Kasahara okina)*, from the series *Modern Parodies of Genji*, chapter 29 (*Miyuki*), 1863.

宮本無三四政名
笠原翁
一恵斎芳幾画

TSUBA
鍔

大石良雄所
用鍔有相得之
呈籠手田君
（鐵舟居士印）

大石良雄所
用鍔有相得之
呈籠手田君
(鐵舟居士印)

"I ACQUIRED THIS TSUBA THAT BELONGED TO ŌISHI YOSHIO, SO I'LL PRESENT IT TO MR. KOTEDA (YASUSADA)"
(TESSHŪ'S SEAL)

大石 内蔵助

● UNSIGNED
OTHER NAME **SHIHŌ FUTATSU-DOMOE TSUBA**
HEIGHT **9 CM (3 17/32 IN)** - WIDTH **8.6 CM (3 3/8 IN)**
- THICKNESS **3 MM (3/32 IN)**

PERIOD **MID-EDO PERIOD, LATE 17TH C.**
KAWABATA TERUTAKA COLLECTION
TERUTAKA

Right
Tsukioka Yoshitoshi (1839–1892), *Ōishi Kuranosuke Yoshitaka, Leader of the Forty-Seven Loyal Retainers*, from the series *A Mirror of Filial Piety in Japan*, 1881.

Opposite
Tsukioka Yoshitoshi (1839–1892), *Ōishi Kuranosuke Yoshio Leading the Night Attack on Kira's Mansion*, from the series *Twenty-four Accomplishments in Imperial Japan*, 1881.

TSUBA

This *tsuba* is said to have belonged to Ōishi Kuranosuke. The box it is kept in has an inscription written by Yamaoka Tesshū attesting to its authenticity from when he presented it to one of his top students, Koteda Yasusada. It is a blackened iron *tsuba* with gold colored applied metal in the form of stylized *futatsu-domoe* (two comma shape) crest badge in each of the four corners (*shihō*).

ŌISHI KURANOSUKE (1659–1703)

Ōishi (Yoshio) Kuranosuke is famous as the leader of the Forty-Seven Rōnin. His Lord, Asano Naganori of Akō, Harima province (Hyōgo pref.), attacked Lord Kira Yoshinaka, a master of ceremonies, inside the precincts of Edo castle. The act of drawing a sword in the castle was forbidden. Therefore, Asano was forced to give up all his lands and commit *seppuku* (ritual suicide). The story of the Forty-Seven Rōnin is another historical tale that has been distorted by fictional accounts. The story has always been told that Kira was an unpleasant and corrupt individual who had tried to exploit Asano for gifts in order to teach him correct etiquette. When Asano refused, Kira did not teach him properly and Asano lost face at an important event at the castle. In a rage, Asano drew his short sword and attacked Kira. However, supporters of Kira have for many years complained that the story is one sided, and that Kira was not the evil man he is depicted as in the story.

In any case, the facts of Forty-Seven Rōnin are just as worthy as any fiction. Their revenge killing of Kira was against the law. In which case, they should have simply been executed as criminals. However, after a hundred years of peace in Japan, public opinion was in favor of the Akō-Rōnin as they had upheld the samurai codes of ethics. In a compromise, and recognition of their samurai beliefs, they were granted permission to commit ritual suicide.

Kuranosuke's *seppuku* (ritual suicide) took place along with 16 other members at the Hosokawa clan's Edo (Tōkyō) residence in Takanawa (Minato ward). The site is marked with stone monument. The remains of Kira's Edo (Tōkyō) mansion can still be visited in Ryōgoku, Sumida ward.

二十四功
大蘇芳年筆

KATANA

刀

● **KATANA**
SIGNED **NOBUKUNI (ORIKAESHI-MEI)**
CUTTING-EDGE LENGTH **67.7 CM ($26\frac{21}{32}$ IN)**
CURVATURE **1.7 CM ($\frac{21}{32}$ IN)**
PERIOD **ŌEI PERIOD, 15TH C.**
REIMEIKAN ARTS CENTER,
KAGOSHIMA PREFECTURE

● **WESTERN STYLE KOSHIRAE**
PERIOD **MEIJI PERIOD, 19TH C.**
REIMEIKAN ARTS CENTER, KAGOSHIMA PREFECTURE

Right
C. Nakagawa (?-?), *Photographic portrait of Saigō Takamori*, from the book *Kinsei Meishi Shashin* (Photographs of early modern celebrities), vol. 1, 1934–1935.

Opposite
Tsukioka Yoshitoshi (1839–1892), central part of a triptych, *The Ritual Suicide of Saigō Takamori*, 1877.

KATANA and **KOSHIRAE**

This sword is said to have been worn by Saigō Takamori and is the one depicted on his statue in Kagoshima city. The blade has been shortened, but the signature has been preserved by folding it back into the opposite side of the tang (*orikaeshi-mei*). The mountings illustrate Japan's transition from samurai styles to that of western cavalry type sabers of the period. The blade has a two-character signature of Nobukuni. It is a rather slender blade but also has a large point section.

The hilt and scabbard were originally covered in shagreen and it has brass fittings. It is thought that this particular set of mountings was based on similar styles used by the French military.

SAIGŌ TAKAMORI (1828–1877)

Saigō Takamori was a warrior of the Satsuma clan in Kyūshū. He is often referred to as 'The Last Samurai' because of his part in the Satsuma Rebellion and his death at the Battle of Shiroyama that was the basis for the plot of the Hollywood movie of the same name. There is a large statue of him that stands close to the entrance of Tōkyō's Ueno Park. It is a famous landmark and regularly used as a meeting point.

Despite the Tokugawa peaceful surrender and transference of power back to the Meiji Emperor, Saigō wanted more. He desired that they had their land confiscated and status removed. His inflexibility on this point is thought to be the catalyst that led to the Boshin war. The Satchō Alliance (Satsuma and Chōshū clans) fought against Tokugawa forces at Toba-Fushimi in Kyōto, eventually obtaining imperial status, and declaring the Tokugawa forces the enemy of the Emperor. Saigō's forces eventually reached Edo and accepted the surrender of Edo castle from Katsu Kaishū. Meanwhile, the Boshin war continued deep into Aizu, and the final battles with the newly formed Ezo Republic in Hakodate.

Saigō became something of a national hero and accepted a position in the new Meiji government. However, finally becoming disgruntled with the way the government was operating, he resigned and went back to the Satsuma stronghold of Kagoshima. This eventually led to government fears of a Satsuma rebellion. The new government sent warships down to Kagoshima requesting the Satsuma clan to disarm. However, this had the reverse effect of what was intended sparking the Satsuma Rebellion. The final conflict was at Shiroyama in Kagoshima. The Satsuma forces were surrounded and outnumbered by the imperial forces when Saigō took a gunshot to the hip. The popular story is that, realizing his fate, he took a sword and plunged it into his stomach to commit *seppuku* and a comrade stepped in to take his head. However, accounts are mixed and whether he actually cut his own stomach is unclear. He remains a popular hero in Japan today.

西郷吉之助隆盛

KATANA

刀

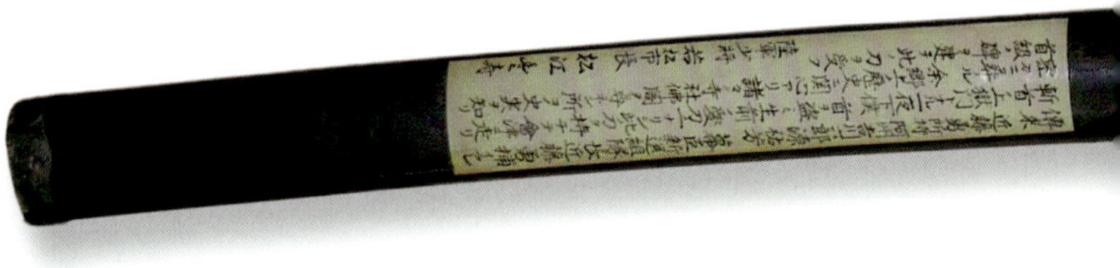

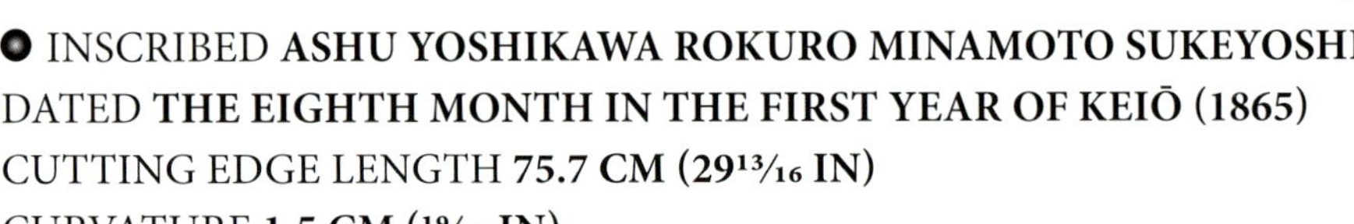

● INSCRIBED **ASHU YOSHIKAWA ROKURO MINAMOTO SUKEYOSHI**
DATED **THE EIGHTH MONTH IN THE FIRST YEAR OF KEIŌ (1865)**
CUTTING EDGE LENGTH **75.7 CM (29 13/16 IN)**
CURVATURE **1.5 CM (19/32 IN)**

PERIOD **EDO PERIOD, 19TH C.**
RYŌZEN MUSEUM OF HISTORY, KYŌTO

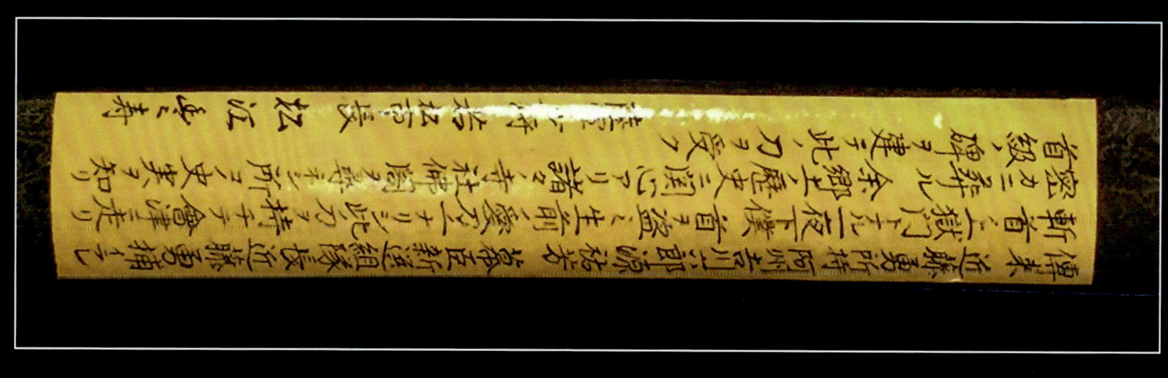

● **KATANA KOSHIRAE** (FOR SUKEYOSHI BLADE))
PERIOD **EDO PERIOD, 19TH C.**
RYŌZEN MUSEUM OF HISTORY, KYŌTO

Right
Anonymous, Photographic portrait of Kondō Isami, pre-1868.

Opposite
Tsukioka Yoshitoshi (1839–1892), *Kondō Isami with Sword*, from the series *New Tales of Honor*, 1875.

KATANA and KOSHIRAE

This sword has a *sayagaki* written by former Major-General Matsue Toyohisa who was the Mayor of Aizu-Wakamatsu, Fukushima prefecture, in the late Taishō era. Matsue was a scholar of the Boshin war, and used to pay his respects by visiting the graves of famous warriors. He heard of Kondō Isami's grave in Tennei-ji temple, Wakamatsu city. When he went to visit it, the priest told him that in the spring of 1868, someone had stolen Kondō's head from Sanjō Bridge in Kyōto and brought it with Kondō's sword to the temple. They buried Kondō's head and entrusted his sword to the temple. The sword was acquired by, and is on display, at the Ryōzen Museum of History in Kyōto that is dedicated to the heroes of the Bakumatsu era and the Meiji Restoration.

The scabbard is black *ishime* (stone ground) lacquer with heavenly clouds motif. The *fuchi/kashira*, *menuki* and *kojiri* are all matching with chrysanthemum designs. The *tsuka* (hilt) is wrapped in white ray-skin (*samekawa*) with a further wrap of black silk cord. The *tsuba* is in a four-leaf clover design. If you look carefully at the *tsuba* of the *wakizashi* in the portraits of Kondō, you can see that it is similar to the one on this sword.

KONDŌ ISAMI (1834–1868)

Kondō Isami was born Miyagawa Katsugoro in Kamiishihara village (Chōfu city, Tōkyō). He was a practitioner of Tennen-Rishin-Ryū swordsmanship. Katsugoro caught the attention of the third headmaster of the school, Kondō Shusuke, after he successfully defeated a group of thieves who had tried to break into his home. Shusuke adopted him as his son and heir. He went on to become the fourth headmaster of the school and changed his name to Kondō Isami. Later, he was employed by the Tokugawa shogunate in 1863 as part of a group known as the 'Rōshigumi.'

This group eventually came under the command of the Lord of Aizu, Matsudaira Katamori, and was renamed 'the Shinsengumi.' They were directed to police Kyōto, with Kondō becoming the commander of the group. One of their greatest achievements was the Ikedaya Affair, where they successfully fought and arrested a group plotting against the shogunate. It was in that incident that Kondō was said to have used and praised his Kotetsu sword. The sword's whereabouts is currently unknown, and there is much debate as to whether it was an actual Kotetsu blade. After the fall of the Tokugawa shogunate, Kondō was eventually arrested and beheaded on May 17, 1868, in Itabashi, Tōkyō.

大蘇芳年

KATANA
刀

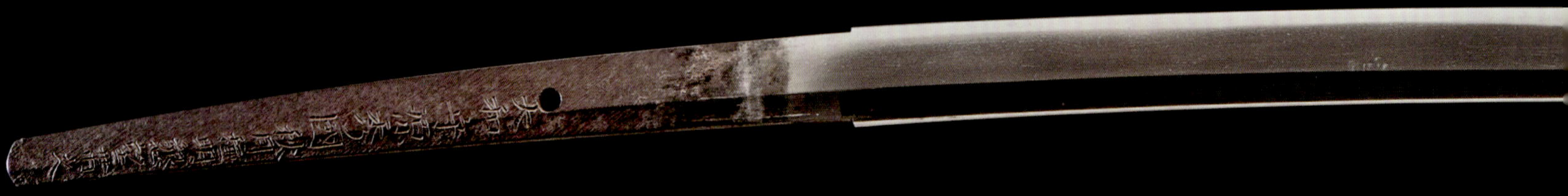

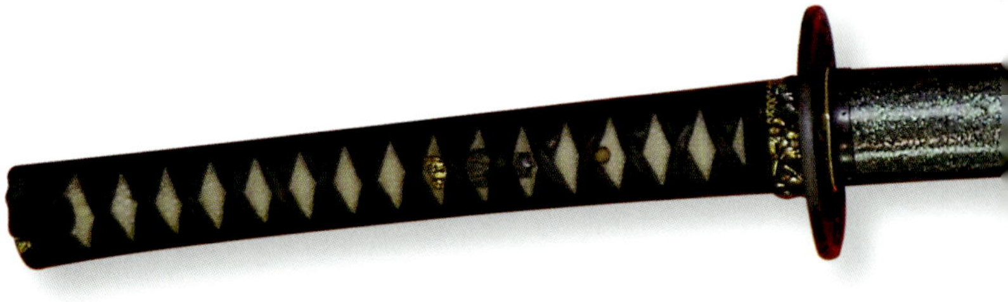

SODE-SHŌ (SHOULDER INSIGNIA)
PERIOD **LATE EDO PERIOD, 19TH C.**
RYŌZEN MUSEUM OF HISTORY, KYŌTO.

INSCRIBED
STRAIGHT **YAMATO NO KAMI MINAMOTO NO HIDEKUNI, AKIZUKI TANEAKI KONBŌ KORE WO TAISU**
REVERSE **KEIŌ NI NEN HACHI GATSU HI, BAKUFU SAMURAI HIJIKATA YOSHITOYO SENTŌ, AKIZUKI KUN YUZURIUKE TAKAHASHI TADAMORI KORE WO TAISU**
DATED **THE EIGHTH MONTH, IN THE SECOND YEAR OF KEIŌ (1866)**

HIJIKATA TOSHIZŌ
土方 歳三

CUTTING-EDGE LENGTH **68.7 CM (27 1/32 IN)**
CURVATURE **1.4 CM (9/16 IN)**
PERIOD **EDO PERIOD, 19TH C.**
RYŌZEN MUSEUM OF HISTORY, KYŌTO

● **KATANA KOSHIRAE** (FOR HIDEKUNI BLADE)
PERIOD **EDO PERIOD, 19TH C.**
RYŌZEN MUSEUM OF HISTORY, KYŌTO

Right
Anonymous, Photographic portrait of Hijikata Toshizō, ca. 1866–1869. The Western-style dress the samurai wears in this photograph is the same as the image sent to his brother-in-law Satō Hikogorō shortly before his death.

KATANA, KOSHIRAE and SODE-SHŌ

This sword is well known for being one of the treasured swords of the Shinsengumi vice-commander, Hijikata Toshizō. The sword was passed to Aizu clan samurai, Akizuki Taneaki, who had fought alongside Hijikata. It was later owned by civil rights activist, Muramatsu Benjirō, of Fuchū, Tōkyō. Later in 1903 (Meiji 36), Muramatsu gave it to his comrade, Yoshino Tainosuke. The blade has a *ko-itame hada*, with a *suguha, nioi-deki hamon*. It is inscribed with Hijikata's birth name of Yoshitoyo. It is one of a very small number of swords that has been proven to actually have been worn by a member of the Shinsengumi. The mountings have the warrior monk, Benkei, and plum blossom designs. The scabbard is decorated with sprinkled crushed shell and *urushi* lacquer. The *tsuba* is iron with pierced (*sukashi*) dragon design. The *tsuka* (hilt) has white ray skin that is wrapped with black silk cord in the *moro-tsumami* style. The *sode-shō* (shoulder insignia) were worn by members of the Shinsengumi to identify each other during a skirmish. It is thought that the *sode-shō* were widely used in place of a uniform that would immediately notify their enemies that they were approaching. Contrary to popular belief, the famous *haori* were rarely worn. In fact, there is not a single extant example.

HIJIKATA TOSHIZŌ (1835–1869)

Hijikata Toshizō was born in Ishida Village (Hino City, Tōkyō) in 1835. He originally worked for his family business selling medicine. His brother in law, Satō Hikogorō, ran a Tennen-Rishin-Ryū kenjutsu *dōjō*. Satō had also been a student of Kondō Shusuke. Hijikata was introduced to Kondō Isami and eventually enrolled into Kondō's Shieikan dōjō. When the Rōshigumi was formed, many members of the Tennen-Rishin-Ryū school signed up, Hijikata and Kondō included. Hijikata went on to become the Vice-Commander of the Shinsengumi. He and Kondō were appointed as Hatamoto in 1867. However, shortly after, the Shogunate fell and Kondō was executed.

Despite the Tokugawa surrender, Hijikata and some other surviving members of the Shinsengumi went north continuing to fight against the new government as part of the newly formed Ezo Republic (Hokkaidō). He was killed in the final battle of the Boshin War at Hakodate. The burial site of his body remains unknown. He is said to have sent his photograph, a sword and a lock of his hair back to Satō Hikogorō. The photograph shows, even by today's standards, what a handsome young man he was. This photograph has become very famous and reproduced many times. However, if you look closely at his right hip in this original photo, you can see that as well as having a sword he also has a holstered revolver.

According to the Hijikata family, the chain mail armor on the right was worn by Hijikata Toshizō during the Ikeda-ya Incident in Kyotō where the Shinsengumi thwarted the plans of a group of Sonnō Jōi Rōnin (masterless samurai) activists who were allegedly intending to set fire to Kyōto. Following the Shinsengumi's success in this raid their reputation soared.

KUSARI KATABIRA
(CHAIN MAIL ARMOR)
HELMET WEIGHT **3½ LBS (1.6 KGS)**
SLEEVES WEIGHT **10½ OZ (300 GRAMS)**
PERIOD **EDO PERIOD, 19TH C.**
HIJIKATA TOSHIZŌ MUSEUM,
HINO, TŌKYŌ

KATANA

● SIGNED **YOSHIYUKI**
CUTTING-EDGE LENGTH **66.7 CM (26¼ IN)**

PERIOD **LATE EDO PERIOD, 19TH C.**
KYOTO NATIONAL MUSEUM, KYŌTO

SAKAMOTO RYŌMA
坂本 龍馬

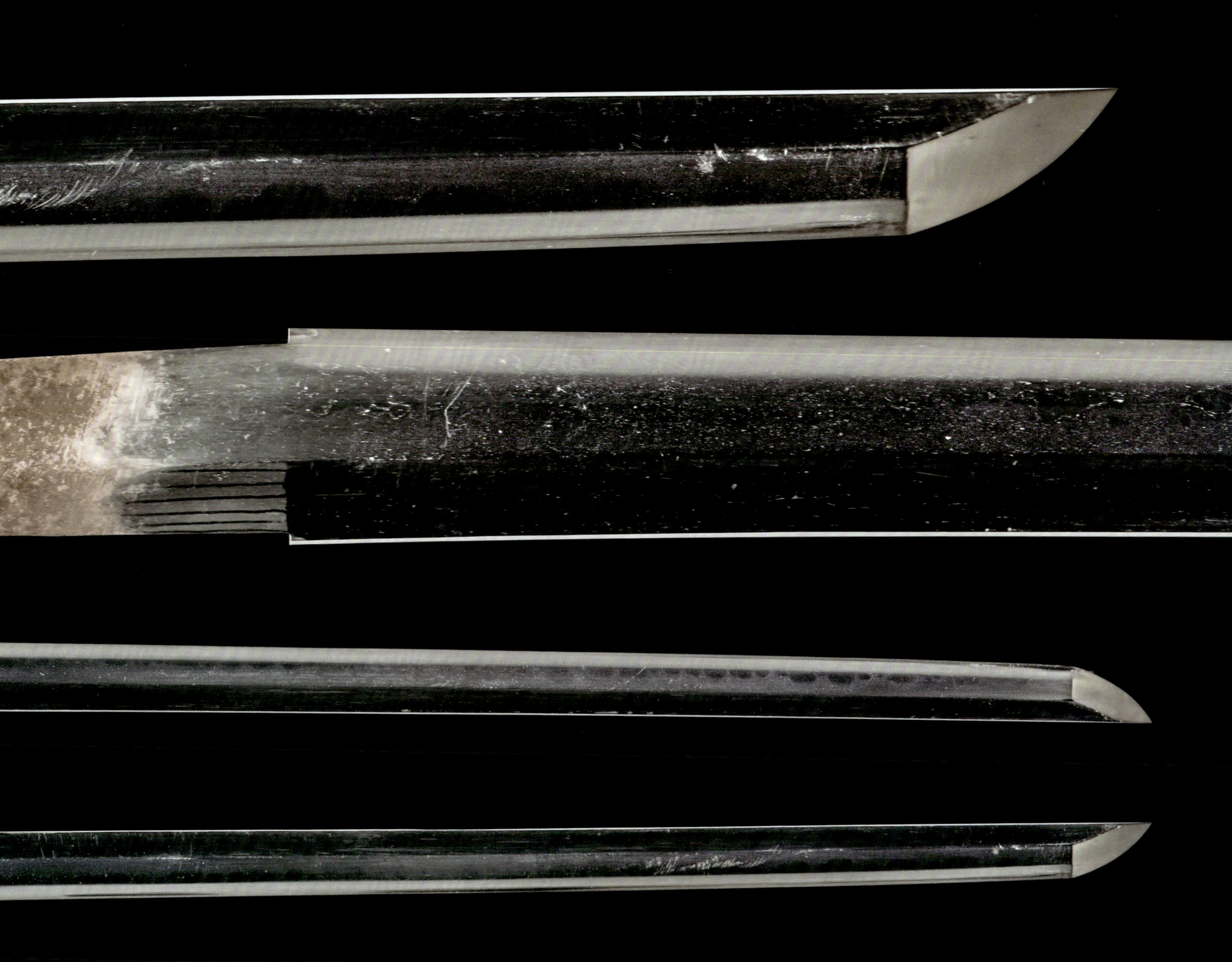

(Enlargement on pages 195–196–197–198)

Right
Anonymous, Photographic portrait of Sakamoto Ryōma seated, shot at the photographic studio of Ueno Hikoma (1838–1904) or in Fukui, 1867.

Opposite
Shunzō Inoue (?–?), Photographic portrait of Sakamoto Ryōma posing in his favorite Western-style shoes, ca. 1866.

坂本龍馬

KATANA

This *shinogi-zukuri* construction *katana* was unfortunately in fire. In addition to being irreparably damaged, the mountings were completely lost in the fire. It is attributed to the work of Mutsu no Kami Yoshiyuki (Yoshiyuki, Lord of Mutsu Province: Fukushima, Miyagi, Iwate and Aomori Prefectures) a swordsmith from Settsu (Ōsaka) who moved to the Tosa domain (Kōchi Prefecture). It was presented to Ryōma by his older brother, and said to be the sword that he had with him when he was assassinated. After his death, it was passed down within the Sakamoto line as a family treasure for several generations until they gifted it to Kyoto National Museum. In 2016, a document was discovered that gave the details of the sword being damaged in a fire in which its *hamon* and curvature were lost.

SAKAMOTO RYŌMA (1836-1867)

Sakamoto Ryōma was a lower tier samurai of the Tosa clan. He was already an accomplished swordsman while living in Tosa, but gained permission to travel to Edo (Tōkyō) where he enrolled in Hokushin Ittō-Ryū Hyōhō Chiba Dōjō where he was eventually awarded *shihan* (senior instructor) status.

Originally a follower of the Tosa faction of Sonnō Jōi ('Revere the emperor, Expel the Barbarians') movement, he decided that he should assassinate the Tokugawa modernist and reformer, Katsu Kaishū. However, Kaishū managed to persuade him into becoming his own student. As Sakamoto became a strong advocate of reformation in Japan he attracted the ire of both Tokugawa and anti-Tokugawa forces. He is also credited with negotiating the famous treaty between the Satsuma and Chōshū forces that created the Satchō-Alliance that eventually forced the Tokugawa surrender.

Sakamoto was assassinated along with his friend, Nakaoka Shintarō, in the Ōmi-ya, Soy sauce shop, that they were staying at in Kyōto. The site is now a Hoshino Coffee shop, in the Kawaramachi area of Kyōto. The shop has a small shrine on the second floor around the area where they were assassinated, and is decorated in their respective family crests. The *wakizashi* that is alleged to be the one that was used to kill Sakamoto was owned by Katsura Hayanosuke. It is signed, 'Echigo no Kami Kanesada', and is on permanent display at the Ryōzen Museum of History in Kyōto.

Sakamoto Ryōma and Nakaoka Shintarō's graves are close by in the mountainside of Ryōzen Gokoku Shrine, overlooking Kyōto.

KATANA
刀

● CONVERTED TACHI
UNSIGNED **ATTRIBUTED TO MASAMUNE**
OTHER NAME(S) (MEIBUTSU) **MUSASHI MASAMUNE**

PERIOD **LATE KAMAKURA PERIOD, 14TH C.**
THE JAPANESE SWORD MUSEUM, SUMIDA (TŌKYŌ)
Important Art Object

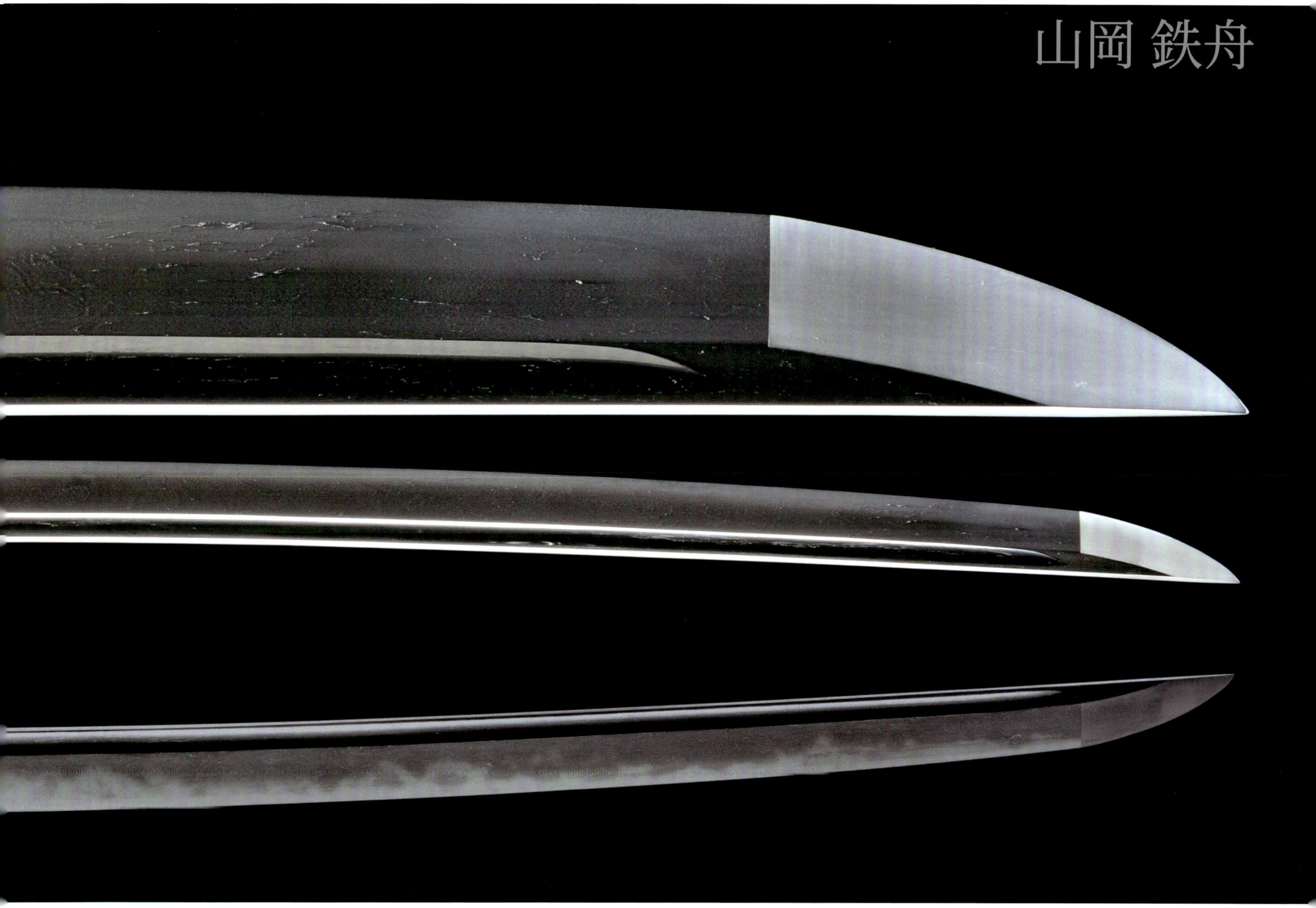

● **UCHI-GATANA KOSHIRAE** DENCHŪ-KOJIRI STORK LEG-SKIN WRAPPED SAYA
PERIOD **LATE EDO PERIOD, 19TH C.**
THE JAPANESE SWORD MUSEUM, SUMIDA (TŌKYŌ)

Right
Anonymous,
Photographic portrait of Yamaoka Tesshū at an older age, pre-1888.

Opposite
Anonymous,
Photographic portrait of Yamaoka Tesshū at a younger age.

KATANA (Converted Tachi) and **KOSHIRAE**

This unique *tachi koshirae* is almost '*kabuki*-esc' in its dimensions and appearance. It is also unique in that the scabbard is wrapped in stork's leg-skin, lacquered and decorated with *aoi-mon*. Tesshū was given this *tachi* by the last *shōgun*, Tokugawa Yoshinobu, for whom he worked as a bodyguard. It was later passed to Iwakura Tomomi.

This *ō-suriage* blade is attributed to Masamune and is recorded in the *Kyōhō Mei-butsu chō* as Musashi Masamune. It is a wide blade that is *shinogi-zukuri* in construction, with a *mitsu-mune*, a rather shallow curvature and a large point section. It has an *itame-hada* with thick *ji-nie*, *chikei* and *yubashiri*. The *hamon* is *ko-notare* with *gunome*, and lots of activies such as *ashi*, *sunagashi*, *kinsuji*, and some *tobi-yaki*.

YAMAOKA TESSHŪ (1836–1888)

Yamaoka Tesshū was an amazing character of the late Edo period. He was a master swordsman and founder of the Ittō Shōden Mutō-ryū (no-sword) style of swordsmanship.
He was born Ono Tetsutarō. His father was a retainer in the Tokugawa shogunate, and his mother was the daughter of a priest from Kashima shrine. He learned various styles of swordsmanship from a young age, eventually joining the Yamaoka Seizan school of spearmanship. Seizan passed away not long after Tesshū joined the school, so he married Seizan's sister and took the Yamaoka name to continue the school. Tesshū was also instrumental in the negotiations with Saigō Takamori and eventual surrender of Edo castle.

It is said that Tesshū split his day into four parts. Six hours sleeping, six hours swordsmanship, six hours calligraphy and six hours drinking. There are many examples of Tesshū's calligraphy that remain today. It is also said that he once tamed a wild horse without any prior experience. When he was asked how he did it, he replied, "I was rather drunk at the time and felt more confident than usual". There is a buckwheat noodle bar in Uguisudani Tōkyō, that serves Tesshū Soba. It is said that he gave the recipe to the original owner and wrote the calligraphy for the shop's *kanban* (shop sign). He died aged just fifty-two from stomach cancer. It is said that he faced death by first writing his death poem, then sitting in *seiza* (formal kneeling position). His death poem reads, *My stomach tightens from the pain inside, the sound of the morning crows.*

Toyohara Chikanobu (1838–1912), left and center parts of a triptych,
Record of the Subjugation of the Kagoshima Uprising, 1877.

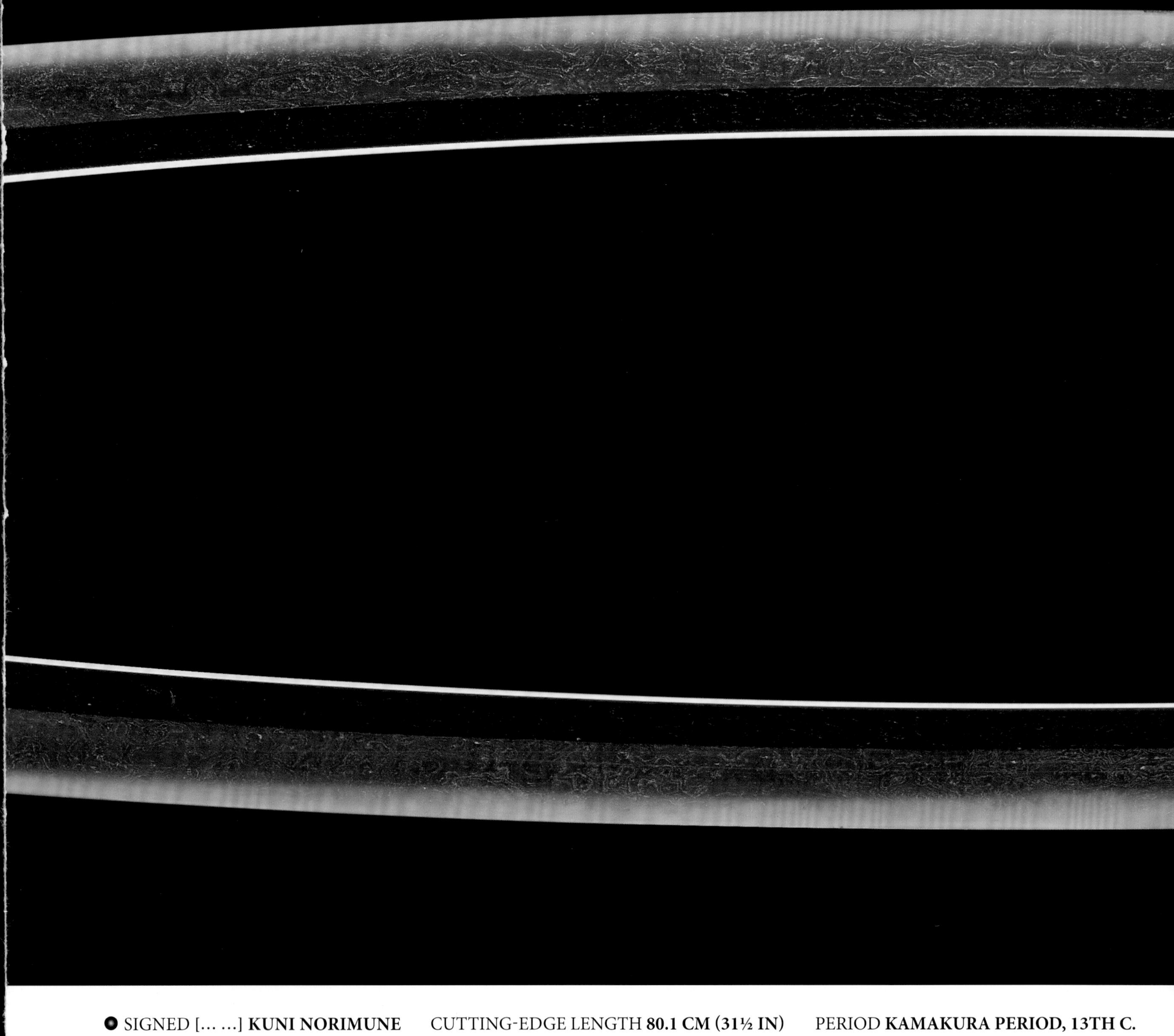

● SIGNED [… …] **KUNI NORIMUNE**
OTHER NAME(S) **SASA-MARU**

CUTTING-EDGE LENGTH **80.1 CM (31½ IN)**
CURVATURE **2.7 CM (1 IN)**

PERIOD **KAMAKURA PERIOD, 13TH C.**
Important Cultural Property

TACHI
太刀

94.3 %

太刀拵

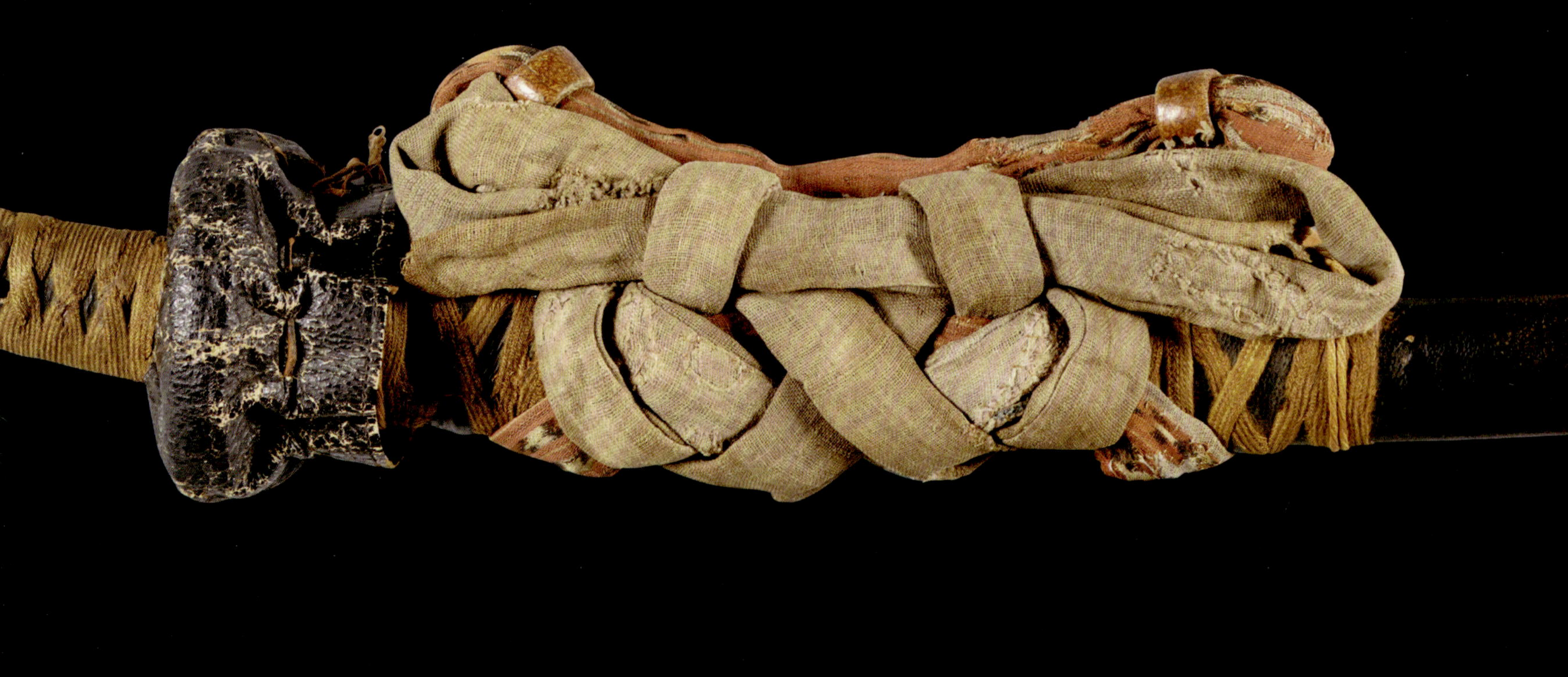

● KOSHIRAE FOR THE TACHI SIGNED [… …] **KUNI NORIMUNE** WHICH BELONGED TO **ASHIKAGA TAKAUJI**

PERIOD **NANBOKUCHŌ PERIOD, 14TH C.**
ATAGO SHRINE, KYŌTO

KATANA
刀

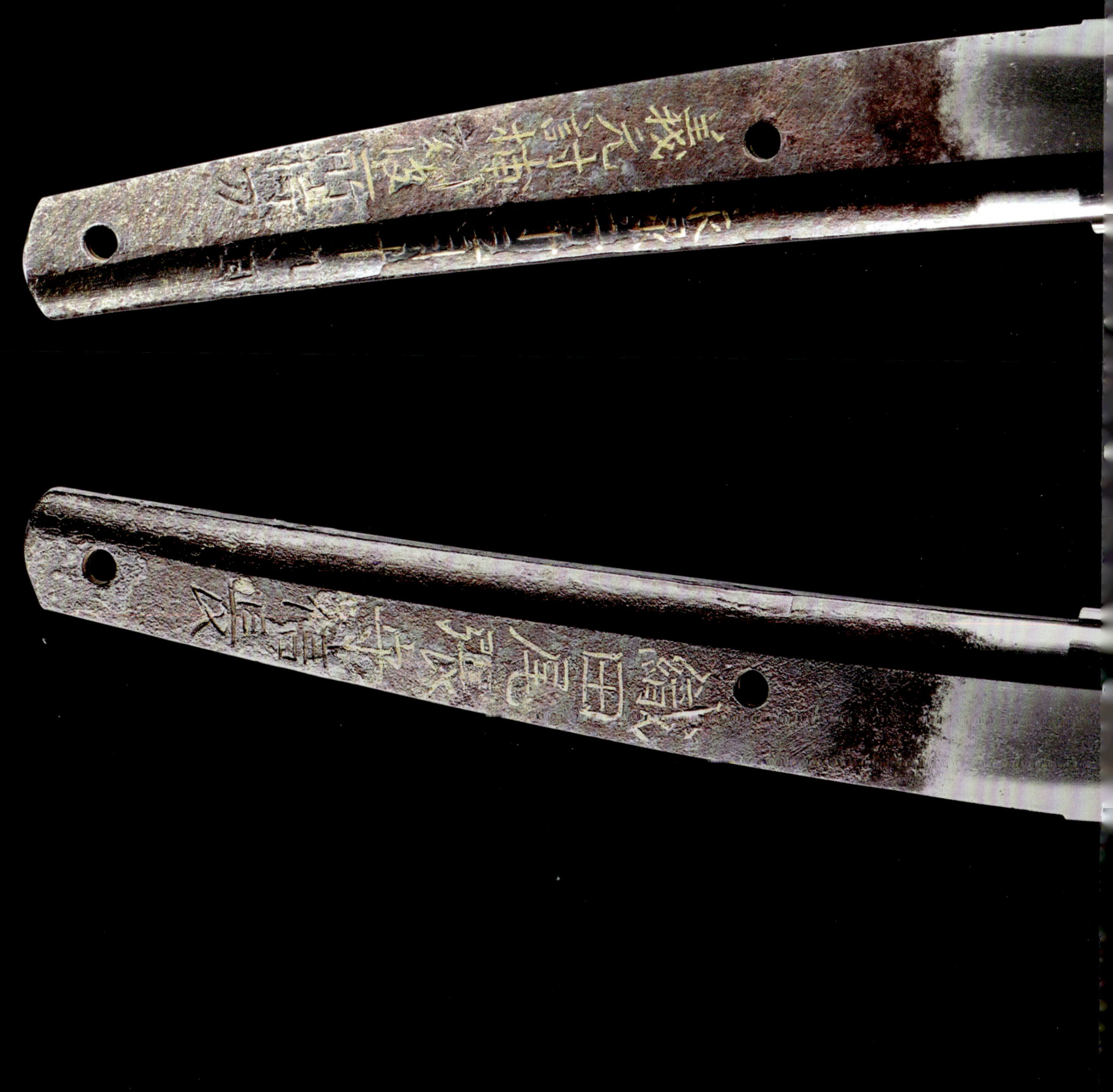

100%

ASHIKAGA TAKAUJI
足利 尊氏

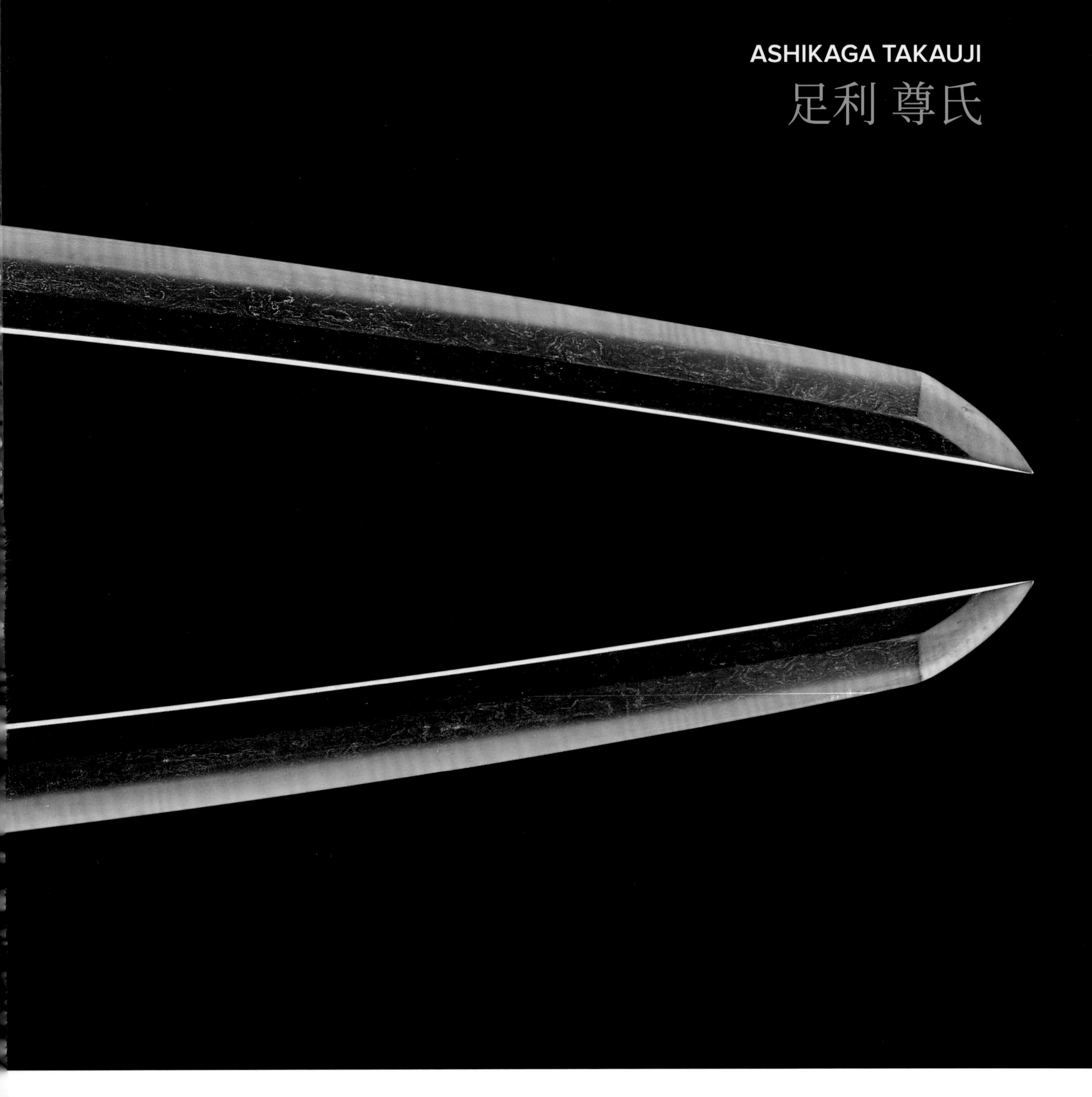

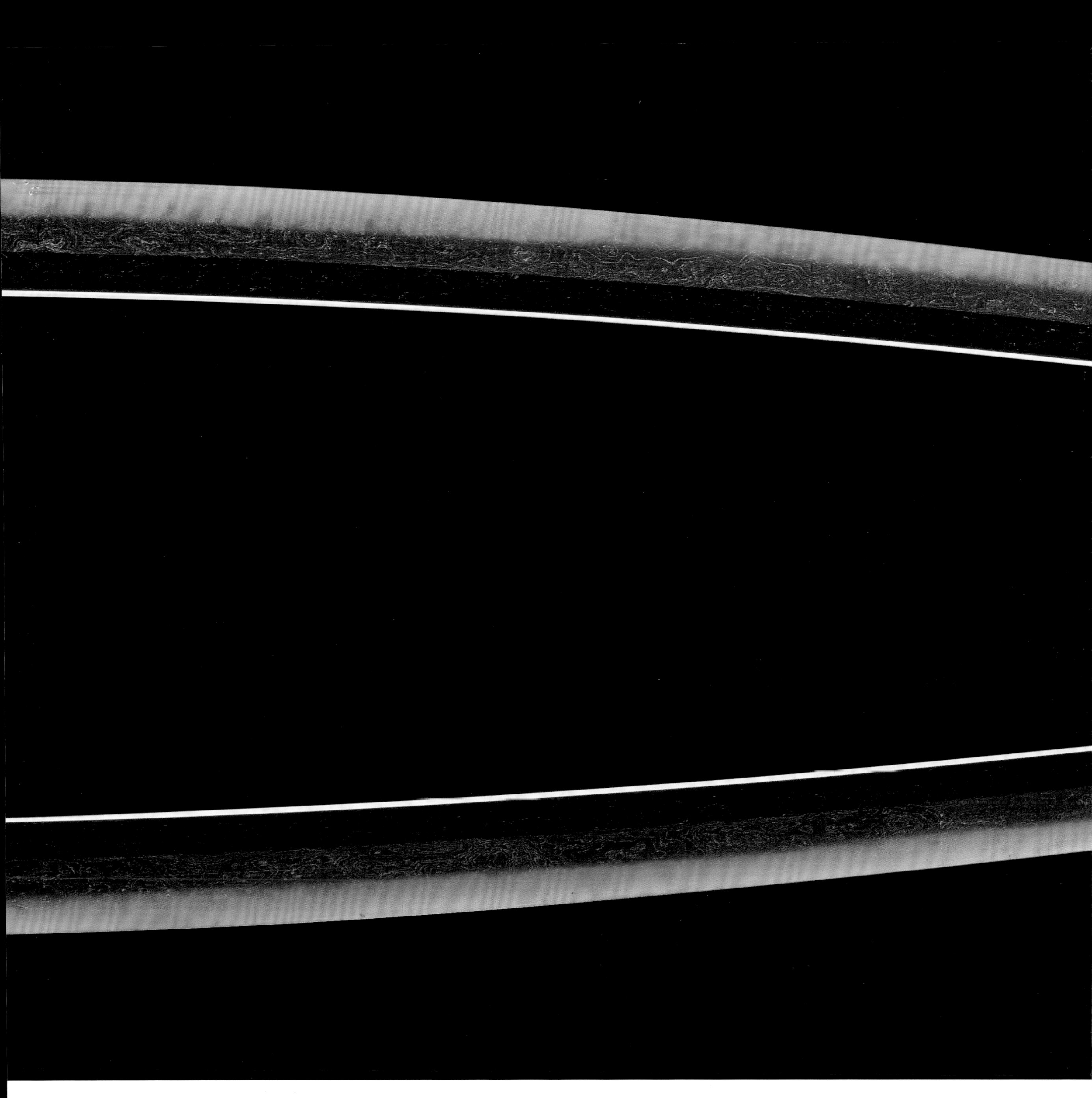

(Enlargement of pages 78–79)

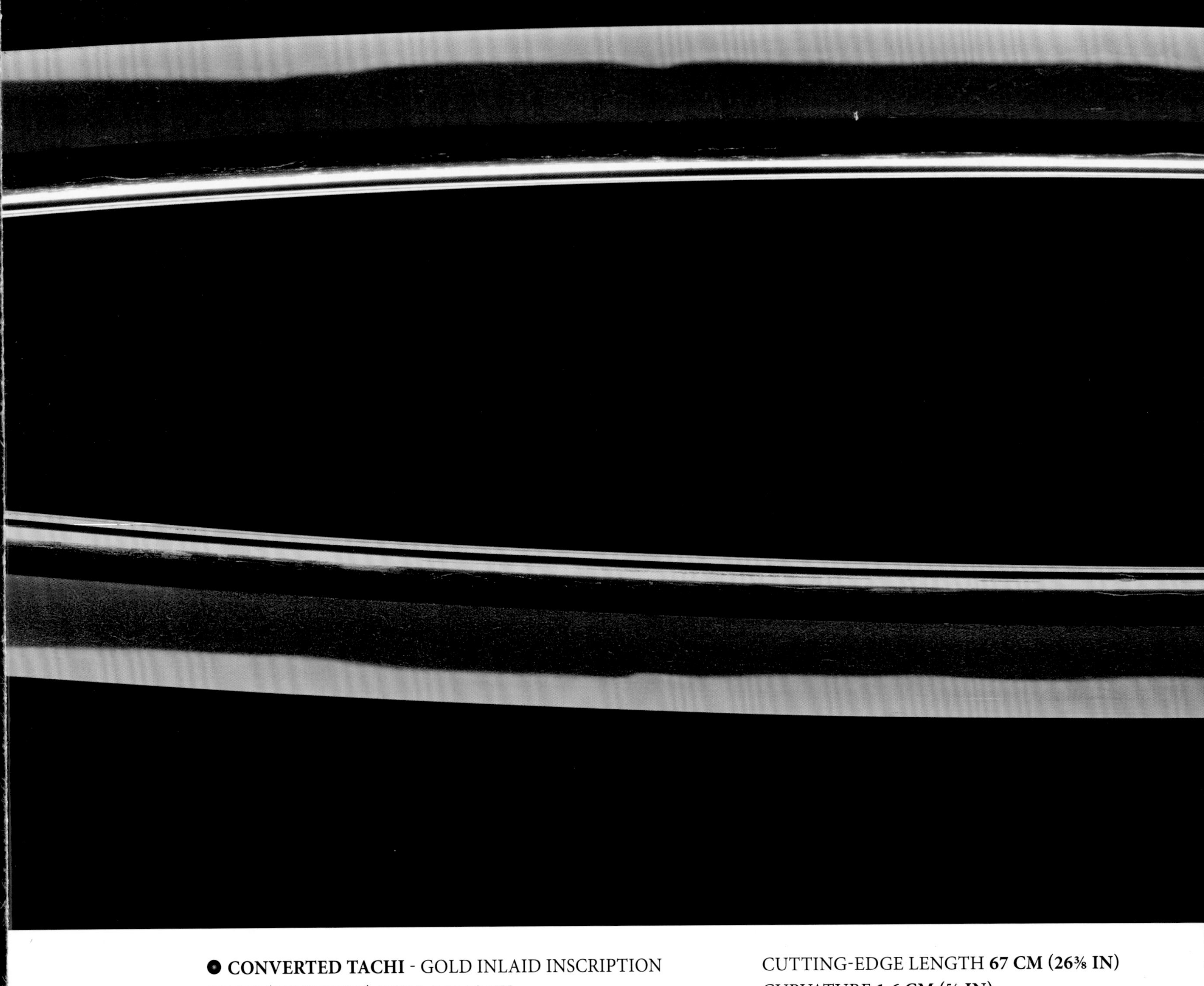

● **CONVERTED TACHI** - GOLD INLAID INSCRIPTION
NAME (MEIBUTSU) **SOZA SAMONJI**
OTHER NAME **YOSHIMOTO SAMONJI**

CUTTING-EDGE LENGTH **67 CM (26⅜ IN)**
CURVATURE **1.6 CM (⅝ IN)**

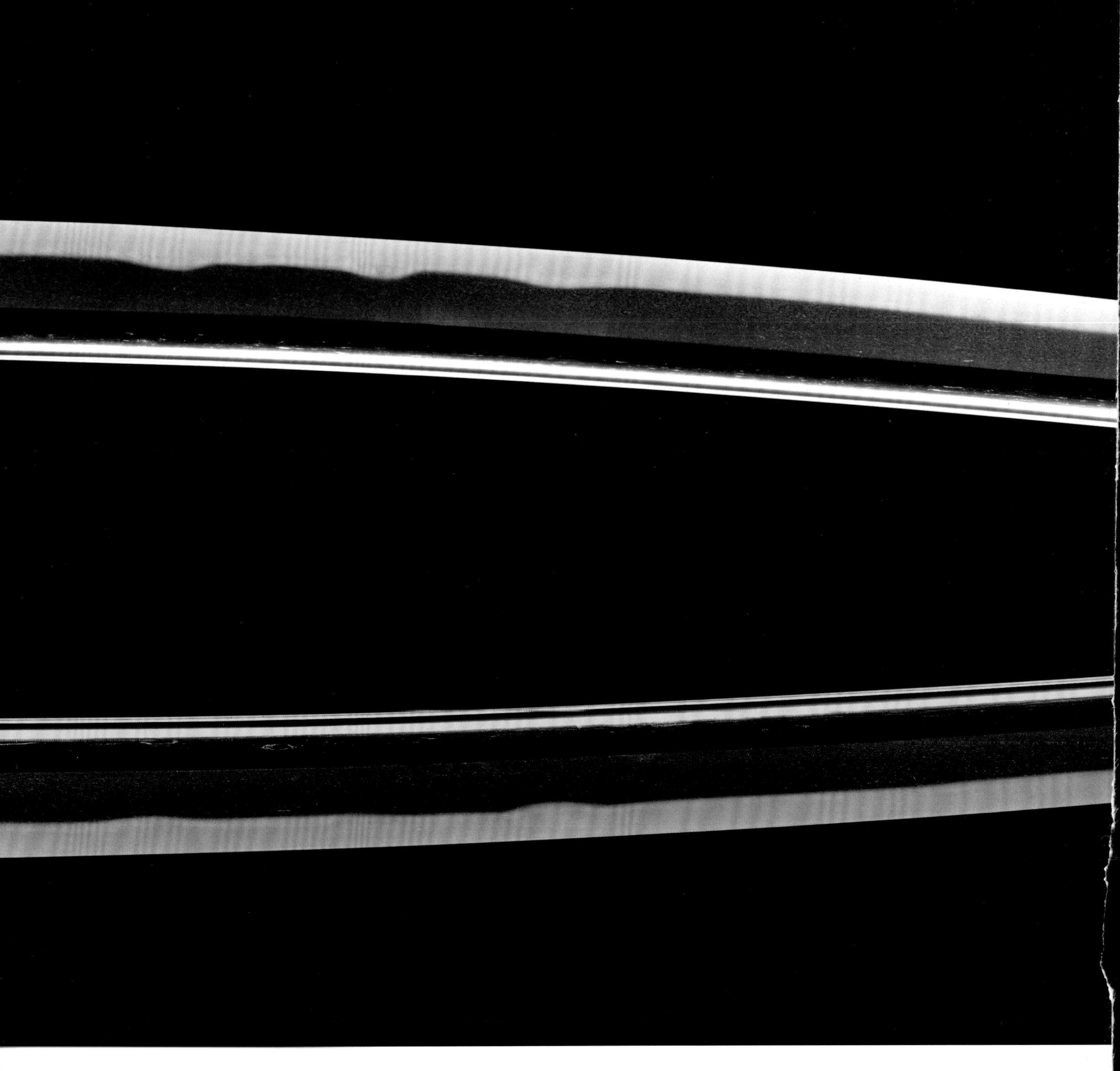

PERIOD **NANBOKUCHŌ PERIOD, 14TH C.**
KENKUN (OR TAKEISAO) SHRINE, KYŌTO
Important Cultural Property

(Enlargement of pages 98–99)

● SIGNED **YOSHIYUKI** PERIOD **LATE EDO, 19TH C.**
CUTTING-EDGE LENGTH **66.7 CM (26¼ IN)** KYOTO NATIONAL MUSEUM, KYŌTO

(Enlargement of pages 176–177)

KATANA
刀

100%

ODA NOBUNAGA
織田 信長

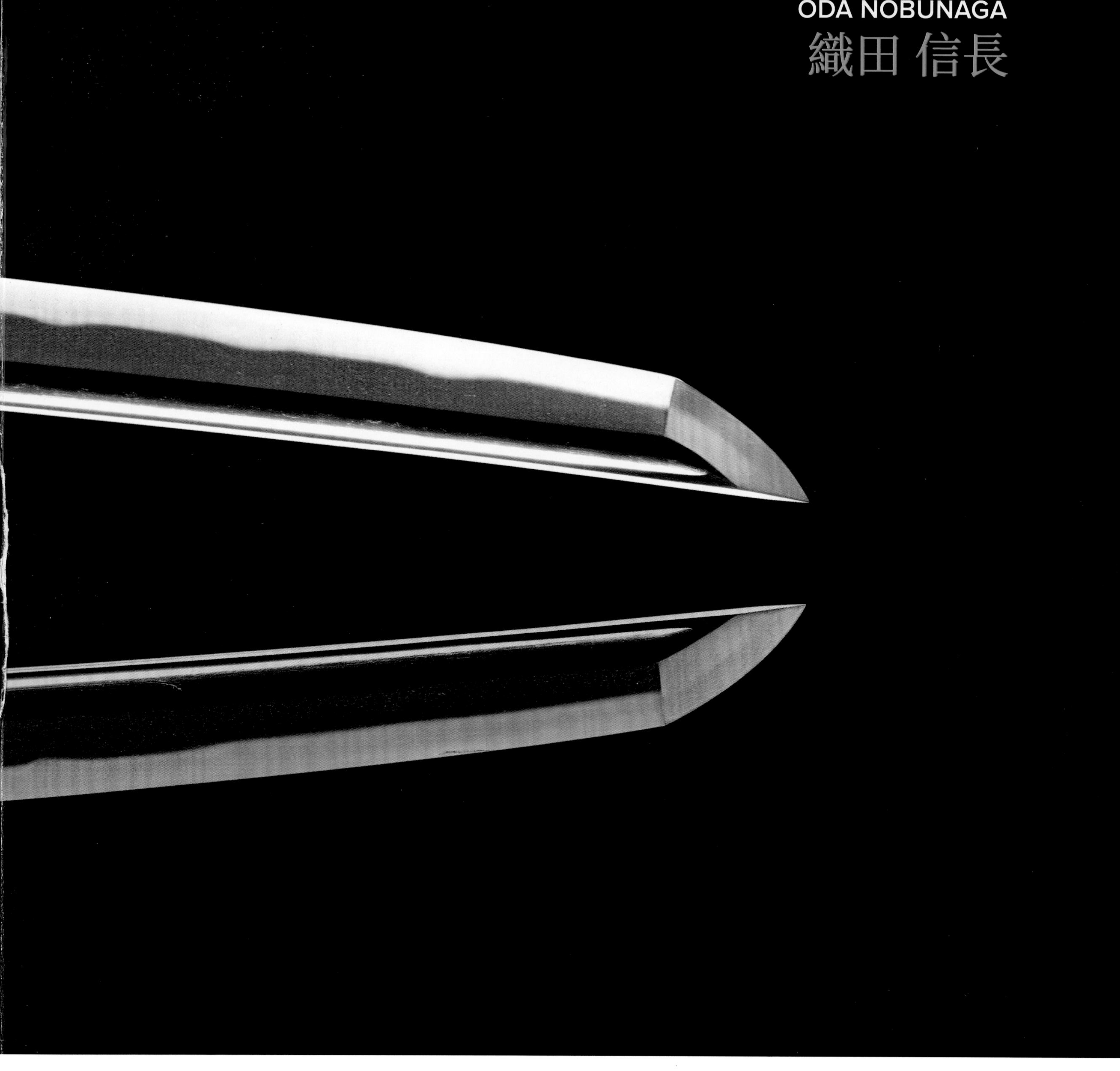

Page 199
Utagawa Kuniyoshi (1798-1861), right part of a triptych, *Ise no Kami Yoshitsune and Kumai Tarō preparing to defend Horikawa Palace against the attack of Tosabō Shōshun*, ca. 1834–1835.

伊豫守義經
一勇斎國芳画

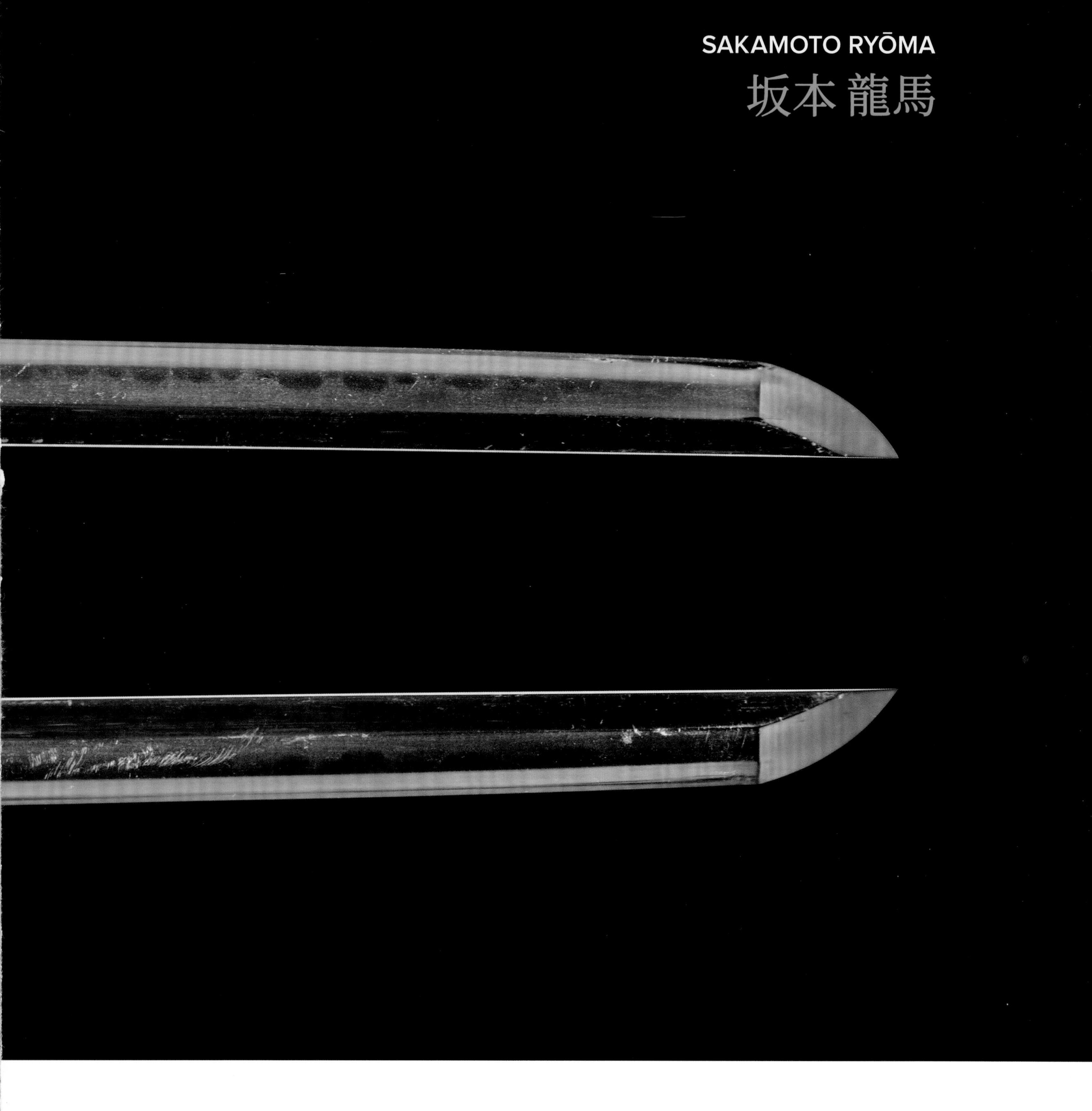

SAKAMOTO RYŌMA
坂本 龍馬

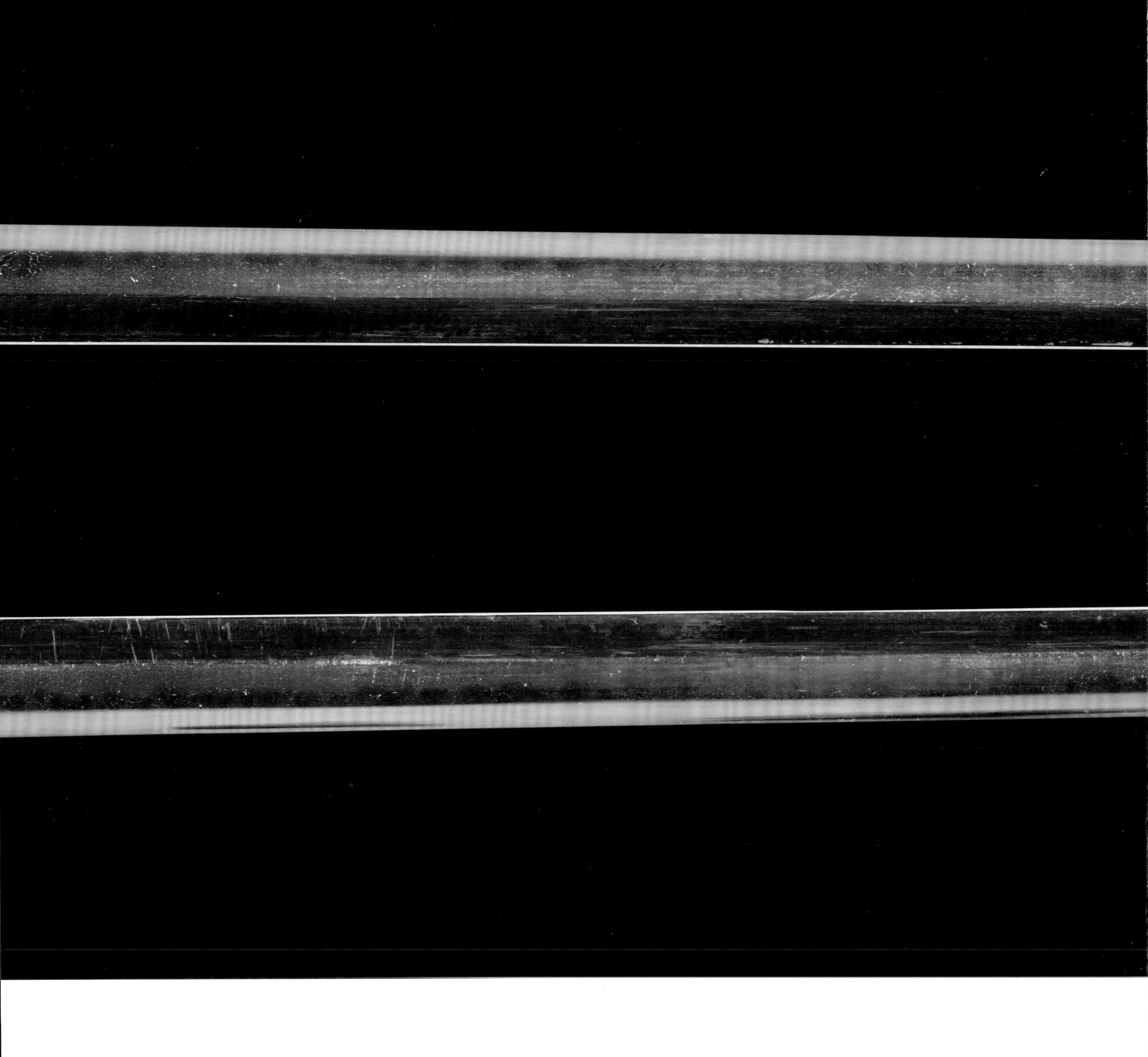

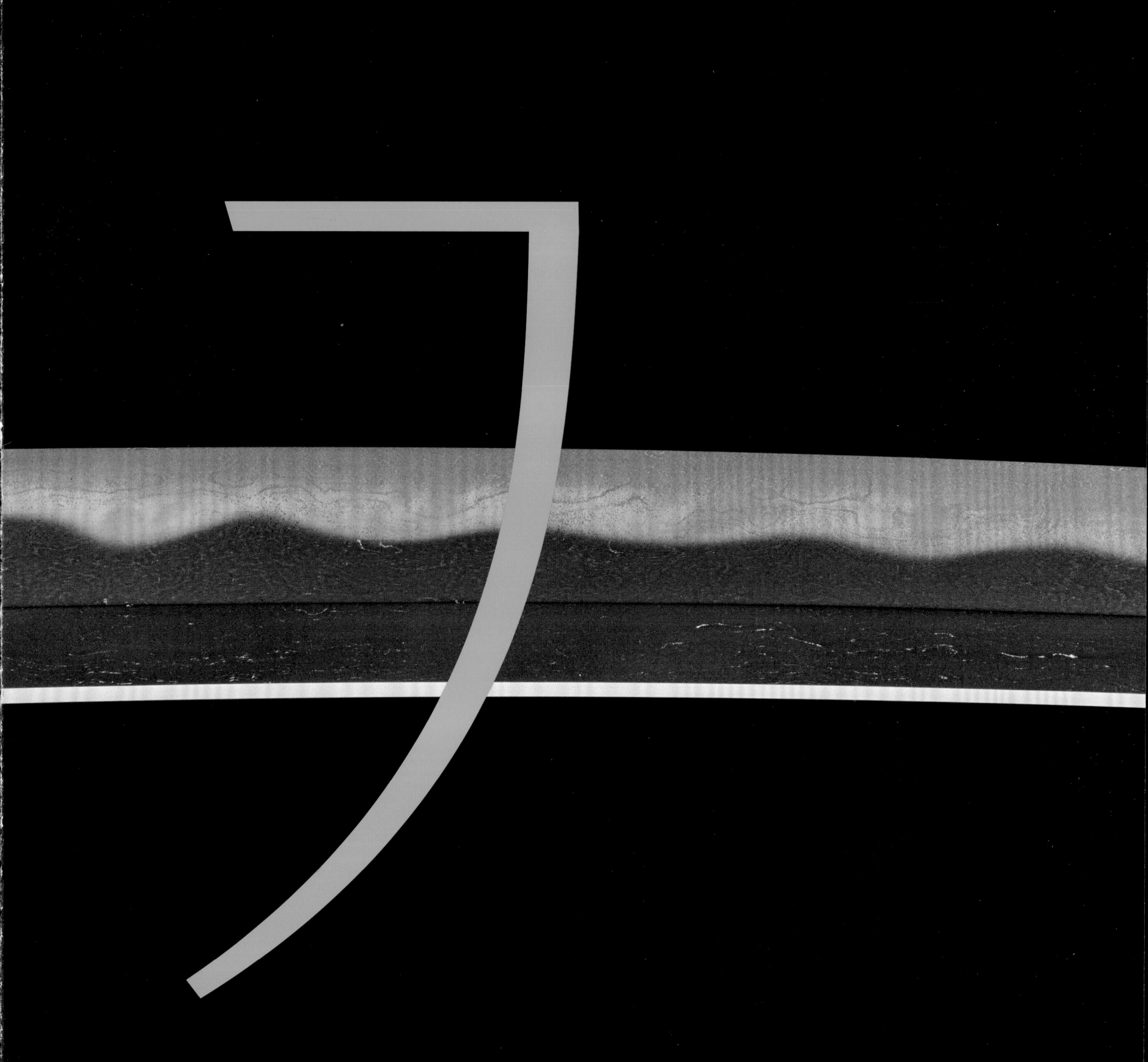

TERMINOLOGY

用語解説

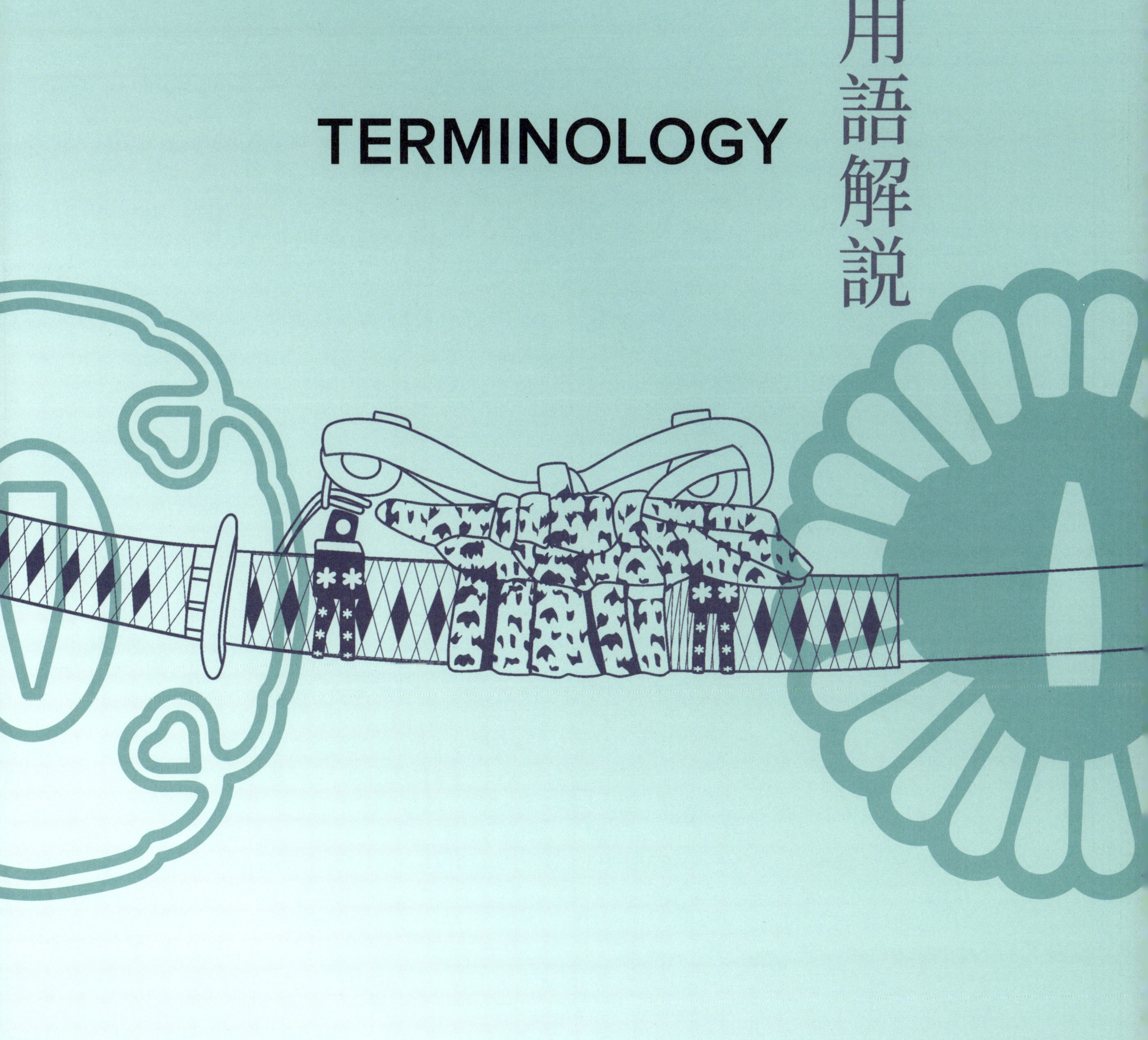

BLADE TERMINOLOGY AND MEASUREMENTS

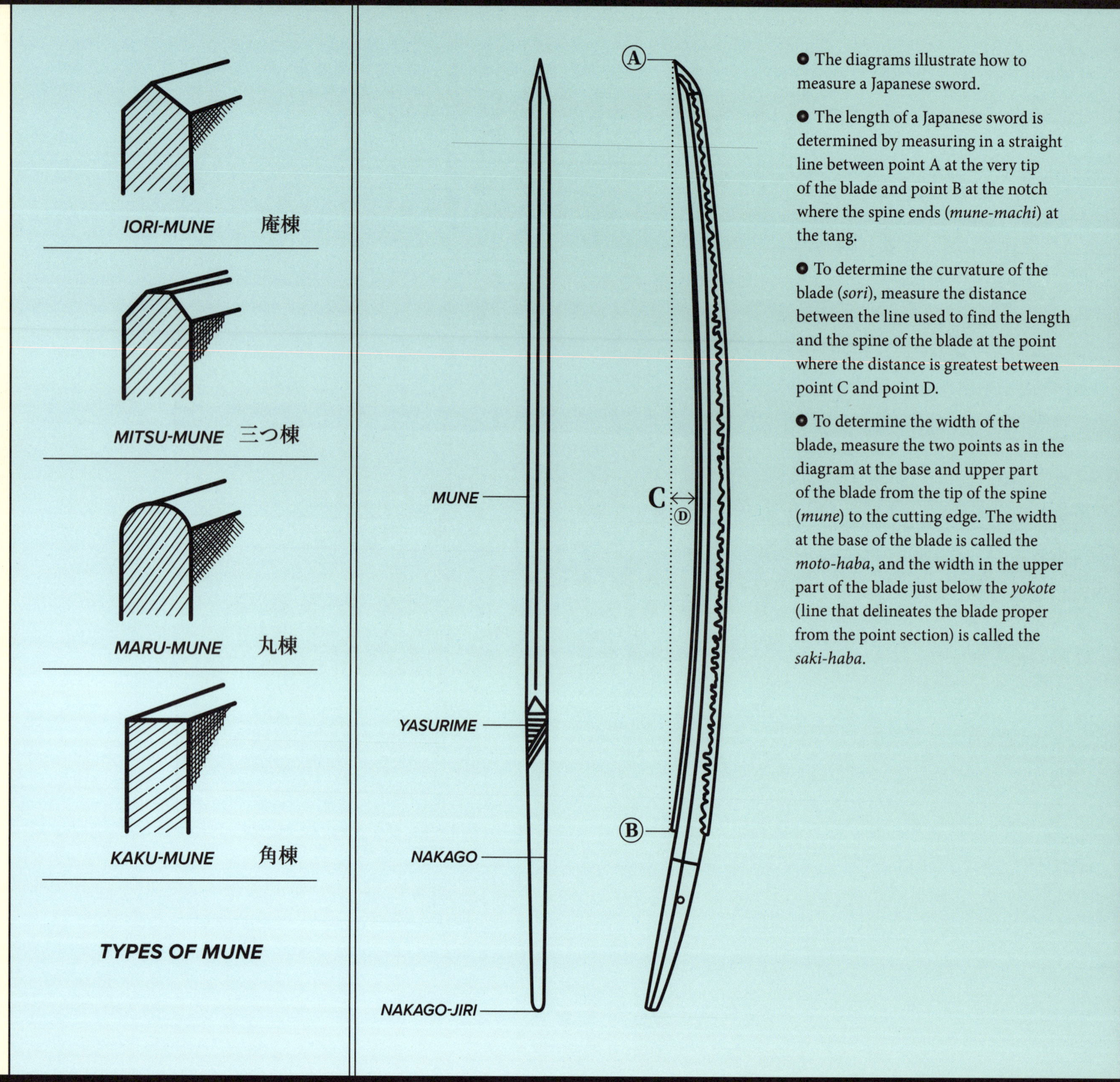

- The diagrams illustrate how to measure a Japanese sword.
- The length of a Japanese sword is determined by measuring in a straight line between point A at the very tip of the blade and point B at the notch where the spine ends (*mune-machi*) at the tang.
- To determine the curvature of the blade (*sori*), measure the distance between the line used to find the length and the spine of the blade at the point where the distance is greatest between point C and point D.
- To determine the width of the blade, measure the two points as in the diagram at the base and upper part of the blade from the tip of the spine (*mune*) to the cutting edge. The width at the base of the blade is called the *moto-haba*, and the width in the upper part of the blade just below the *yokote* (line that delineates the blade proper from the point section) is called the *saki-haba*.

● To determine the thickness of the blade, measure at the same points as the *moto* and *saki-haba*, but measure across the spine (*mune*) of the blade: the distance between the two shoulders of the *mune* (*mune-kado*). At this point, you might want to also take note the of width of the blade at the *shinogi* (ridgeline).

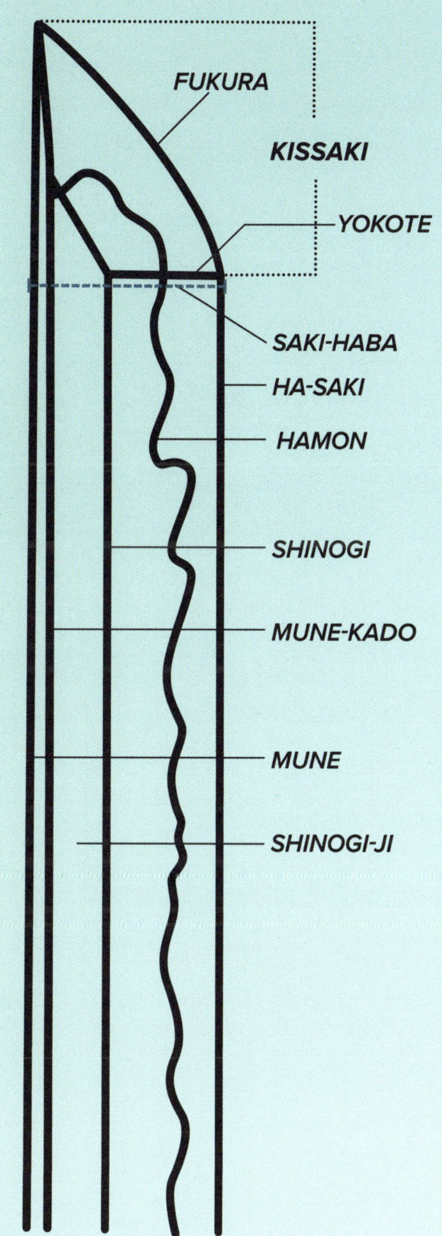

TYPES OF KISSAKI AND BŌSHI

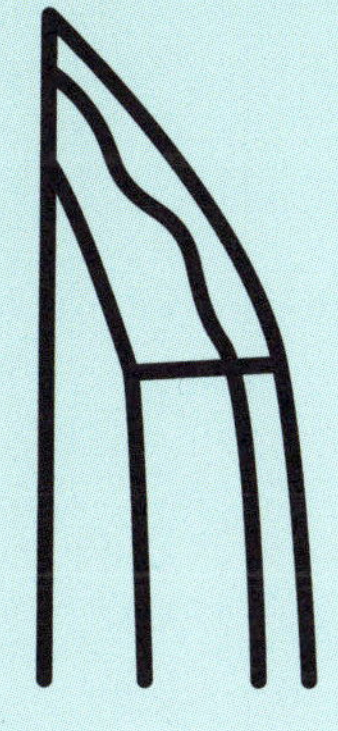

KO-KISSAKI with *yakizume bōshi*

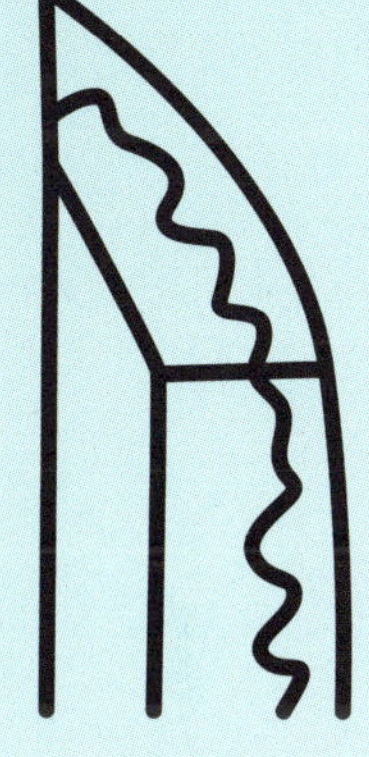

IKUBI-KISSAKI with *midare-komi bōshi*

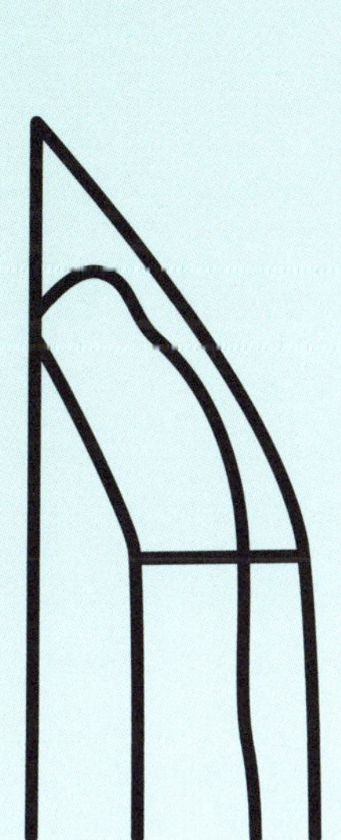

CHU-KISSAKI with *ko-maru bōshi*

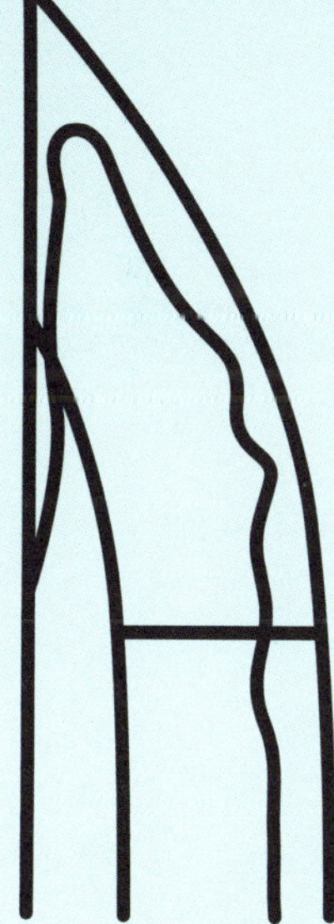

Ō-KISSAKI with *jizō bōshi* and long *kaeri*

BLADE CLASSIFICATION

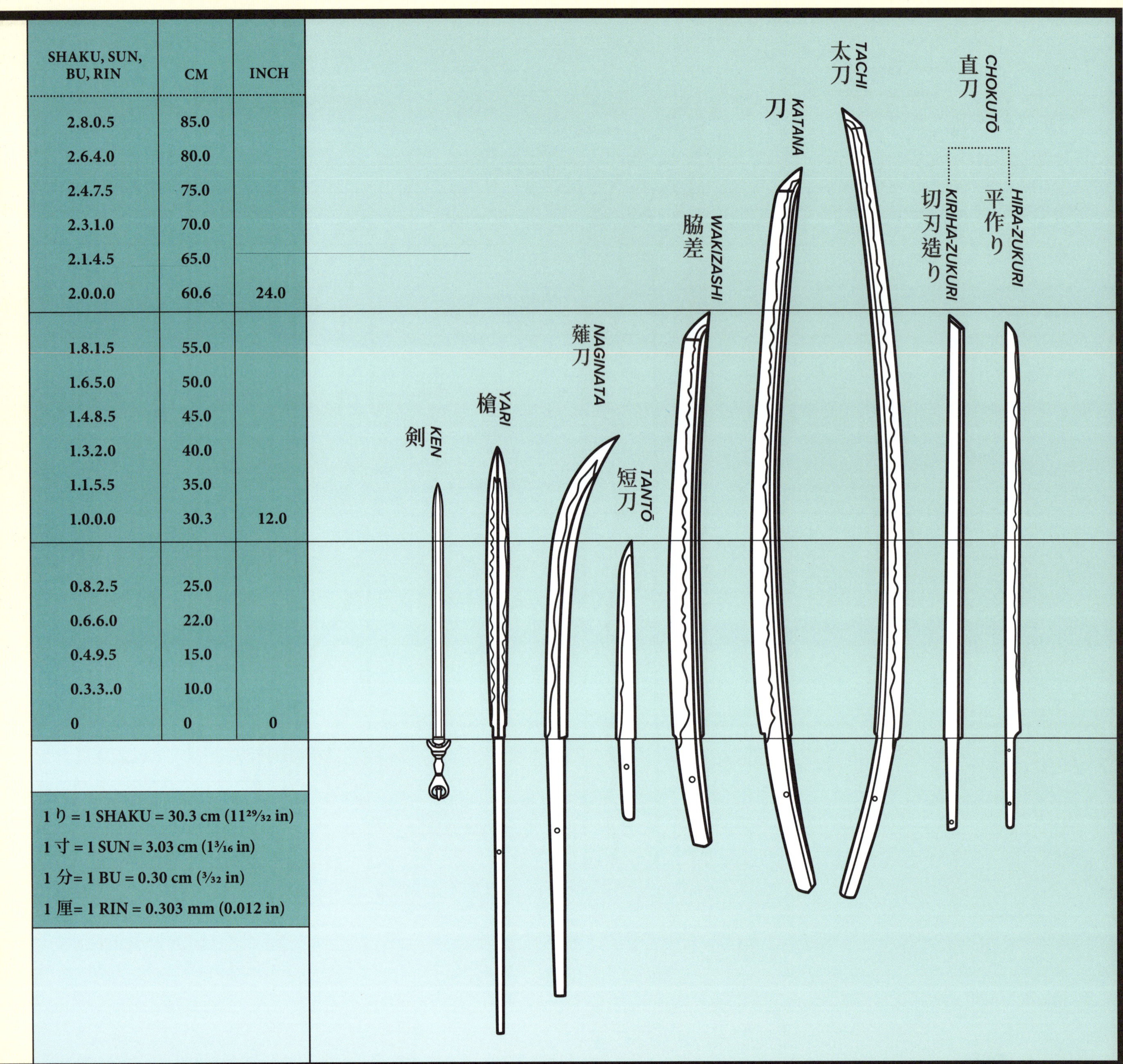

SHAKU, SUN, BU, RIN	CM	INCH
2.8.0.5	85.0	
2.6.4.0	80.0	
2.4.7.5	75.0	
2.3.1.0	70.0	
2.1.4.5	65.0	
2.0.0.0	60.6	24.0
1.8.1.5	55.0	
1.6.5.0	50.0	
1.4.8.5	45.0	
1.3.2.0	40.0	
1.1.5.5	35.0	
1.0.0.0	30.3	12.0
0.8.2.5	25.0	
0.6.6.0	22.0	
0.4.9.5	15.0	
0.3.3..0	10.0	
0	0	0

1 り = 1 SHAKU = 30.3 cm (11 29/32 in)
1 寸 = 1 SUN = 3.03 cm (1 3/16 in)
1 分= 1 BU = 0.30 cm (3/32 in)
1 厘= 1 RIN = 0.303 mm (0.012 in)

用語解説

MAIN SHAPES OF THE BLADE

- ***CHOKUTŌ*** are straight, single edged blades. There are two types; *hira-zukuri* (no ridgeline) and *kiriha-zukuri* (the ridgeline is close to the cutting edge). Blades of this type usually have a cutting edge of over 60 cm (23⅝ in) in length, and were popular prior to the Heian period (794–1185).
- ***TACHI*** are blades that are over 2 *shaku* (60.6 cm/ 23²⁷⁄₃₂ in) in length. They were mainly used from the end of the Heian period (794–1185) through to the early part of the Muromachi period (1392–1573) when cavalry warfare was popular. *Tachi* were worn suspended from the belt with the cutting edge down so that the end of the sword pointed upwards so as to avoid contact with the rear of the horse.
- ***KATANA*** are blades of 2 *shaku* (60.6 cm/23²⁷⁄₃₂ in) and over in length. They are worn thrust through the sash with the cutting edge upper-most. This style of sword was popular from the early Muromachi period through to the Edo period (1600–1867). *Katana* are generally shorter and have less curvature than *tachi* as a result of the shift from cavalry warfare to large infantry battles.
- ***WAKIZASHI*** are blades over 1 *shaku* (30.3 cm/ 11²⁹⁄₃₂ in), but no longer than 2 *shaku* (60.6 cm/ 23²⁷⁄₃₂ in) in length. They were often used as a companion sword to the *katana*.
- ***TANTŌ*** are daggers that are less than 1 *shaku* (30.3 cm/11²⁹⁄₃₂ in) in length.
- ***NAGINATA*** are halberds that were attached to long poles. They vary in length and curvature depending on period of manufacture, but are on average around 40 cm (15¾ in) in length.
- ***YARI*** are spears that were mounted on long poles. There are various types of *yari* including socket types. Long *yari* are called *ōmiyari*.
- ***KEN*** are double edges blades mostly used for esoteric Buddhist activities. Some larger ones have been excavated from ancient Japanese burial mounds.

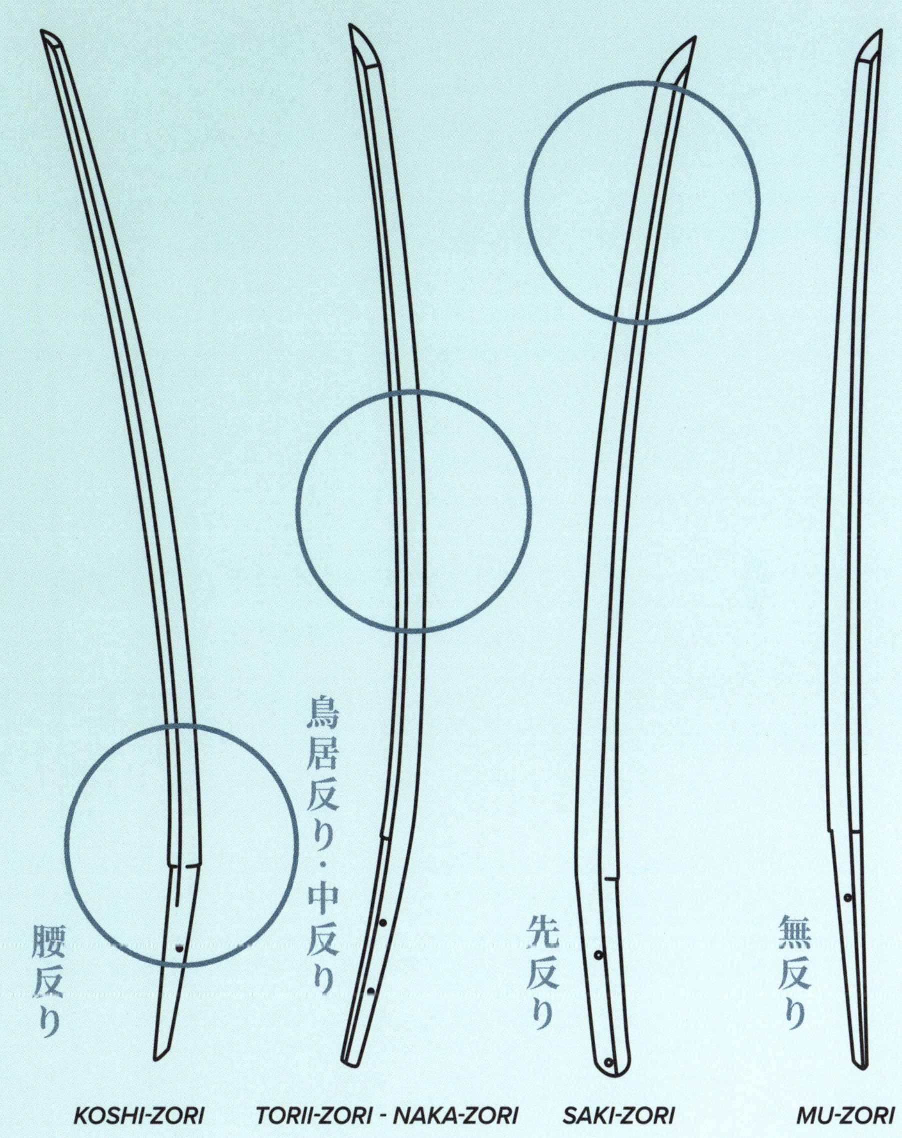

There are four basic shapes of long sword (from left to right):

❶ ***KOSHI-ZORI*** the deepest part of the curvature in the lower half of the blade.

❷ ***TORII-ZORI - NAKA-ZORI*** the deepest part of the curvature is around the center of the blade.

❸ ***SAKI-ZORI*** the deepest part of the curvature is in the upper part of the blade.

❹ ***MU-ZORI*** little or no curvature (straight). Usually used for *tantō*, but can also be used for blades of the Kanbun era (c. 1661).

THE TANG (*NAKAGO*)

● The *nakago*, or tang, can contain lots of clues as to the age or maker of the blade. There may be an inscription by the maker that includes a date of manufacture. However, one must proceed with caution as it is rather common to find spurious inscriptions that are best verified by an official organization.

● Additionally, even if a blade has no inscription, specialists can determine if it has been shortened or adjusted by the condition of the tang. As well as inscriptions, many tangs have the original maker's file marks. These are usually performed at an angle or direction customarily done by a particular smith or school. It is also a good point to bear in mind that old files were handmade (as opposed to modern production files) and also left distinctive types of filemarks.

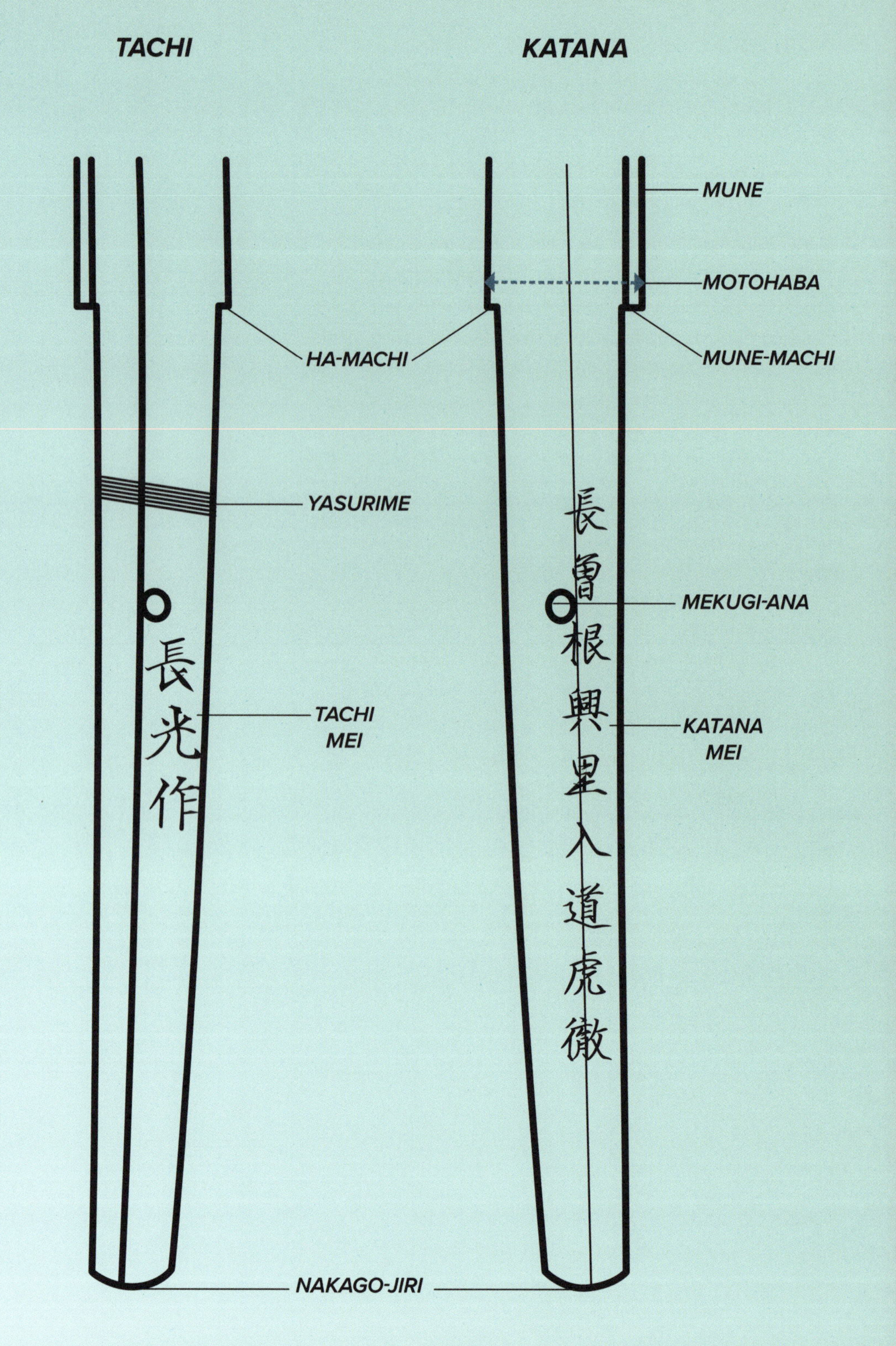

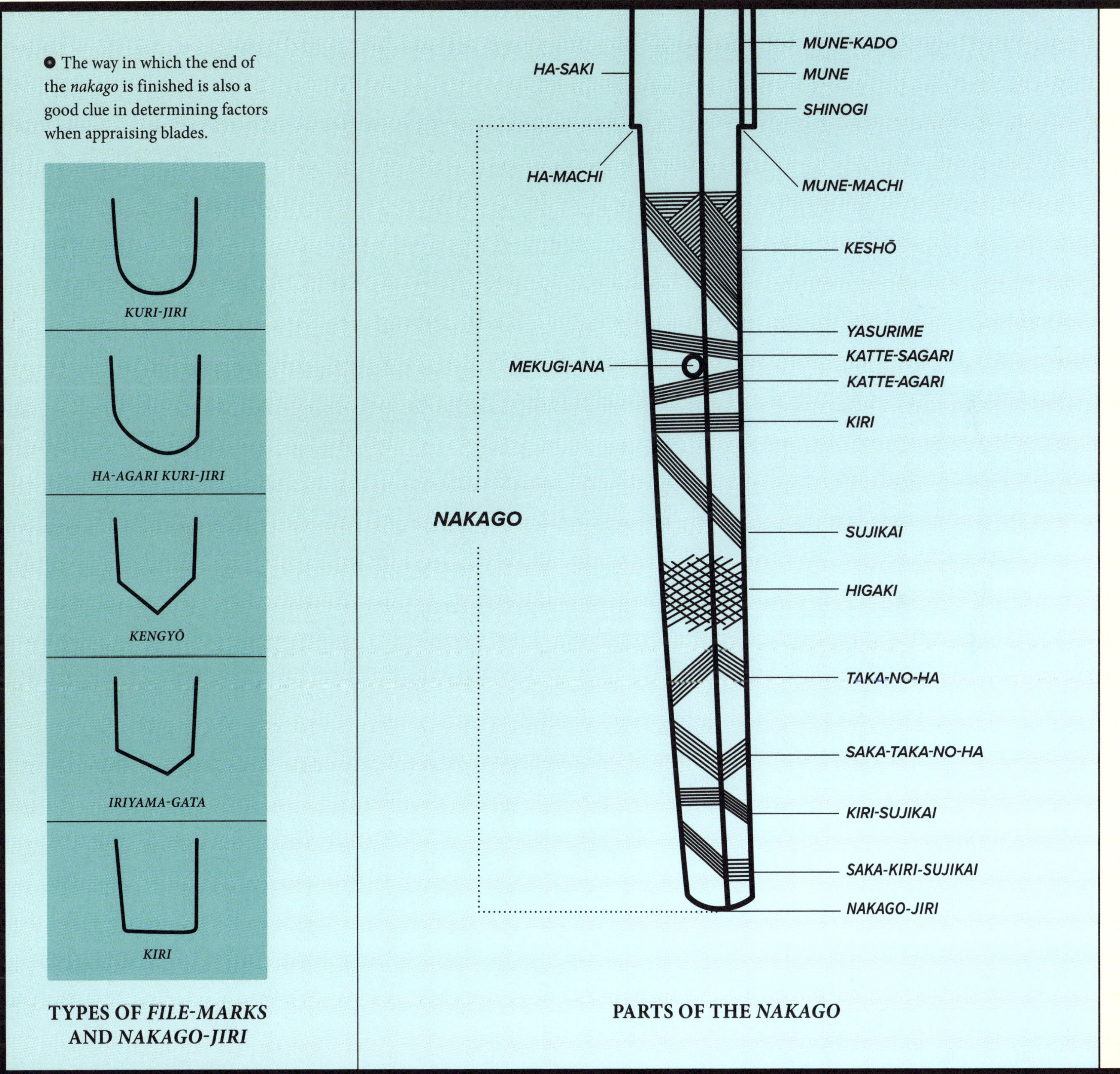
The way in which the end of the *nakago* is finished is also a good clue in determining factors when appraising blades.
KURI-JIRI
HA-AGARI KURI-JIRI
KENGYŌ
IRIYAMA-GATA
KIRI
TYPES OF FILE-MARKS AND NAKAGO-JIRI
HA-SAKI
MUNE-KADO
MUNE
SHINOGI
HA-MACHI
MUNE-MACHI
KESHŌ
YASURIME
KATTE-SAGARI
MEKUGI-ANA
KATTE-AGARI
KIRI
NAKAGO
SUJIKAI
HIGAKI
TAKA-NO-HA
SAKA-TAKA-NO-HA
KIRI-SUJIKAI
SAKA-KIRI-SUJIKAI
NAKAGO-JIRI
PARTS OF THE NAKAGO

CHANGES IN THE SHAPE OF THE JAPANESE SWORD

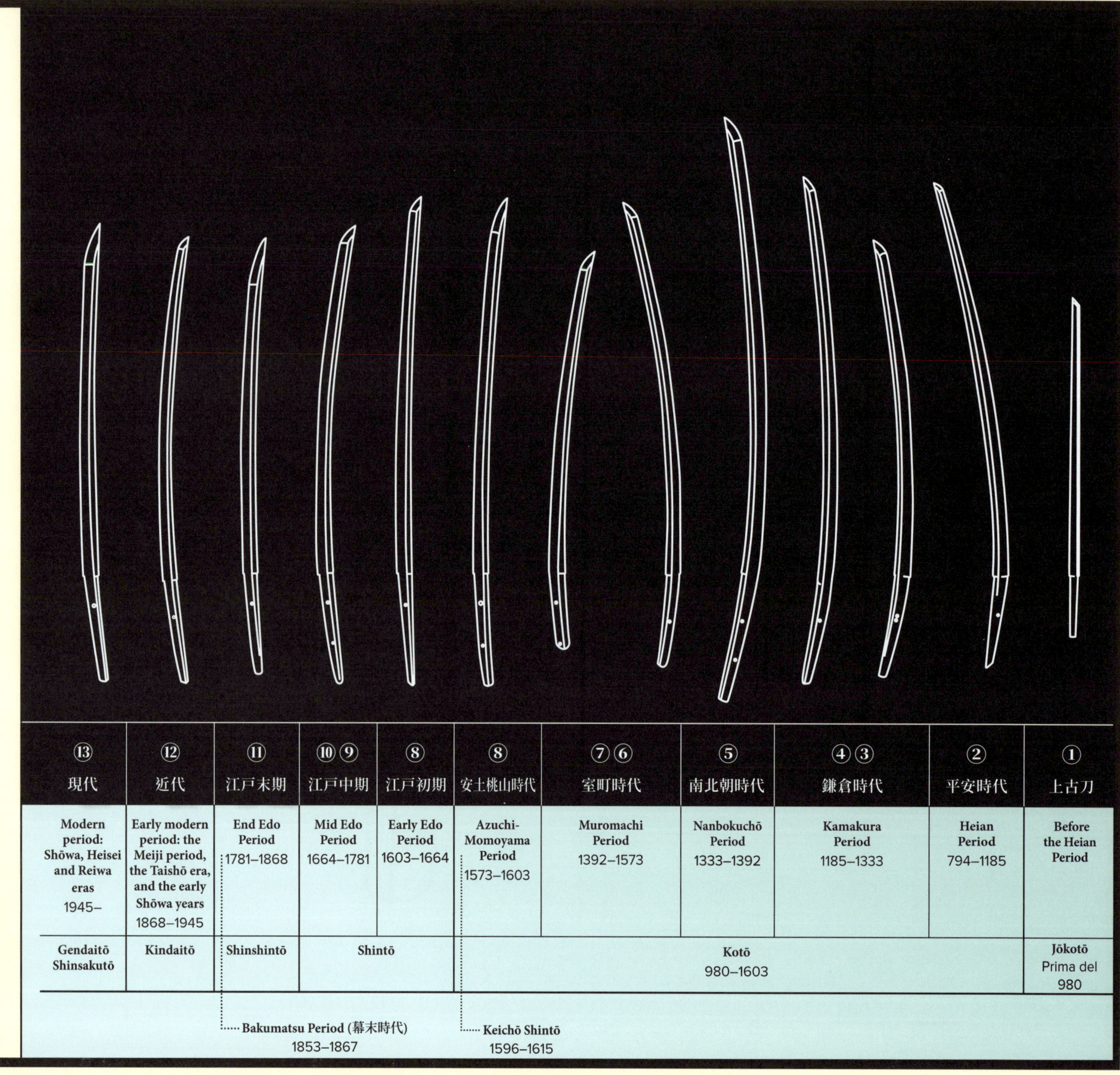

⑬ 現代	⑫ 近代	⑪ 江戸末期	⑩⑨ 江戸中期	⑧ 江戸初期	⑧ 安土桃山時代	⑦⑥ 室町時代	⑤ 南北朝時代	④③ 鎌倉時代	② 平安時代	① 上古刀
Modern period: Shōwa, Heisei and Reiwa eras 1945–	**Early modern period: the Meiji period, the Taishō era, and the early Shōwa years** 1868–1945	**End Edo Period** 1781–1868	**Mid Edo Period** 1664–1781	**Early Edo Period** 1603–1664	**Azuchi-Momoyama Period** 1573–1603	**Muromachi Period** 1392–1573	**Nanbokuchō Period** 1333–1392	**Kamakura Period** 1185–1333	**Heian Period** 794–1185	**Before the Heian Period**
Gendaitō Shinsakutō	**Kindaitō**	**Shinshintō**	**Shintō**		**Kotō** 980–1603					**Jōkotō** Prima del 980

Bakumatsu Period (幕末時代) 1853–1867

Keichō Shintō 1596–1615

The curved Japanese sword was perfected at the end of the Heian period (974–1185) in the mid 10th century. Since that time the curvature and the geometry of the blade has undergone many changes according to the requirements of the various historical periods. Understanding these changes is an important part of Japanese sword appraisal. This chart illustrates the changes in shape in the different historical eras.

❶ *Jōkotō*: Swords of the Ancient Period

Before the emergence of the curved tachi, continental style straight blades called *chokutō* were originally brought to Japan from the Asian continent. Later, during the Kofun period (300–538 AD) sword making began to flourish in Japan with makers continuing the manufacture of straight swords in similar styles. They are usually constructed in the *hira-zukuri* and *kiriha-zukuri* styles. Many of these straight blades have been excavated from Kofun period tombs, and some were stored in the Shōsōin Imperial Repository, Nara.

❷ Late Heian to Early Kamakura Periods

This shape represents the earliest curved Japanese swords. Long swords of this era are generally referred to as *tachi*. It is thought that the shift from straight blades to Japanese swords with curvature happened around the mid-tenth century. They are quite slender blades with the curvature concentrated between the handle and base of the blade. This shape is called *koshi-zori*. They are *shinogi-zukuri* (ridgeline) construction, wide at the base of the blade while narrowing acutely towards the small point section (*ko-kissaki*).

From midway towards the point there is generally very little curvature. The average length of the cutting edge of blades of this period is usually around 75.8–78.8 cm ($29\frac{27}{32}$–$31\frac{1}{32}$ in).

❸ Mid-Kamakura Period

At the zenith of the warrior class's power during the Kamakura period, the blades become rather thicker (*kasane*) and wider and take on magnificent *tachi* shape. There is not much difference between the width of the *moto-haba* and the *saki-haba*. The blades still have *koshi-zori*, but the center of the curvature has moved slightly further along the blade. The *kissaki* has become a compact *chu-kissaki* (*ikubi*). The *hamon* has developed into a flowing gorgeous *chōji-midare*. Around this time, *tantō* production also appears.

It is thought that the Mongol invasions of 1274 and 1281 had an influence on not only the thickness of *tachi*, but also the manufacture of *tantō* due to the difficulty in cutting thick leather Mongol armor.

❹ Late Kamakura Period

Tachi at the end of the Kamakura period have developed into blades with magnificent shapes. There are two types: one style is wide throughout its length and the point section is similar to the mid-Kamakura period *kissaki*, but slightly extended. The other is quite slender and similar in appearance to the late Heian, early Kamakura shapes. However, when you look further along the blade, the center of curvature has moved slightly further up the blade.

❺ Nanbokuchō Period

For reasons that are unclear, many over-sized blades of 90.9 cm ($35\frac{25}{32}$ in) and longer with large point sections (*ō-kissaki*) were made during the Nanbokuchō period. Large size *tantō* were also commonly produced. Among these were extremely long blades called *ō-dachi* and *no-dachi*. To compensate for the extra length, blades of this period were rather thin in construction, or have a *bō-hi* (groove) cut into the *shinogi-ji* area to lighten the blade. Many *tachi* from this period were shortened (*ō-suriage*) to regular sword lengths in later periods as they were difficult to wield. Consequently, many extant blades from the Nanbokuchō period are unsigned due to being shortened.

❻ Early Muromachi Period

Blades of the early part of the Muromachi period are reminiscent in shape to the blades of the early Kamakura period. Compared to the shape of Nanbokuchō period blades, the design has completely changed and no longer includes *ō-kissaki*. They are quite narrow and deeply curved with a medium-sized point section. The length of the cutting edge is generally between 72.7 cm ($28\frac{5}{8}$ in) and 75.7 cm ($29\frac{13}{16}$ in). They may appear somewhat similar in shape to Kamakura period blades, but on closer inspection they are somewhat *saki-zori* character.

CHANGES IN THE SHAPE OF THE JAPANESE SWORD

❼ Late Muromachi Period

By the late Muromachi period, fighting methods had changed from cavalry to mass infantry style warfare. Shorter blades, known as *uchigatana*, with a cutting edge of around 63.6 cm (25 1/32 in) in length that were intended for one-handed use became popular. As opposed to *tachi* that were worn suspended from the belt, *uchigatana* were worn thrust through the sash with the cutting edge uppermost. Following the Ōnin war, conflicts broke out in many places prompting the mass-production of blades (*kazu-uchi*) that were inferior in quality to regular Japanese blades. However, specially ordered blades of excellent quality (*chūmon-uchi*) were still also produced at this time. The provinces of Bizen (Okayama prefecture) and Mino (Gifu prefecture) became major places of production. Many blades produced in this period have with strong *saki-zori*, with either a *chu-kissaki* or an extended *chu-kissaki.*

❽ Momoyama and Early Edo Periods

Swords produced up to the Keichō era (1596–1614) are classified as Kotō (old-swords). Blades made during and after the Keichō era are classified as Shintō (new-swords). As peace began to spread throughout Japan during the Momoyama period, many smiths moved gathered in major cities, or castle towns of influential *daimyō*. Many blades from around this period tend to mirror the shape of that of shortened Nanbokuchō blades with a large or extended medium sized point section. They have a cutting edge of around 72.7 cm (28 5/8 in) to 75.8 cm (29 27/32 in) in length. Unlike their shortened earlier counterparts, they retain the maker's signature on the *katana-omote* and have a thicker *kasane* than Nanbokuchō period blades.

❾ Edo Period; Kanbun Era

Swords of the Kanbun period have a noticeably shallow curvature. The *saki-haba* is relatively narrow when compared to the *moto-haba*, and have a rather small to medium-sized point section. They have an average cutting-edge length of around 69.7 cm (27 7/16 in). This particular type of construction is usually referred to as Kanbun-shintō and was generally produced around the middle of the Kanbun (1661–1673) and Enpō (1673–1681) eras.

Japan had been at peace for about 50 years, and in that time many Japanese fencing *dōjō* had been established. It is thought that as Japanese swordplay moved into the *dōjō* and became popular, that it affected the shape of the Japanese sword. Up to this point, deeply curved swords had been popular as they were extremely effective for slashing. However, deeply curved swords are also very difficult to fence and perform thrusting techniques with. As fencing tip to tip in the smaller confines of practice halls (as opposed to the battle field) grew in popularity, a shape of sword was produced that allowed swordsmen to utilize this way of fighting and use thrusting techniques proficiently. This was also a period in which dueling was not uncommon.

❿ Edo Period; Genroku Era

The change in shape of Japanese swords between the Jōkyō (1684–1688) and Genroku (1688–1704) eras reflects the transition of shape from Kanbun-shintō blades to the beginning of the Shin-shintō (New new-sword) period of sword manufacture. As it was a very peaceful period in Japanese history, rather flamboyant *hamon* appear. In this era, there was a revival movement to recreate blades of older periods. Unlike the previous Kanbun era blades, the curvature once again becomes quite deep. The shape somewhat resembles that of *tachi* of earlier eras, but they are generally signed on the *katana-omote.* A pioneer of the movement was Suishinshi Masahide.

⓫ Edo period; Bakumatsu

Bakumatsu blades are shallow in curvature, have a thick *kasane*, a wide *haba* throughout, and an *ō-kissaki*. They generally have a cutting-edge length of 75.7–78.7 cm (29 13/16–31 in). The revival movement of making blades in older shapes continues but in heavier thicker blades. One of Suishinshi Masahide's noteable students was Taikei Naotane. Minamoto Kiyomaro also led a revival aimed at Sōshū-den and Mino-Shizu workmanship.

⓬ Meiji up to 1945

In 1876, Haitorei decree was issued banning civilians from wearing swords, resulting in a steep decline in the need for swords. Blades from this time until present day are referred to as *gendaitō* (modern swords). However, in 1906 the swordsmiths Gassan Sadakazu and Miyamoto Kanenori were designated 'Tei-shitsu Gigei-in' (craftsmen by imperial appointment). Another resurgence of swordmaking took place from the 1930's up until the end of the Second World War.

⓭ 1945 to Present Day

Following Japan's defeat in the Second World War, sword making and martial arts were banned during the Allied Occupation of Japan. When sword making resumed in 1953, licensing systems for not only swords, but also swordsmiths was introduced. Today sword making is recognized as a traditional Japanese craft and continues to this day. Modern swordsmiths try to recreate works based on the workmanship of eminent smiths or schools of every period while including their own characteristics and originality.

THE FIVE BASIC TRADITIONS (*GOKADEN*)

There is a relatively modern system that uses five basic types of manufacture and names each tradition, or '*den*', after the province from which it originates. It is called the Gokaden, and refers to the archaic provinces of Yamato (Nara), Yamashiro (Kyōto), Bizen (Okayama), Sagami (Kanagawa), commonly referred to as Sōshū, and Mino (Gifu). The common traits of these original main centers of sword production have long been used as a teaching basis for appraisal, but they were formalized into the Gokaden system that is now in common use by Hon'ami polishers Kōson and Ringa in the Meiji era.

● Yamato-den

Yamato-den (Nara province) is is said to be the oldest of all the traditions and the origins of them all. According to old documents, Amakuni was the founder of the tradition around 701–704 (Nara period), but no extant signed examples of his work exist. The tradition is split between five major schools all with their own style. However, general characteristics of Yamato blades include: a relatively thick *kasane* with a high *shinogi*, and a graceful curvature. They have a flowing *itame-mokume-hada* with *masame*, or in the case of the Hōshō school: pure *masame* with *chikei*. The *hamon* are *suguha* based, with *hotsure*, strong *nie* and lots of *masame* based activities inside the *hamon*: *kinsuji*, *sunagashi*, *kuichigaiba*, and *niju-ba*. The *bōshi* is often *yakizume*, with *hakikake*.

● Yamashiro-den

Yamashiro-den originated around the center of government, Kyōto, around the mid Heian period (987–989). The oldest Yamashiro smith with extant works is thought to be Sanjō Munechika. Characteristics: blades have an even graceful curvature called *torii-zori* also known as *kyō-zori* because of their Kyōto origins. The steel surface appears to be rather clear with a *hada* texture of *nashiji*, or more noticeable *mokume*. *Nie-utsuri* can often be seen. The *hamon* are *suguha* based, with fine *nie*. *Horimono* in the designs of short *koshi-bi*, or *suken* finished in *kaki-nagashi* can also be seen.

● Bizen-den

Ko-Bizen Tomonari along with Masatsune are accredited with being the founders of Bizen-den in the late Heian period. During the Kotō (old sword) era of swordmaking, Bizen became a mecca of sword making. The characteristics change slightly depending on period of manufacture and sub-group, but the main characteristics are dynamic shapes with deep *koshi-zori* (also called Bizen-zori), prominent *utsuri* in different forms (*midare utsuri*, peony *utsuri*, *bō-utsuri*). The *hada* is *itame*, often flowing or with patches of *masame*. There are various types of *hamon*, but the most famous is *chōji midare*, the *juka-chōji* of the Kamakura period, and *gunome-chōji midare*.

● Sōshū-den

The founder of Sōshū-den is said to be Shintōgo Kunimitsu. His student Masamune is said to have perfected the tradition in the late Kamakura period. Blade shapes tend to be in keeping with the styles of the late Kamakura to Nanbokuchō eras of large, and over-sized, *tachi* that are wide in the upper part of the blade are common with an extended medium, or large sized point section. Many have *mitsu-mune*. The *hada* is a bright *itame* with lots of prominent *nie* (*nie deki*). *Hamon* are *notare-gunome* and *hitatsura hamon* are also common.

● Mino-den

Mino-den is the last of the five traditions. The founder is said to be, Shizu Saburō Kaneuji, who is said to have evolved from Yamato-den via Sōshū-den. Later Mino-den have a reputation for practicality over beauty. Many Mino blades have a *saki-sori* shape, reflecting their prosperity during the Muromachi period. The *hada* is a flowing *itame* mixed with *masame* reflecting their Yamato roots, and display a prominent pale *utsuri*. The *hamon* has pointed (see *sanbon-sugi*) or rounded *gunome*. The Mino *chōji* and *gunome hamon* tend to have rounded valleys and a tight *nioi-deki nioi-guchi*. The *bōshi* often has a Jizō (Kṣitigarbha) shape.

JIGANE AND *HADA*: THE SURFACE STEEL OF THE BLADE

Strictly speaking, *hada* or *jihada* are terms used to describe the resulting grain pattern on the surface of the steel from the repeated folding process, and *jigane* is a term used to describe the condition of the surface steel itself.

Although, the appearance of the *jigane* can be affected by the polisher's techniques to a large degree, it is an important aspect of *kantei* (sword appraisal). When viewing the *jihada* and *jigane* of a sword in a reasonably polished condition it is possible to assess where in Japan the blade was manufactured, the period of production, school, or even the maker.

The *hada* pattern comes in four basic forms, *itame-hada*, *mokume-hada*, *masame-hada*, and *ayasugi-hada*. However, it is not uncommon for the blade surface may contain one or more of these different types of *hada*. The patterns are produced during the fold-forging process of the steel billet that is used for the *kawagane* (jacket steel), or surface steel of the blade. When the steel billet is folded repeatedly the resulting layers gradually get stretched out becoming thinner and thinner until the hammer eventually punches through the top layers producing a rather natural looking wood grain type pattern.

Generally, *itame* or *mokume-hada* can be observed on the top and bottom surfaces of the billet. Whereas, if you turn the billet on its side and hammer it down, it exposes the lines of the layers, exposing a straight wood grain type *masame-hada* pattern. *Ayasugi-hada* is the least natural looking out of the four basic patterns as it repeats along the blade giving a more man-made appearance. However, the terminology used to describe it, (a row of) cedar trees hada, still greatly alludes to nature.

ITAME-HADA
板目肌

MOKUME-HADA
杢目肌

MASAME-HADA
柾目肌

AYASUGI-HADA
綾杉肌

ITAME AND *MOKUME-HADA*

Distinguishing between *mokume-hada* and *itame-hada* can be rather difficult, as both patterns generally contain an element of the other. *Itame-hada* contains predominantly elliptical shapes, whereas *mokume-hada* contains predominantly circular shapes. It is also possible to create contrived *mokume* shapes in a *hada* by puncturing holes in the surface of the billet and the hammering the surface until it is flat again.

MASAME-HADA

For pure *masame-hada*, during forging the steel billet is turned on its side, and then hammered into the block. The oldest school known for this technique is the Yamato Hōshō school of the Kamakura period.

AYASUGI-HADA

Ayasugi-hada is waves of continuous undulating lines punctuated by *mokume* type shapes. This type of *hada* appeared in sections of Heian and Kamakura blades of the Hōju, Mogusa, Naminohira and Gassan schools, but the perfected uniform style of *ayasugi-hada* is associated with the Gassan school and is subsequently commonly referred to as 'Gassan-*hada*'.

VARIOUS TYPES OF *HAMON*

The *hamon* is the result of the differential hardening process. The crystals in the steel expand and group and while it is being heated in a charcoal fire. They are then frozen in place by rapidly cooling the red-hot blade in a bath of tepid water creating a visible pattern in the crystalline structure of the steel that runs along the cutting edge of the blade.

The swordsmith can control the overall shape of the *hamon* by an application of clay to the blade, which is either applied along the whole blade and scraped off along the cutting edge, or a thicker layer of clay is applied to the back of the blade with a thinner of layer applied along the cutting edge. The clay is then dried before the heating and quenching process.

Hamon of the same types can be produced. However, the process produces a *hamon* that distinguishes each blade completely from all other blades. It can be compared to the uniqueness of fingerprints or DNA. Crystals that are individually distinguishable in the steel with the naked eye are called *nie* (lit. boiling), while crystals that appear like clouds (as they are not individually distinguishable), are called *nioi* (lit. fragrance). The various combinations of crystals create different shapes that all have specific terms applied to them, and are often likened to that of natural phenomena.

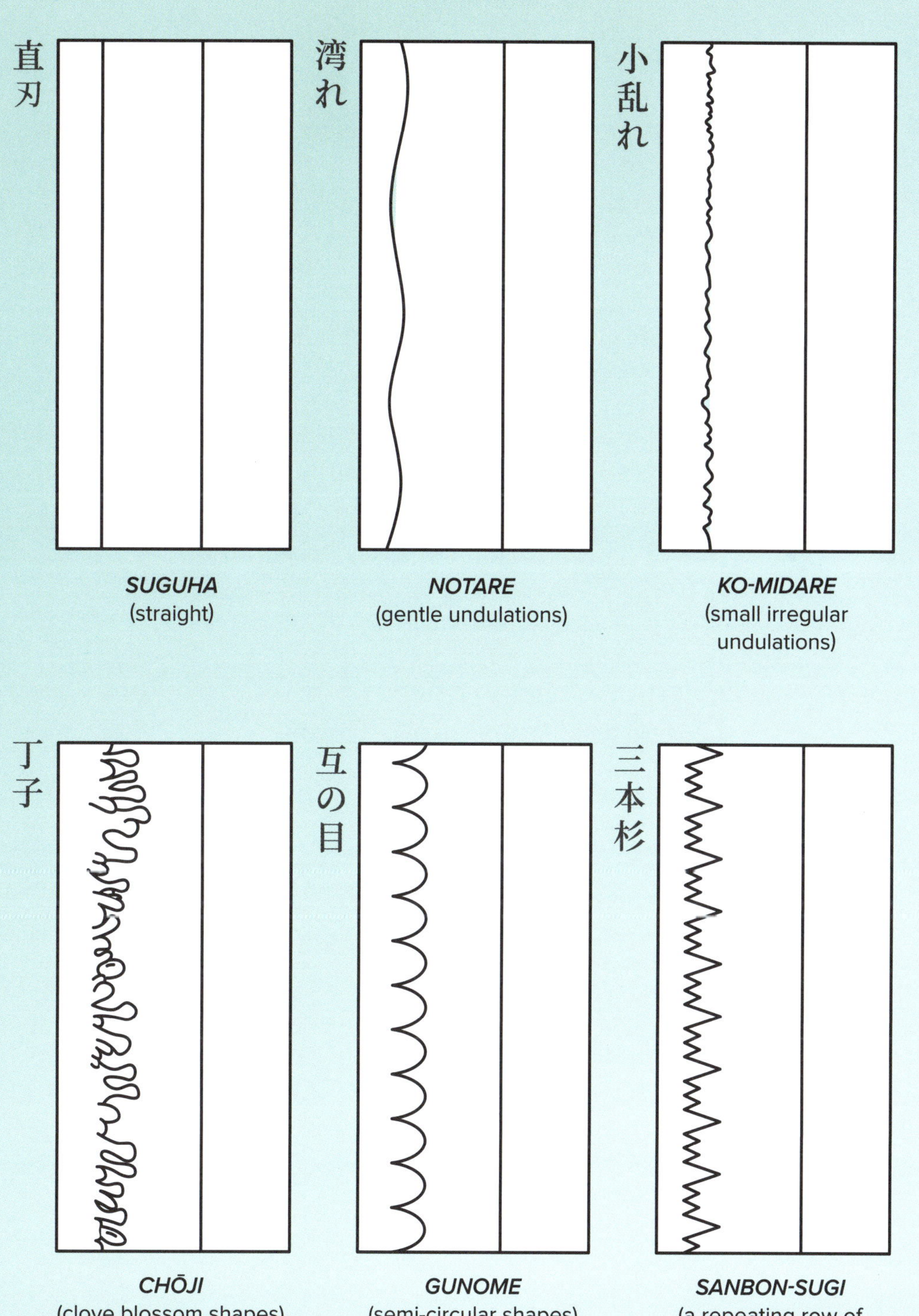

SUGUHA (straight)

NOTARE (gentle undulations)

KO-MIDARE (small irregular undulations)

CHŌJI (clove blossom shapes)

GUNOME (semi-circular shapes)

SANBON-SUGI (a repeating row of three cedar trees)

ACTIVITIES WITHIN THE STEEL (*HATARAKI*)

働き

Hataraki, i.e. crystalline activities in the steel, come in all different forms. As the raw materials for Japanese swords is a type of bloom steel, even with several rounds of the fold-forging process the steel is still not homogenized. Therefore, retains a somewhat inconsistency in its make-up. Therefore, when the blade is heated ready for differential hardening process called *yakiire* (a system of coating the blade in clay of different thicknesses to create a hard steel capable of holding a sharp cutting edge, while at the same time, allowing the back of the blade to retain a more flexible condition) before it is plunged into a bath of tepid water to rapidly cool the steel and freezing the various crystal combinations in place. As the blade heats up, the crystals group and form in relation to the forging pattern of the *hada*. Therefore, it is typical to associate some *hataraki* with certain types of workmanship. For example, *niju-ba* and *kuichigai-ba* are associated with blades that have *masame-hada* in them. However, these various combinations come in all different forms and are often named with terms that allude to natural phenomena.

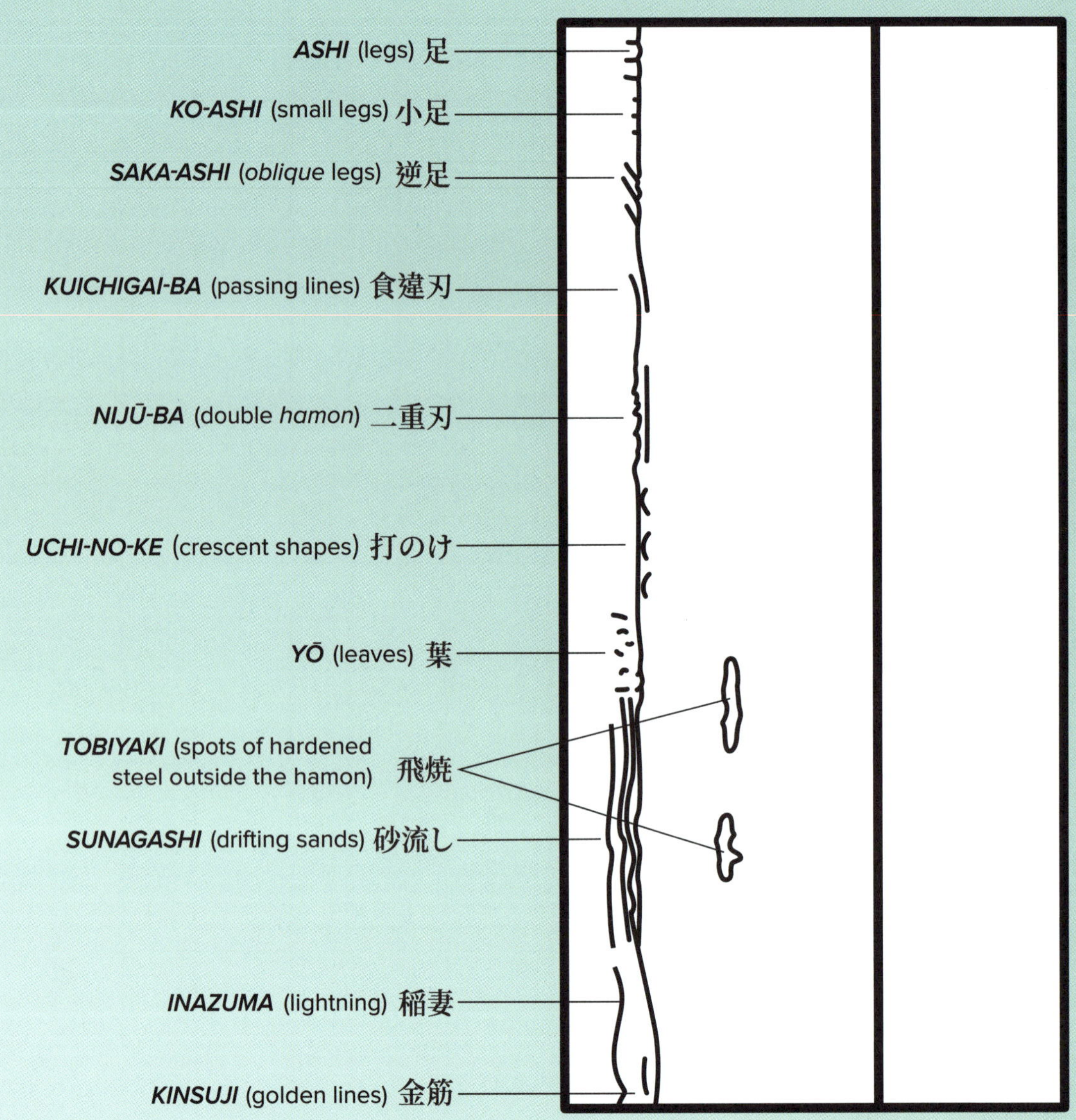

彫物

***Horimono* as various kinds of carving into the blade.** Some are for practical reasons, such as weight decrease or balance. Others are for decorative or spiritual reasons. Early decorative *horimono* tend to have religious meaning. Later *horimono* gradually became more flamboyant and have various meanings including wishes for prosperity.

The most common *horimono* is a long groove called a *hi*, or *bō-hi*, that is cut into the length of the *shinogi-ji*. In some cases, this has earned the misnomer of 'blood groove'. However, it is simple weight decreasing technology the same as your typical I-beam, or railroad rails.

A common theme of decorative *horimono* are the many different representations of the Buddhist deity, and foremost of the Kings of Light, Fudō-Myō-ō the Immoveable. Encapsulated in a halo of flames, he has a fierce expression. He holds a rope in his left hand, and a double-edge *ken* in his right. The rope is to bind the enemies of enlightenment, while the sword is used to cut through the illusionary world to the ultimate reality. He is depicted in various forms, either sitting, or standing under a waterfall, and in various other ways such as a simple Sanskrit character, a solitary double-edge *ken*, or a pair of ritual chopsticks called *gomabashi* that are used in a Buddhist fire ritual in which Fudō-Myō-ō is invoked. His indomitable spirit is to what Japanese swordsmen aspire, therefore he is the patron deity of swordsmen.

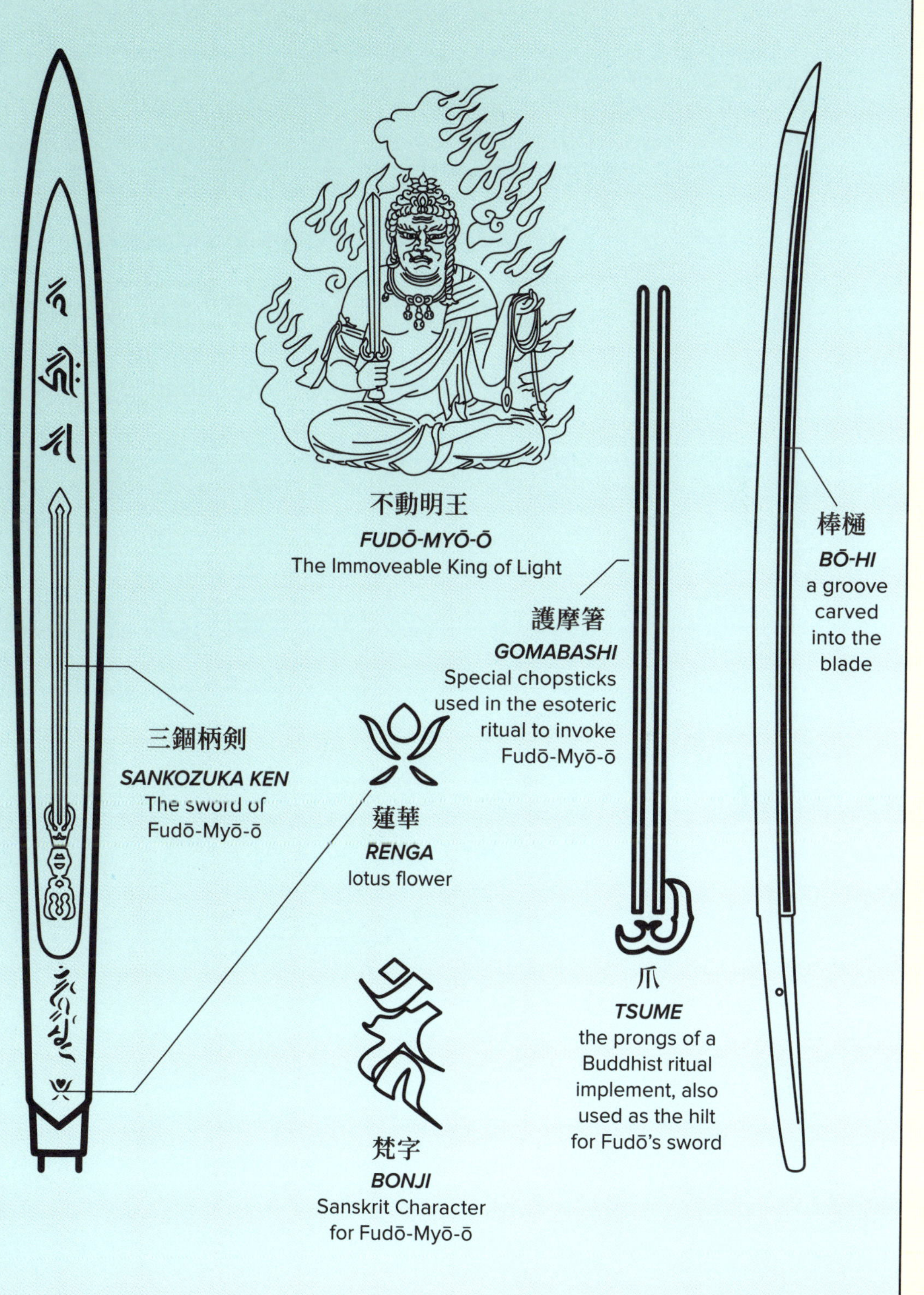

BASIC TYPES OF MOUNTINGS (*KOSHIRAE*)

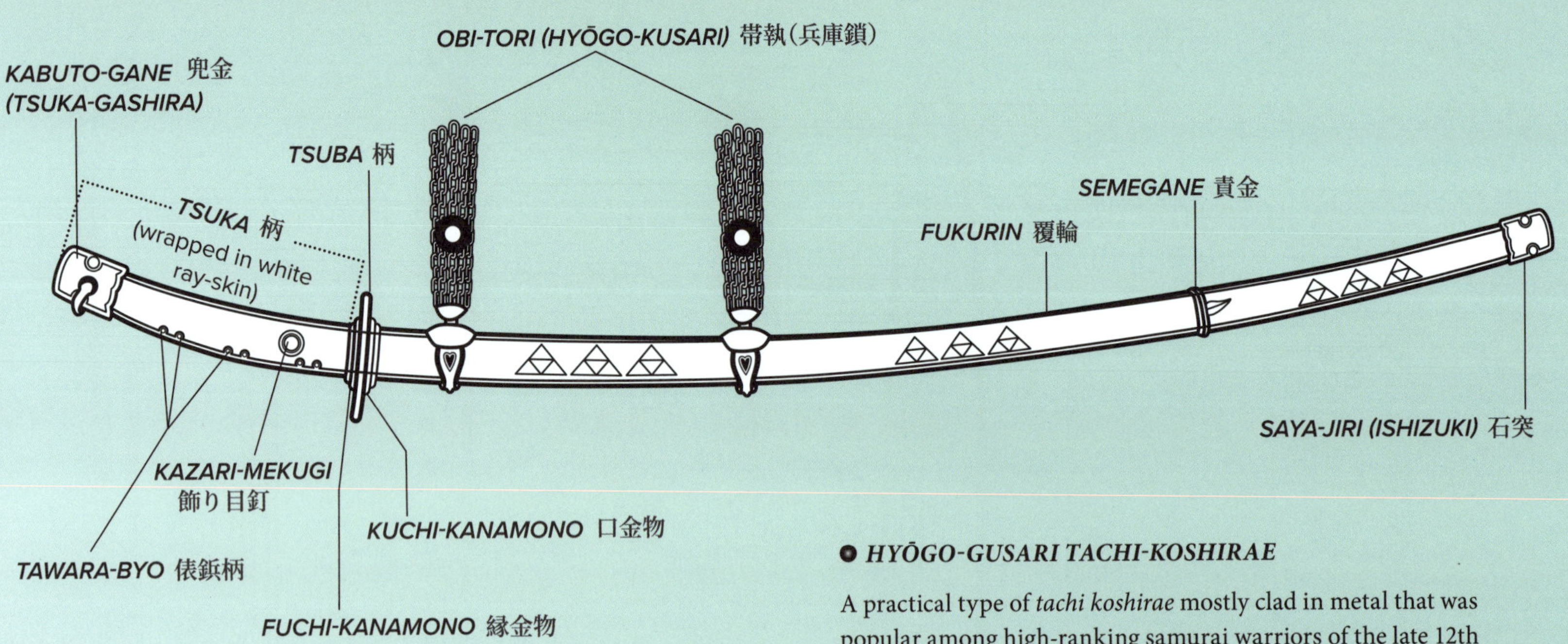

HYŌGO-GUSARI TACHI-KOSHIRAE

A practical type of *tachi koshirae* mostly clad in metal that was popular among high-ranking samurai warriors of the late 12th century. A distinguishing trait of *hyōgo-gusari koshirae* is that the *ashi* are constructed from chain.

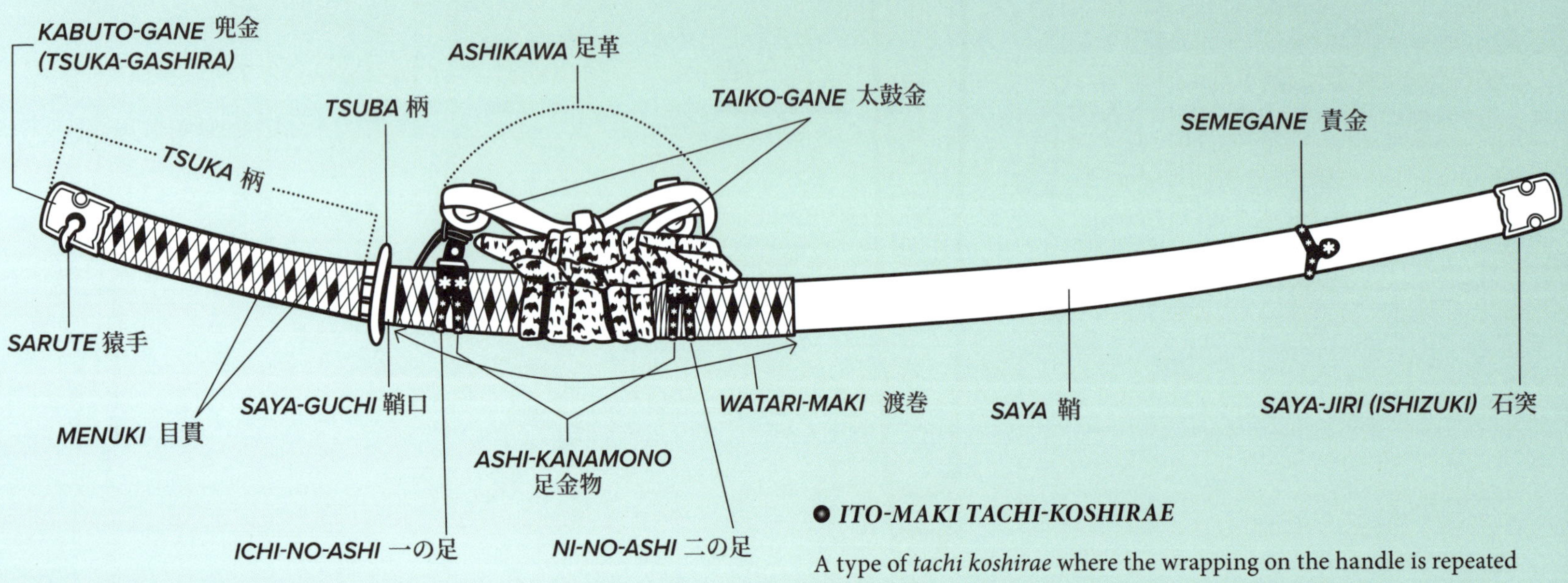

ITO-MAKI TACHI-KOSHIRAE

A type of *tachi koshirae* where the wrapping on the handle is repeated on the upper part of the *saya* (*watari-maki*). It can be seen on some formal mountings of the Kamakura period (12th to 14th centuries). From the late 15th century onwards, it became standard formal and ceremonial wear for *daimyō*.

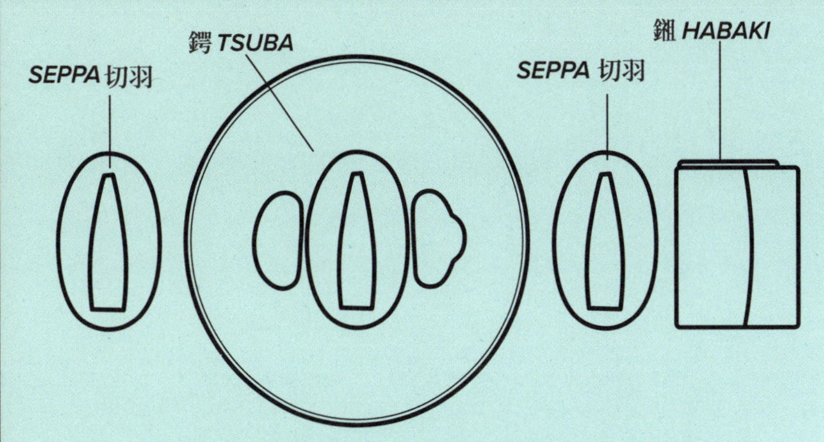

HABAKI

A *habaki* is the collar that is fitted to the base of the blade. Early *habaki* were made of iron, but from around the 14th c. onwards they are usually made of solid copper, silver or gold. They can then be decorated as is, or covered in decorated gold, silver or *shakudō* foil. There are standard types, but *habaki* can also be determined by area of manufacture. The *habaki* not only functions as a stopper to secure the blade into the scabbard, but it also acts as a base on which the tsuba is sandwiched between two spacers called *seppa* and the hilt.

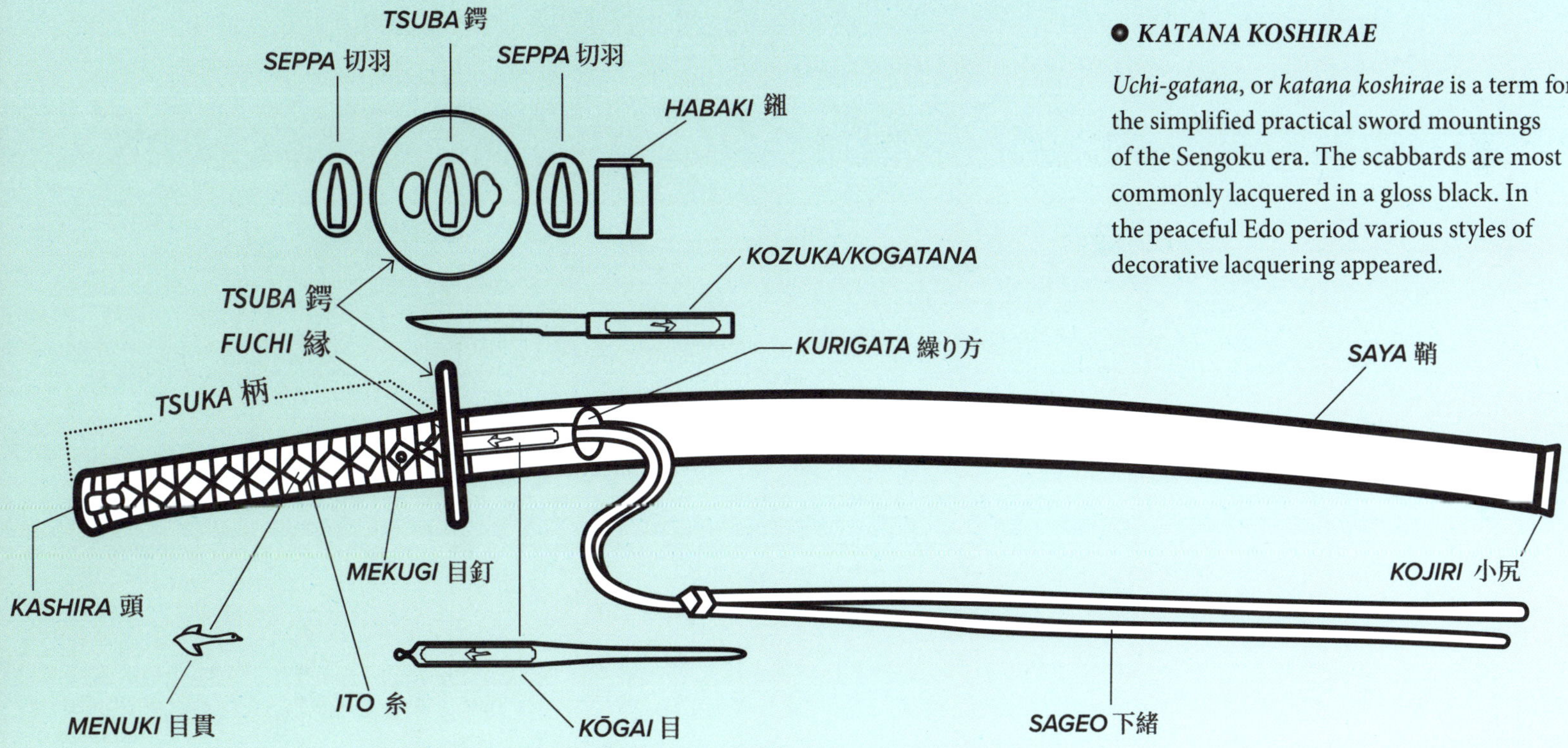

TSUBA 鍔
SEPPA 切羽
SEPPA 切羽
HABAKI 鎺
KOZUKA/KOGATANA
TSUBA 鍔
FUCHI 縁
KURIGATA 繰り方
SAYA 鞘
TSUKA 柄
MEKUGI 目釘
KOJIRI 小尻
KASHIRA 頭
MENUKI 目貫
ITO 糸
KŌGAI 目
SAGEO 下緒

KATANA KOSHIRAE

Uchi-gatana, or *katana koshirae* is a term for the simplified practical sword mountings of the Sengoku era. The scabbards are most commonly lacquered in a gloss black. In the peaceful Edo period various styles of decorative lacquering appeared.

MENUKI

Menuki started out as decorative heads for the *mekugi* (securing pegs) for the hilt on early *koshirae*. They later became a separate fixture as decorative hand-grips. Their placement on the hilt differs between *tachi* and *katana*, and the preferences of various clans and schools of swordsmanship. They come in a wide range of designs, including family crests, and are usually made from the same various soft metals and alloys as the other fittings.

TSUBA

鍔

Tsuba are sword guards that are mounted on the blade between the hilt section (_tsuka_) and the _habaki_ (retaining collar). They are usually secured in place using two spacers, or washer type discs, called _seppa_.

Tsuba are generally rather small offering little protection. It is thought that one of their functions was to also stop the user's hands from sliding onto the blade.

Early sword guards were made from compressed leather that was encased with a metal rim called *fukurin*. Many early iron *tsuba* were made by swordsmiths and are referred to as *tōshō-tsuba*. Ones made by armorers are referred to as *katchū-tsuba*. Later, sword guards gradually became more elaborate with decorative designs with specialist schools of fittings makers appearing in the Edo period.

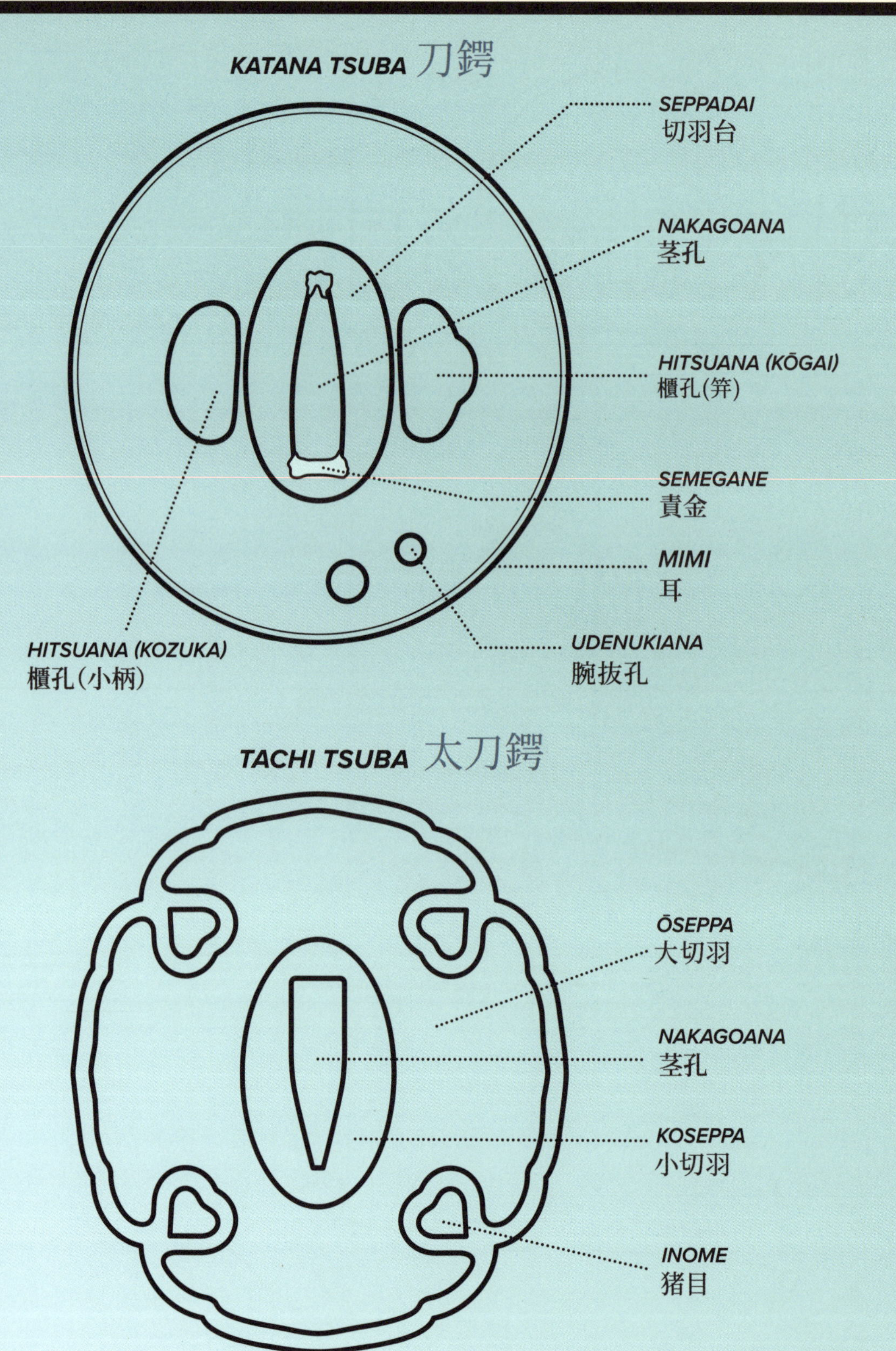

VARIOUS SHAPES OF *TSUBA*

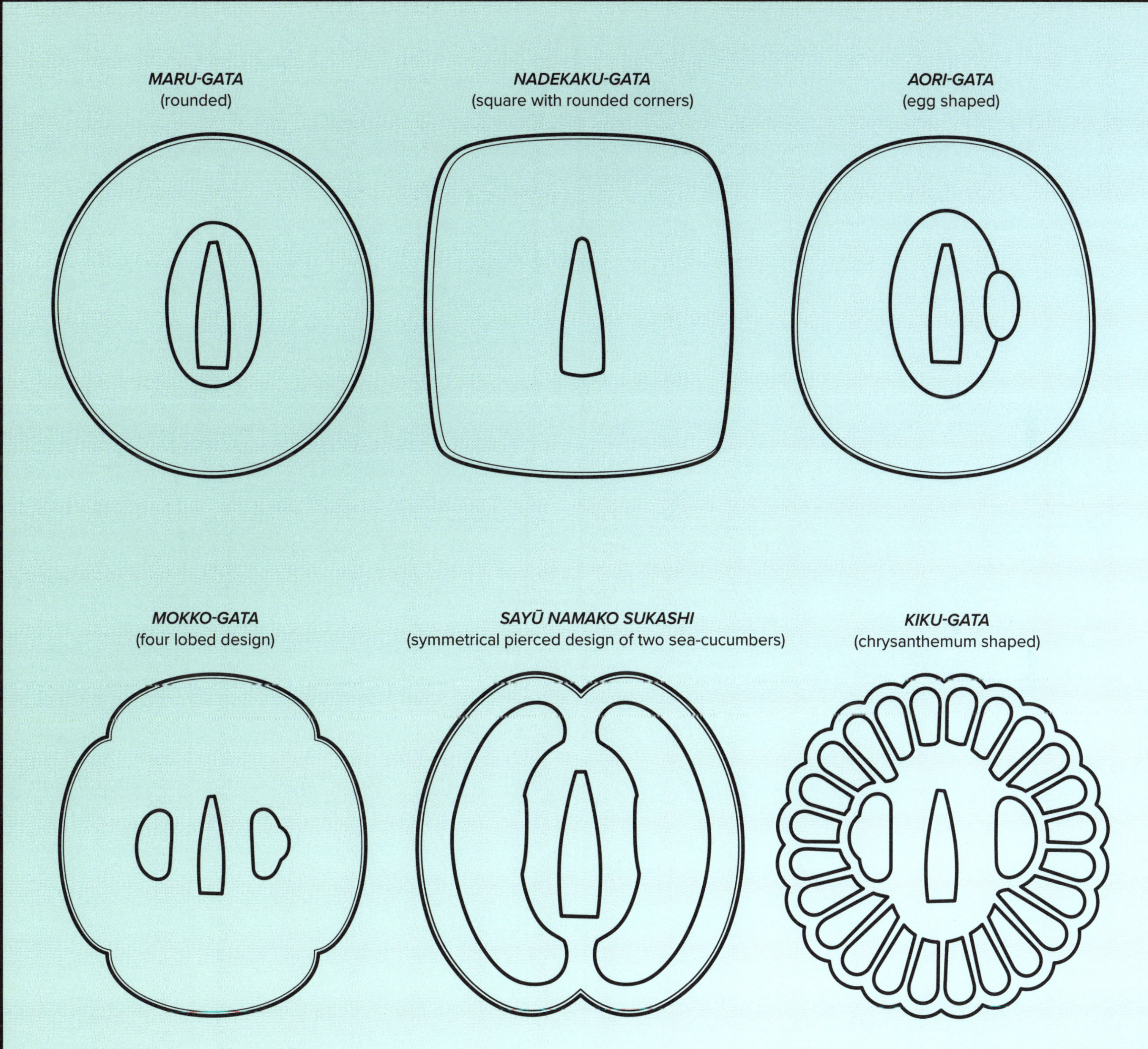

小柄

● **A *kozuka is* a decorative handle** that fits onto a small utility knife called a *kogatana*, which fits into a small pocket on the side of the scabbard that faces the wearer. It is common for either word to be used to describe both of them when they are joined together.

笄

● **A *kōgai* is a small decorative bodkin type grooming utensil** that fits into a small pocket on the side of the scabbard that faces outwards from the wearer. Much like the sumo wrestlers of today, samurai would wear a wax type product in their hair. To avoid getting this on their hands, the *kōgai* was used to fix their hair, tie the top-knot, or just to scratch their head. The scoop at the other end of the *kōgai* is an ear cleaner. It was common for a *kozuka* and *kōgai* to have matching designs.

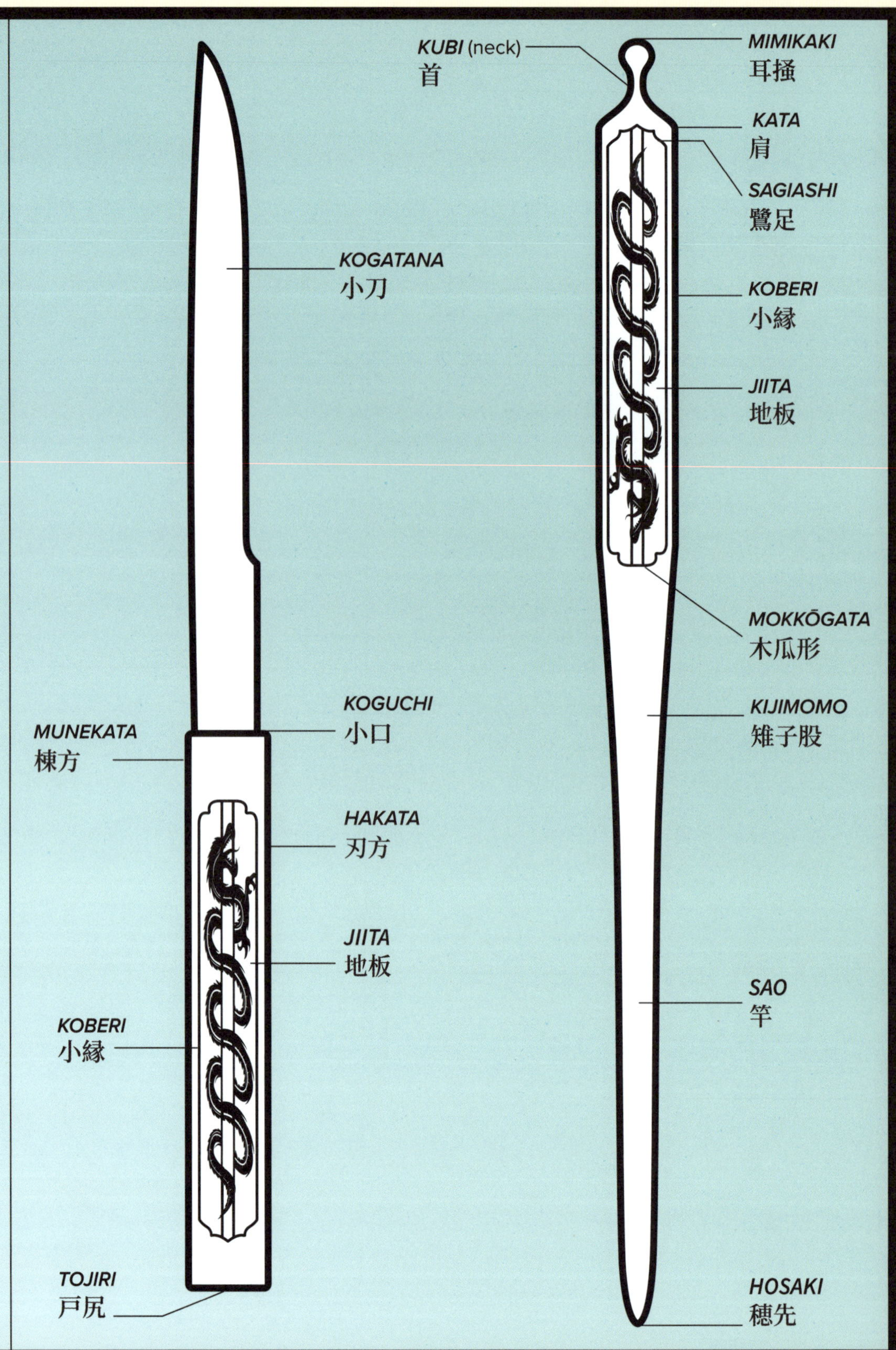

Early types include *ō-yoroi*, which were gradually replaced by the more popular *haramaki* and *dō-maru* types.

Over time, more parts were added, leading to the development of the *tōsei-gusoku* armor by the late 16th c. An armor can consist of a combination of several components: helmet (*kabuto*), cuirass (*dō*), shoulder guards (*sode*), sleeves (*kote*), facemask (*menpō*), thigh guards (*haidate*) and shin-guards (*suneate*).

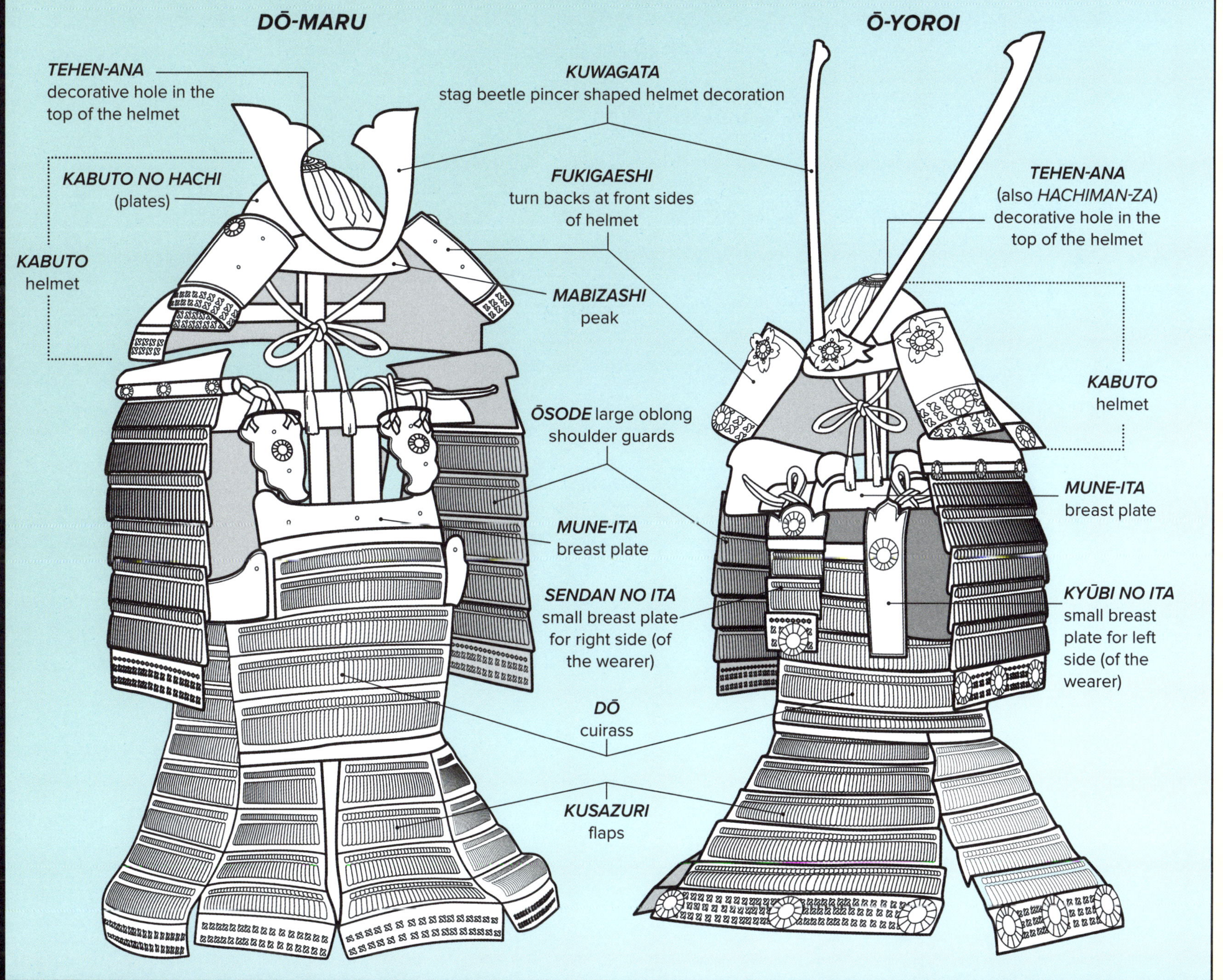

GLOSSARY 用語集

A

Ashi (1) (lit. legs) An activity in the *hamon*, usually *nioi*, that extend from the *nioi-guchi* towards the cutting edge.

Ashi (2) Fittings attached to the scabbard of a *tachi* that connects to other parts in order to secure it to the waist.

Ayasugi-hada An undulating grain pattern in the *ji* resembling a row of Japanese cedar trees.

B

Bakufu The Shogunate (military government).

Bakumatsu (lit. End of the Shogunate / bakufu) The very last part of the late Edo period 1853–1867.

Bizen Archaic province of Japan, modern day Okayama prefecture.

Bizen-tō Swords produced in Bizen province.

Bizen-zori Deep curvature close to the tang area of the sword; also known as *koshi-zori*.

Bō-hi A groove carved into the blade for decoration or weight decreasing purposes.

Bonji Sanscrit characters carved into the blade invoking Buddhist deities.

Bōshi Literally 'cap', the *hamon* formed within the *kissaki*.

Bō-utsuri A straight formation of *utsuri*.

Bu Japanese imperial form of measurement (10 *bu* = 1 *sun*).

Bushi Another term for samurai—the warrior class.

C

Chikei A curved line of *nie*, seen in the *ji*.

Chogi A swordsmith of Osafune famous for So-den Bizen workmanship.

Chōji-abura Oil used for preserving blades with clove fragrance.

Chōji-ashi Clove-shaped *ashi*.

Chōji-midare A *hamon* consisting of *chōji* shapes.

Chōji-utsuri *Utsuri* in a *chōji* pattern.

Chokutō A straight sword, but similar in construction to the *tachi*.

Chu-kissaki A medium sized *kissaki*, in relation to the overall size of the blade.

Chu-suguha A medium-sized straight *hamon*.

D

Daimyō provincial samurai lords.

Daishō A pair of swords in matching fittings worn together: *dai-* being the long sword, and *shō-* being the shorter companion sword. Only the samurai were permitted to wear them during the Edo period.

Dewa Archaic name for region in present-day Akita & Yamagata Prefectures.

Dō-maru A type of cuirass that opens on the right side and wraps around the torso.

E

Eto Animal zodiacal calendar often used for date inscriptions on swords.

F

Fuchi-kashira (also, *fuchigashira*) Matching pommel (*kashira*) and base collar (*fuchi*) fittings for the hilt of a sword.

Fudō Myō-ō A Buddhist deity, the immovable King of Light. Patron deity of swordsmen. Commonly used for *horimono*.

Fukigaeshi The protruding turn backs either side of the peak of the helmet. They often are decorated with clan crests. Sizes vary according to period of manufacture.

Fukura The line of the curved edge of the *kissaki*.

Funagata A type of *nakago* shaped like the bottom of a boat.

Funbari Used to describe a blade when it noticeably tapers from the base.

Futasuji-hi Two parallel grooves carved into the blade.

G

Genpei War A civil war between the Minamoto (Gen) and Taira (Hei→Pei) clans from 1180–1185.

Gobankaji The swordsmiths summoned to work with the Cloistered Emperor Gotoba.

Goka-den The five main styles of sword-making that originate in the Kotō (old-sword) period of swordmaking (794–1603).

Goki-shichido The five home provinces and seven main roads. Originally used for units of governmental administration. Currently used for classifying swordsmiths by region and style.

Gomabashi A *horimono* in the form of the ritual chopsticks used in both Shintō and Buddhist rites.

Gomaidō A cuirass made of five-sections for a Japanese armor.

Gunome A type of *hamon* that undulates in a series of semi-circles.

Gusoku Another word for armor.

H

Habaki The small metal collar (often decorated) that buffers the *tsuba* and secures the blade into the *saya*.

Habaki-moto The part of the blade that sits under the *habaki*.

Hachō Length of the cutting edge (also see *nagasa*).

Hada The steel skin of the blade, also called *jihada*.

Hadōri A polishing technique which highlights the *hamon*, also known as *keshō*.

Hagire A hairline crack in the blade rising up from the cutting edge.

Haitōrei The law administered in Japan 1876, banning the wearing of swords in public.

Hakikake Similar to *sunagashii*, activities that resemble brush strokes.

Ha-machi The notch that separates the cutting-edge of the blade from the *nakago*.

Hamon The pattern of the crystalline structure which forms along the cutting edge of a blade as a result of the hardening process.

Han-dachi (lit. Half-*tachi*) A style of *katana koshirae* that includes elements similar to that of a *tachi koshirae*.

Ha-saki The cutting edge.

Hatamoto A rank designated to senior vassal samurai of the Tokugawa shogunate.

Hataraki The various crystalline activities within the *hamon*.

Ha-watari See *nagasa*.

Hi A groove carved into the blade for decoration or weight decreasing purposes.

Hira-zukuri A sword made without any ridgelines, flat on both sides.

Hiro-suguha A wide *suguha hamon*.

Hitatsura A type of *hamon* with *tobiyaki* liberally spread across the width of the blade.

Horimono Decorative blade carvings.

Hoso-suguha A narrow straight *hamon*.

Hotsure The edge of the *nioi-guchi* appears frayed.

Hyōgo-gusari Tachi Koshirae A practical type of *tachi koshirae* clad in metal with *ashi* constructed from chain.

I

Ichimai-bōshi A *bōshi* that covers or almost covers the entire point section.

Ichimonji School A 13th c. school of swordsmiths working in the Bizen tradition.

Ikubi kissaki A stout *kissaki* which is shorter in length than it is wide.

Inazuma (literally, lightning) A line of *nie* inside the *hamon* resembling lightning.

Iori-mune A two-sided *mune* resembling the roof of a house.

Iriyama-gata A type of *nakago jiri* shaped like a lop-side mountain. The longer side is on the same side as the cutting edge.

Itame-hada A wood grain pattern in the skin steel of the blade with predominantly elliptical shapes.

Ito Thread or cord.

Ito-maki Tachi Koshirae A type of *tachi koshirae* where the hilt and part of the scabbard are wrapped in maching cord (*ito*).

Iyozane A small fork shaped type of platelet used for some Japanese armor.

J

Ji The surface area of the blade between the *shinogi* and the *hamon*.

Jifu-utsuri Discontinuous *utsuri*.

Jigane The surface steel of the blade.

Jihada The surface pattern of the blade, see *hada*.

Juka-chōji Multiple grouped *chōji* pattern.

Ji-nie *Nie* in the *ji*.

Jitetsu See *hada* and *jigane*.

Jizō A type of *bōshi* similar to a *midare komi*, but with a narrow *kaeri* that makes it resemble a statue of the Bodhisattva Jizō seen in profile.

K

Kabuto A Japanese helmet.

Kaen A type of *bōshi* that resembles burning flames.

Kaeri The part of the *bōshi* that turns back towards the tang, along the *mune*.

Kaki-nagashi A groove that ends by tapering within the tang.

Kaki-toshi A type of groove that continues through the tang to the end.

Kakudome A groove end that is square, usually stops just before the *habaki*.

Kanbun Shintō Blades made around the Kanbun era 1661–1673.

Kanmuri-otoshi-zukuri A blade shape in which a few centimeters from the *habaki* the *shinogi-ji* becomes beveled and continues in that condition right through the point section (*kissaki*).

Kantō Kanrei The *shōgun*'s chief adviser for eastern Japan. There was also a Kyōto Kanrei, the *shōgun*'s adviser for western Japan.

Kantei Sword appraisal.

Kantei-shō A certificate given to swords expressing an opinion of authenticity.

Kasane The thickness of the blade.

Kashira The pommel at the end of the hilt (see *fuchi-kashira*).

Kataochi-gunome Flat topped gunome that slant in the same direction like saw teeth

Katana Curved blades worn thrust through the sash with the cutting edge uppermost.

Katchū Generic term for Japanese armor.

Katte-agari-yasuri File marks on the tang that slant downward to the left.

Katte-sagari-yasuri File marks on the tang that slant downward to the right.

Kawagane (lit. skin-steel) The higher carbon steel used for the outer surface of the blade.

Kawazuko-chōji Tadpole shaped *chōji*.

Kazu-uchimono Mass produced blades of little artistic quality.

Ken A straight double-edged ritual Chinese style sword, often associated with Fudō Myō-ō.

Kenjutsu-dōjō A place or school dedicated to the practice of swordsmanship.

Keichō era 1596–1615.

Keichō Shintō Blades produced around the Keichō era (1596–1615) at the start of the Shintō sword period.

Keshō See *Hadōri*.

Kijimomo Pheasant thigh (shaped).

Kiku-go-saku Swords attributed to the hand of Emperor Gotoba.

Kiku mon Crest in the shape of a chrysanthemum flower. Later used by the Imperial family.

Kinsuji A small shiny line of *nie* inside the *hamon*, similar to *inazuma*.

Kiriha-zukuri A sword made with the *shinogi* close to the cutting edge.

Kiri-jiri The end of a *nakago* that has been cut straight across.

Kiri-yasuri Horizontal file marks.

Kissaki The point section of the blade.

Kissaki-moroha-zukuri A blade made with a double edge in the *monouchi* area.

Ko Prefix, meaning small (example, *ko-nie*—small *nie*).

Ko-ashi Small *ashi*.

Ko-bushigata chōji Fist shaped *chōji*.

Kogarasu-maru zukuri A type of blade created in the Heian period where the upper section is sharp on both sides.

Kogatana Utility knife.

Kōgai A bodkin like grooming utensil.

Koi-guchi The mouth of the *saya*.

Ko-itame Small wood grain pattern.

Kojiri A protective cap fitting (chape) on the bottom of the *saya* (scabbard).

Ko-maru A type of *bōshi* that turns back in a small smooth circular motion.

Ko-nie Small *nie* particles.

Konuka-hada A term used mainly for Hizen blades, commonly referred to as rice grain *hada*.

Koshi-ba A flamboyant section of *hamon* at the base when compared to the rest of the blade.

Koshi-bi A short type of groove carved in the blade close to the tang.

Ko-shinogi The part of the *shinogi* that runs from the *yokote* to the tip in the *kissaki*.

Koshi-no-hiraita Wide based undulations that slope gently, usually with *chōji*.

Koshirae A full set of sword mountings.

Koshi-zori Swords with the deepest part of the curve near to the tang.

Kotō (Old swords) Swords made in the pre-Edo period.

Ko-wakizashi A short *wakizashi*.

Kozuka A decorative knife handle for the *kogatana* (utility knife) that fits into a pocket on the side of the scabbard.

Kuichigaiba A section of *hamon* that appears to break and overlap, like the lines are passing by each other.

Kurijiri Round-ended type of *nakago*, similar to the shape of a chestnut.

Kurikara A *horimono* of a dragon wrapped around a *ken*, a representation of Fudō Myō-ō.

Kusazuri The skirt of Japanese armor made from rows of iron or leather plates laced together using silk or leather cord.

M

Machi-okuri The notches at the base of the blade are moved further along the blade, decreasing the cutting-edge length, but not the overall length of the blade.

Maedate Decorative appendage on the front of a helmet (*kabuto*).

Maki Wrap/wrapped (example, *tsuka-maki*: hilt wrapping).

Makie A Japanese technique where items are decorated using various colored traditional *urushi* lacquers to produce images and designs on lacquered items including arms and armor.

Makura Pillow. Small ones are used to keep the tip of the swords elevated.

Marudome A carved groove end that is rounded.

Marumune A *mune* that is rounded.

Masame-hada A straight grain pattern in the *hada*.

Mei Signature or inscription on the tang.

Mekugi The bamboo peg used to secure the handle onto the tang.

Mekugi-ana The hole on the tang where the *mekugi* (retaining peg) is inserted.

Mekugi-nuki A tool for removing the *mekugi*.

Menuki Decorative hand grips made of soft metals placed on either side of the hilt.

Midare *Hamon* of irregular shape; this characteristic affects all types of *hamon* except *suguha*.

Midare-komi A *bōshi* where the irregularity of the *hamon* continues in the *kissaki*.

Midare-utsuri *Utsuri* of irregular form.

Mihaba The width of a blade: measured from the *mune* to the cutting edge.

Mitsukado The place where the *shinogi* meets the *ko-shinogi* and the *yokote*.

Mitsumune A *mune* with three planes.

Mokume-hada A grain pattern in the *hada* with predominantly round shapes.

Monouchi One-third of the blade from the *yokote* towards the tang.

Moroha-zukuri A blade with a cutting edge on both sides.

Moto-haba The width of the base of the blade just above the *ha-machi* and *mune-machi*.

Mukansa A grade awarded to swordsmiths whose work is recognized to be above the regular ranking systems.

Mumei Unsigned. A blade or fittings that lack an inscription or have lost maker's signature.

Mune The spine of the blade.

Mune-machi See *machi*.

Mune-yaki When sections or the entire of the length of the spine has been hardened.

Mu-zori A blade with little or no curvature.

N

Nagare-hada A *hada* that flows along the blade.

Nagasa The blade length; measured between the tip and the *mune-machi*.

Naginata A Japanese halberd.

Nakago The tang of a blade.

Nakago-jiri The tip of the tang.

Namako sukashi A symmetrical pierced *tsuba* in the design of two sea-cucumbers.

Nanbantetsu A general term for foreign steel.

Nashiji A type of *hada* that resembles the skin of Japanese pears.

Nie Small martensite crystals individually visible to the naked eye.

Nie-deki A blade with a predominantly *nie hamon*.

Nihon Bijutsu Tōken Hozon Kyōkai The Society for the Preservation of Japanese art Swords (NBTHK).

Nihontō Japanese swords (including *ken*, *tantō*, *naginata* and *yari*).

Nihontō Bunka Shinkō Kyōkai The Society for the Promotion of Japanese Sword Culture (NBSK).

Nijū-ba A line of *nioi* or *nie* that runs parallel to the *hamon*, giving the appearance of a twin *hamon*.

Nioi Martensite crystals not individually distinguishable to the naked eye, like the clouds of the Milky Way in appearance.

Nioi-deki A sword with a *hamon* consisting mainly of *nioi*.

Nioi-guchi The transitional border of the *hamon* and the *ji*.

No-dachi Swords of a much greater size than standard.

Notare Gently undulating *hamon*.

Notare-komi A notare type of *bōshi*.

O

Ō Prefix, denoting large (example, *ō-gunome*—large *gunome*).

Ō-chōji midare Large sized *chōji* (clove like pattern) type *hamon*.

Ō-dachi A large-sized *tachi* with a cutting edge that exceeds 3 *shaku* (91 cm/35²⁶⁄₃₂ in).

Omote The front side of a blade.

Orikaeshi-mei When a blade has been shortened (*suriage*), but the original *mei* (signature/inscription) has been preserved by folding it back, and inserting into the opposite side of the tang.

Ōsasaho A type of *yari* (spear) that resembles a large bamboo leaf.

Oshigata A rubbing taken of the tang and outline of a blade. The *hamon* and activities are then drawn by hand.

Ōsode Large oblong shoulder guards.

Ōsuriage A blade that has been greatly shortened from the *nagako* (tang) end of the blade.

Ō-Yoroi A term for earlier style Japanese armor of the Heian and Kamakura periods.

S

Saiha A blade that has had its cutting edge re-hardened.

Saka ashi Oblique *ashi*.

Saka chōji Oblique *chōji*.

Saki-haba Width of the blade at the *yokote*.

Saki-zori When the curvature is centered in the upper part of the blade.

Saku (Suffix) 'made by'. See also *Zukuri*.

Samekawa Stingray-skin. Often mistaken for shark-skin, it is used to wrap hilts, scabbards and other items. It can be lacquered and polished flat. It has larger nodules around the center of the back that are placed usually towards the top on the obverse of the hilt.

Samurai The warrior class of Japan.

Sanbon-sugi A type of *hamon* that resembles three cedar trees repeated along the blade.

Sankozuka-ken A straight double-edge blade (*ken*) with a Buddhist ritual implement (*vajra*) as the hilt.

Sashikomi An older style of Japanese polish where the area between the *shinogi* and the *ha-saki* is polished in the same finish (as opposed to *keshō*).

Saya Scabbard.

Sayagaki A description or appraisal of the blade written directly onto the scabbard.

Shaku Japanese imperial form of measurement (1 *shaku* = 30.3cm/11 29/32 in).

Shakudō-nanako *Shakudō* is an alloy of gold and copper. *Nanako* is a pattern that resembles fish roe.

Sengoku jidai Age of the warring states (1493–1573).

Seppa Washer like spacers placed either side of the *tsuba* between the *habaki* and the base of the hilt.

Shikoro The neck protector made of several layers of shaped strips made of iron or leather, and attached to the bowl of a Japanese helmet (*kabuto*).

Shinogi The ridge line that that runs from the *yokote* to the end of the *nakago*.

Shinogi-ji The area between the *shinogi* and the *mune*.

Shinogi-zukuri A sword manufactured in the ridgeline construction method.

Shinsakutō (Newly made swords) Swords made by contemporary smiths.

Shintō New-swords made between 1600 and 1781.

Shin-shintō New-new swords made between 1781 and 1868.

Shirasaya A plain wooden sleeping scabbard and handle to protect the blade. Plain wooden sleeping scabbard made from *honoki* (magnolia wood) for preservation of the blade.

Soe-bi A smaller carved groove that runs parallel to the large groove.

Sori The curvature of the blade.

Sōshū-den The tradition of swordmaking originating from the archaic province of Sagami (Kanagawa Prefecture).

Suaca Japanese copper.

Sudare-ba A *hamon* that resembles brush strokes, or a bamboo curtain.

Sugata The shape of the blade.

Suguha A straight *hamon*.

Suji-kabuto A helmet constructed from plates that were joined form ridgelines.

Sujikai-yasuri Acutely slanted file mark pattern on the *nakago*.

Sukehiro A swordsmith of the Osaka Shintō school credited with inventing *toran-ba*.

Suken Also known as a *ken*, straight ritual double-edged sword, often associated with Fudō Myō-ō.

Sun Japanese imperial form of measurement (1 *sun* = 3.03 cm/1 3/16 in, 10 *sun* = 1 *shaku*).

Sunagashi An activity in the *hamon* that resembles drifting sands.

Sunobi-tantō An oversized *tantō*.

Suriage A process where the blade is shortened from its original length.

Suriage nakago A *nakago* that has been adjusted/reformed after a blade has been shortened.

T

Tachi Swords made to be worn with the cutting edge down, suspended from the belt.

Tachi-mei A signature on a blade on the side of the tang that faces outward when worn with the cutting edge downward.

Tachi koshirae A set of sword mountings that are worn slung from the hip for use on horseback.

Tamahagane Archaically produced Japanese steel, used in the manufacture of Japanese swords.

Tantō (Dagger) Blades with a cutting-edge length shorter than 30 cm (11 13/16 in).

Tenshō era 1573-1592.

Tobiyaki Spots of hardened steel independent from the main *hamon*.

Togariba Pointed shapes protruding from the *hamon.*

Toran-ba A type of *hamon* that resembles the waves of the sea.

Torii-zori A blade with an even curvature.

Tsuba Sword guard.

Tsuchioki The clay applied to the blade before the hardening (*yaki-ire*) process.

Tsuka The hilt.

Tsuka-ito A special type of cord usually made from silk, leather, and occasionally whale beard that is used to bind the *tsuka* (hilt).

Tsurugi Alternate Japanese word for sword.

U

Ubu Original, usually used when referring to the *nakago*.

Ubu-ha An area of the cutting edge from the *ha-machi*, which has not yet been sharpened. This is typical with new blades.

Uchi-gatana Blades produced for one-handed use during the Muromachi period.

Uchi-no-ke Small crescent shapes appearing like *nijū-ba* in the *ji* close to the *hamon*.

Uchi-zori The back of the blade curves toward the cutting edge.

Ura The reverse side/back.

Utsuri (Reflection) A white misty formation that runs parallel to the *hamon* in the *ji*.

Utsushi-mono Facsimile of past masterpieces (not to be confused with forgeries).

W

Wakizashi Blades over 30 cm (11¹³⁄₁₆ in) in length, but shorter than 60 cm (23⅝ in). Often a companion sword to the *katana*.

Y

Yakidashi A part of the *hamon* which starts off straight at the *ha-machi*, but turns into a different *hamon* several centimetres along the blade.

Yaki-ire The differential hardening process of the blade where it is heated and quenched in water.

Yaki-otoshi A *hamon* which starts further along the blade, about 3–5 cm (1³⁄₁₆ in–1³¹⁄₃₂ in) from the *ha-machi*.

Yakizume A type of *bōshi* without a turn-back.

Yari A Japanese spear usually mounted on a long shaft.

Yamagata Mountain shaped.

Yasurime File markings.

Yō An activity in the *hamon* that resembles leaves.

Yokote A dividing line between the *kissaki* and the body of the blade.

Yōroi Japanese armor.

Yōroi-doshi Armour piercing (*tantō*).

Yubashiri A concentration of *nie* in the *ji*.

Z

Zaimei An item with an original signature.

Zukuri (Suffix) 'made by'. See also *Saku*.

PHOTOGRAPHIC CREDITS

Where not otherwise specified, art images are all prints or diptychs / triptychs of prints.

Cover: top © TNM Image Archives / center © Agency for Cultural Affairs - Bunkachō / bottom © Lord Takeda Shingen Treasure House, Kōshū, Yamanashi Prefecture

Back cover: top © Kawabata Terutaka Collection - Photographs by Ikeda Nagamasa / bottom © Courtesy of Kyoto National Museum

p. 1 © Akama Shrine, Yamaguchi Prefecture

pp. 2–3 and 20 © The British Museum, Londres, Dist. RMN-Grand Palais / The Trustees of the British Museum - 1962,1013,0.2

p. 5 © Molteni & Motta / UIG / Bridgeman Images

p. 6 © Luisa Ricciarini / Bridgeman Images

p. 8 © Izu City, Shizuoka Prefecture

p. 9 © Public domain, Rijksmuseum, Amsterdam - Object Number: RP-P-1991-541 - Gift of J.H.W. Goslings, Epse

p. 11 © Public domain, The Cleveland Museum of Art - Accession number: 1919.914 - Gift of Ralph King - https://clevelandart.org/art/1919.914

p. 12 © The Hiratsuka Museum of Art, courtesy of Yukio Yasuda

p. 13 © The National Museum of Modern Art, Tōkyō - MOMAT / DNPartcom

p. 14 left © Dipper Historic / Alamy Foto Stock

p. 14 center © Public domain, via Wikimedia Commons

p. 14 right © Public domain, via Wikimedia Commons

p. 15 © Harvard Art Museums / Arthur M. Sackler Museum - Bequest of William S. Lieberman - Accession number: 2007.214.92.1 - Photo credit: President and Fellows of Harvard College - Persistent link: https://hvrd.art/o/318754

pp. 16–17 © Museum of Fine Arts, Boston - William Sturgis Bigelow Collection - Accession number: 11.34998.101a-c - www.mfa.org

pp. 18–19 © Philadelphia Museum of Art - Purchased with funds contributed by the E. Rhodes and Leona B. Carpenter Foundation, 1989 - Accession number: 1989-47-134a--c

pp. 20–27 © Terebi Setouchi Create

p. 28 © Imperial Household Agency

p. 29 © Fair Use

pp. 30–31 bottom © TNM Image Archives

p. 32 © Collection of the Honolulu Museum of Art - Purchase, 2000 (9398.1)

p. 33 © Museum of Fine Arts, Boston - William Sturgis Bigelow Collection - Accession number: 11.20494 - www.mfa.org

p. 34 © Museum of Fine Arts, Boston - William Sturgis Bigelow Collection - Accession number: 11.16451 - www.mfa.org

p. 35 © Utagawa Kuniyoshi / National Museum of Asian Art - Smithsonian Institution - Arthur M. Sackler Collection - The Pearl and Seymour Moskowitz Collection, S2021.5.572a-c

pp. 36–37 top © Kitano Tenmangū Shrine, Kyōto

pp. 36–37 bottom © TNM Image Archives

p. 38 © Public domain, via Wikimedia Commons (Jingoji, Kyōto)

p. 39 © Torii Kiyonaga / National Museum of Asian Art - Smithsonian Institution - Freer Study Collection - Gift of Alan, Donald, and David Winslow from the estate of William R. Castle, FSC-GR-133

p. 41 left © Ōyamazumi Shrine, Ehime Prefecture - Sogeisha

p. 41 right © Public domain, Rijksmuseum, Amsterdam - Accession number: RP-P-1958-451 - J.A. Bierens de Haan Bequest, Amsterdam - Acquisition: bequest 1958 - Persistent URL: http://hdl.handle.net/10934/RM0001.COLLECT.45892

pp. 42–43 © Ōyamazumi Shrine, Ehime Prefecture - Sogeisha

pp. 44–45 © Toyohara Chikanobu / National Museum of Asian Art - Smithsonian Institution - Arthur M. Sackler Collection - Robert O. Muller Collection, S2003.8.2622 (Detail)

p. 46 © Utagawa Hiroshige / National Museum of Asian Art - Smithsonian Institution - Arthur M. Sackler Collection - S Bequest of Charles H.W. Verbeck, 2010.18.147

p. 47 © Museum of Fine Arts, Boston - William Sturgis Bigelow Collection - Accession number: 11.16466 - www.mfa.org

pp. 48–49 © Ōyamazumi Shrine, Ehime Prefecture - Sogeisha

p. 51 left © Public domain, Rijksmuseum, Amsterdam - Accession number: RP-P-1977-101 - Purchased with the support of the F.G. Waller-Fonds - Acquisition: purchase 1977 - Persistent URL: http://hdl.handle.net/10934/RM0001.COLLECT.45408

p. 51 right © Public domain, Rijksmuseum, Amsterdam - Accession number: RP-P-1956-663 - Purchased with the support of the Vereniging Rembrandt and the Ministerie van Onderwijs, Kunsten en Wetenschappen - Acquisition: purchase 1956 - Persistent URL: http://hdl.handle.net/10934/RM0001.COLLECT.45611

p. 52 © Museum of Fine Arts, Boston - William Sturgis Bigelow Collection - Accession number: 11.14997 - www.mfa.org

p. 53 © Philadelphia Museum of Art - Gift of Mrs. David Klein, 1971 - Accession number: 1971-180-62

p. 54 © Daikakuji, Kyōto

p. 55 © The Picture Art Collection / Alamy Foto Stock

p. 56 © Museum of Fine Arts, Boston - William Sturgis Bigelow Collection - Accession number: 11.6575 - www.mfa.org

p. 57 © Kasuga Taisha Treasure House, Nara

p. 58 © The Metropolitan Museum of Art - Gift of Estate of Samuel Isham, 1914 - Accession number: JP939 / The Metropolitan Museum of Art / Art Resource / Scala, Firenze

p. 59 © Museum of Fine Arts, Boston - William Sturgis Bigelow Collection - Accession number: 11.37136 - www.mfa.org

pp. 60–61 © Utagawa Yoshitsuya / National Museum of Asian Art - Smithsonian Institution - Arthur M. Sackler Collection - The Anne van Biema Collection, S2004.3.203a-c

pp. 62–63 © The Japanese Sword Museum, Sumida (Tōkyō)

p. 64 © History and Art Collection / Alamy Stock Photo

p. 65 © Library of Congress, Prints & Photographs Division [repr. number: LC-DIG-jpd-00292] (https://www.loc.gov/item/ 2009615282/)

pp. 66–67 © Public domain, via Wikimedia Commons - Claremont Colleges Digital Library

pp. 68–69 © TNM Image Archives

p. 71 © National Diet Library's website (https://www.ndl.go.jp/en/index.html)

pp. 72–73 © Kyoto National Museum / DNPartcom

p. 74 © Public domain, via Wikimedia Commons

p. 75 © Museum of Fine Arts, Boston - Fenollosa-Weld Collection - Accession number: 11.4613 - www.mfa.org

p. 77 © Kasuga Taisha Treasure House, Nara

pp. 78–79 © Courtesy of Kyoto National Museum

p. 80 © Public domain, via Wikimedia Commons

p. 81 © Public domain, The Cleveland Museum of Art - Accession number: 1916.932 - Gift of Mrs. Henry S. Upson - https://clevelandart.org/art/1916.932

pp. 83–84 © Public domain, The Metropolitan Museum of Art - Gift of Bashford Dean, 1914 - Accession Number: 14.100.121b–e

p. 85 © Public domain, The Metropolitan Museum of Art - Gift of Bashford Dean, 1914 - Accession number: 14.100.121a

写真提供

pp. 86–87 © Lord Takeda Shingen Treasure House, Kōshū, Yamanashi Prefecture
p. 89 © Museum of Fine Arts, Boston - Alfred Greenough Collection - Accession number: 08.543.35 - www.mfa.org
pp. 90–91 © The British Museum, Londres, Dist. RMN-Grand Palais / The Trustees of the British Museum - 2008,3037.18311
pp. 92–93 © Terebi Setouchi Create
p. 94 © World History Archive / Alamy Stock Photo
p. 95 © Tsukioka Yoshitoshi / National Museum of Asian Art - Smithsonian Institution - Arthur M. Sackler Collection - The Anne van Biema Collection, S2004.3.311
pp. 96–97 © National Museums Scotland / Bridgeman Images
pp. 98–99 © Courtesy of Kyoto National Museum
p. 100 © Public domain, via Wikimedia Commons
p. 101 © Library of Congress, Prints & Photographs Division [repr. number: LC-DIG-jpd-01508] (https://www.loc.gov/item/2008660170/)
pp. 102–103 © Pictures from History / Bridgeman Images
pp. 104–105 © The Tokugawa Art Museum Image Archives / DNPartcom
p. 107 © TNM Image Archives
p. 108 © TNM Image Archives
p. 109 © Public domain, The Walters Art Museum, Baltimore - Gift of Mr. and Mrs. C. R. Snell, Jr., Maryland Line, Maryland; given to the Walters Art Museum, 1987 - Accession number: 95.196
pp. 110–111 © TNM Image Archives
p. 112 © Public domain, via Wikimedia Commons
p. 113 © Philadelphia Museum of Art - Gift of Sidney A. Tannenbaum, 1978 - Accession number: 1978-129-230a
pp. 114–115 © Ōyamazumi Shrine, Ehime Prefecture
p. 117 © Philadelphia Museum of Art - Purchased with funds contributed by the E. Rhodes and Leona B. Carpenter Foundation, 1989 - Accession number: 1989-47-50
p. 118 © Kikkawa Historical Museum, Yamaguchi Prefecture
p. 119 © Philadelphia Museum of Art - Purchased with funds contributed by the E. Rhodes and Leona B. Carpenter Foundation, 1989 - Accession number: 1989-47-417
pp. 120–121 top, center and bottom left © Fukuoka City Museum / DNPartcom - Photographs by Fumiyasu Kaname
pp. 120–121 bottom right © Fukuoka City Museum / DNPartcom - Photographs by Kenpachi Fujimoto
p. 123 © Fukuoka City Museum / DNPartcom
p. 124 © Morioka History and Culture Museum, Iwate Prefecture
p. 125 © Fukuoka City Museum / DNPartcom - Photographs by Kenpachi Fujimoto
p. 126 left © TNM Image Archives
p. 126 right © TNM Image Archives
p. 128 © TNM Image Archives
p. 129 © TNM Image Archives
pp. 130–131 © Agency for Cultural Affairs - Bunkachō
p. 132 © Sano Art Museum (Yabe Collection), Shizuoka Prefecture
pp. 134–135 © The British Museum, Londres, Dist. RMN-Grand Palais / The Trustees of the British Museum - 1906,1220,0.1616.1-3
pp. 136–137 © TNM Image Archives
p. 139 © The Picture Art Collection / Alamy Stock Photo
p. 140 © TNM Image Archives
p. 141 © Public domain, Rijksmuseum, Amsterdam - Object Number: RP-P-1983-387 - Gift of H. Filedt-Kok Piebenga, Amsterdam - Acquisition: gift 1983 - Persistent URL: http://hdl.handle.net/10934/RM0001.COLLECT.47421
pp. 142–143 © The British Museum, Londres, Dist. RMN-Grand Palais / The Trustees of the British Museum - 1906,1220,0.1615
pp. 144–145 top (*naginata*) © Ekki Bunko Collection, Fukui City History Museum - Photographs by Myōga Akiko
pp. 144–145 center and bottom (*katana* and *koshirae*) © Miyagi Prefecture, Sanada Tetsu Collection - Photographs by Myōga Akiko
p. 147 © Philadelphia Museum of Art - Gift of Sidney A. Tannenbaum, 1978 - Accession number: 1978-129-221
pp. 148–149 © Museo Civico di Sendai, prefettura di Miyagi
p. 151 © Philadelphia Museum of Art - Gift of Sidney A. Tannenbaum, 1978 - Accession number: 1978-129-132
p. 152 © Sendai City Museum, Miyagi Prefecture
p. 153 left © Los Angeles County Museum of Art (LACMA), Los Angeles (CA), USA - Gift of George and Lillian Kuwayama (M.2007.223.3) / Digital Image Museum Associates / LACMA / Art Resource NY / Scala, Firenze
p. 153 right © Sendai City Museum, Miyagi Prefecture
pp. 154 top and 155 © Collezione di Kawabata Terutaka - Photographs by Ikeda Nagamasa
p. 154 bottom © Eisei Bunko Museum, Tōkyō
pp. 156–157 top © Yatsushiro Municipal Museum, Kumamoto Prefecture
pp. 156–157 bottom © Public domain, via Wikimedia Commons - Artelino
p. 158 © Collection of the Honolulu Museum of Art - Gift of Victor S.K. Houston in honor of his wife, Pinao Brickwood Houston, 1941 (11641.36)
p. 159 © Museum of Fine Arts, Boston - William Sturgis Bigelow Collection - Accession number: 11.41122 - www.mfa.org
pp. 160–161 © Kawabata Terutaka Collection - Photographs by Ikuta Kyōko
p. 162 © Public domain, Los Angeles County Museum of Art (LACMA), Los Angeles (CA), USA - Herbert R. Cole Collection (M.84.31.335)
p. 163 © Philadelphia Museum of Art - Purchased with funds contributed by the E. Rhodes and Leona B. Carpenter Foundation, 1989 - Accession number: 1989-47-263
pp. 164–165 © Reimeikan Arts Center, Kagoshima Prefecture
p. 166 © Public domain, via Wikimedia Commons - National Diet Library – Portraits of Modern Japanese Historical Figures - https://www.ndl.go.jp/portrait/e/datas/85/
p. 167 © Philadelphia Museum of Art - Purchased with funds contributed by the E. Rhodes and Leona B. Carpenter Foundation, 1989 - Accession number: 1989-47-36b
pp. 168–169 © Ryōzen Museum of History, Kyōto
p. 170 © The Satō Hikogorō Shinsengumi Museum, Hino (Tōkyō)
p. 171 © Philadelphia Museum of Art - Gift of Sidney A. Tannenbaum, 1978 - Accession number: 1978-129-245
pp. 172–173 © Ryōzen Museum of History, Kyōto
p. 174 © The Satō Hikogorō Shinsengumi Museum, Hino (Tōkyō)
p. 175 © Hijikata Toshizō Museum, Hino (Tōkyō)
pp. 176–177 © Kyoto National Museum
p. 178 © The Kochi Prefectural Sakamoto Ryōma Memorial Museum, Shikoku
p. 179 © The Kochi Prefectural Sakamoto Ryōma Memorial Museum, Shikoku
pp. 180–181 © The Japanese Sword Museum, Sumida (Tōkyō)
p. 182 © Zenshōan, Taitō (Tōkyō)
p. 183 © Fair Use
p. 184 © Toyohara Chikanobu / National Museum of Asian Art - Smithsonian Institution - Arthur M. Sackler Collection - The Elizabeth D. Woodbury collection of prints from Meiji Japan, S1999.82a-c (Detail)
p. 191 © Pictures from History / Bridgeman Images
pp. 192–200 © Courtesy of Kyoto National Museum
pp. 201–221 © Paul Martin - Illustrations by Abdallah Amrain
p. 231 © Photographs by Steve Morin

ERAS OF JAPANESE HISTORY

Kofun ca. 300 – 538
Asuka ca. 538 – 710
Nara 710 – 794
Heian 794 – 1185
Kamakura 1185 – 1333
Nanbokuchō 1333 – 1392
Muromachi 1392 – 1573
Azuchi-Momoyama 1573 – 1603
Edo 1603 – 1868
Meiji 1868 – 1912
Taishō 1912 – 1926
Shōwa 1926 – 1989
Heisei 1989 – 2019
Reiwa 2019 –

BIBLIOGRAPHY

The Book of Five Rings, Miyamoto Musashi, Trans. Victor Harris, The Overlook Press, 1974.

Fukushi, Shigeo, *Tosogu Kansho Gadai Jiten*, Ribun Publishing, 2012.

Ginza Choshuya, *Nihonto Jiten*, Gakken Publishing, 2006.

Inada, Kazuhiko, *The Japanese Sword - A Treasure Celebrated for Over a Thousand Years,* Trans. Paul Martin, NuiNui, 2017.

Jansen, Marius B., *Sakamoto Ryoma and the Meiji Restoration*, Columbia University Press - New York, 1994.

Kasuga Taisha no Katchu to Token, 3rd edition, Kasuga Taisha Museum, 2020.

Kikan Eisei-Bunko, n° 119, Eisei Bunko, 2023.

Kubo, Yasuko, *Swords of Japan*, Trans. Paul Martin, Tokyo Bijutsu, 2016.

Trans. Matsubayashi, Yasuaki, *Jōkyū-ki*, Gendaishicho Publishing, Tokyo 1982.

Nagayama, Kōkan, *The Connoisseur's Book of Japanese Swords*, Trans. Mishina Kenji, Kodansha International, 1997.

Nakahara, Nobuo, *Facts and Fundamentals of Japanese Swords - A Collector's Guide*, Trans. Paul Martin, Kodansha International, 2010.

Ogasawara, Nobuo, *Nihonto no Kansho Kiso Chishiki*, Shibundo, 1994.

Ogasawara, Nobuo, *Omishima no Token*, Sogeisha/Ōyamazumi Jinja.

Ogawa, Morihiro, ed., *Art of the Samurai*, New York Metropolitan Museum, 2009.

Ohama, Kenichi, *Toso no Subete,* Kogei Publishing, 2005.

Ōyamazumi Jinja, Ōyamazumi Jinja, 2015.

Samson, George, *A History of Japan - Vols. I-III* (reprint), WM Dawson and Sons, LTD, 1978.

Sasama, Yoshihiko, *Katchū no Subete*, PHP Kenkyujo, 1997.

Sasano, Masayuki, *Sukashi Tsuba*, Kyuryudo, 1993.

Suekane, Toshikiko, *Swords of Kyoto: Master Craftsmanship from an Elegant Culture*, Trans. Paul Martin and Melissa Rinne, Kyoto National Museum, 2018.

The Taiheiki: A Chronicle of Medieval Japan, Trans. Helen Craig McCullough, Tuttle Publishing, 2004.

The Tale of the Heike, Trans. Helen Craig McCullough, Stanford University Press, 1988.

Uchigatana Koshirae, Tokyo National Museum, 1985.

Varley, Paul H., *A Chronicle of Gods and Sovereigns*, Columbia University Press, New York, 1980.

Watanabe, Taeko, ed., *Bizen Ichimonji*, Sano Art Museum, 2007.

著者・謝辞

ABOUT THE AUTHOR

Paul Martin is a Japanese sword and culture specialist residing in Tokyo. He is a former curator from the Japanese department of the British Museum where he cared for the arms and armor collections. Paul has a Master's Degree in Asian Studies from the University of California, Berkeley. He is currently a Trustee for the Society for the Promotion of Japanese Sword Culture (NBSK), a recognized specialist for the Japanese Ministry of Land Infrastructure, Transport and Tourism (MLIT), and the founder of the Shin-Gobankaji Project. He is also a two-time winner of the sword appraisal competition in Tokyo sponsored by the Japanese Sword Museum. The first non-Japanese to do so. He has provided specialist translations for many Japanese sword exhibitions at major institutions, and produced several leading books and DVDs on Japanese swords. Paul has appeared on TV all around the world (Discovery Channel, History Channel, National Geographic, NHK World, BBC). He was also the Japanese sword lecturer and author of the accompanying texts for two seasons of *Shumi Doki!* on NHK's domestic channel as the main lecturer on Japanese swords in 2022 and 2023. He is a former three times English Karate champion (lightweight: under 65 kgs) and England Team Member, a 4th Dan Kendo, a 5th Dan Iaido and practices Batto-jutsu.

ACKNOWLEDGMENTS

The author thanks: Clara Zanotti · Federica Romagnoli · Fujishiro Tatsuya · Hara Eiji · Hijikata Megumi · Hosokawa Morimitsu · Ishihara Hiroshi · Izumi Koushiro · Kawabata Terutaka · Kimura Takehito · Matsumura Kazuya · Mishima Yasunori · Nakaie Ren · Nakaie Yumi · Ogawa Morihiro · Ōno Yoshimitsu · Ōno Masafumi · Sanada Tetsu · Sato Fukuko · Sato Hirosuke · Shida Satoko · Shimizu Kazumasa · Sugiyama Masao · The Imperial Household Agency · The Society for the Preservation of Japanese Art Swords · The Society for the Promotion of Japanese Sword Culture · Tokita Kōichi

The publisher thanks: ADEAC (Ōta Ryōko) · Agency for Cultural Affairs - Bunkachō (Keita Kawasaki, Meiki Kumagai, Shō Sugimoto) · Bridgeman Images (Pénélope Estrada) · DNP (Yasumichi Kuniya) · Egenolf Gallery (Veronica Miller) · Freer Gallery of Art and Arthur M. Sackler Gallery (Tellie Simpson) · Harvard Art Museums (Britt Bowen, Jeff Steward) · Hiratsuka Art Museum (Shigeru Katsuyama) · Honolulu Museum of Art (Schamarra Smith, Kyle Swartzlender) · Kyoto National Museum (Satoko Sakaguchi) · Museum of Fine Arts, Boston (Carolyn Cruthirds) · Philadelphia Museum of Art (Jonathan Hoppe) · Melissa Rinne · RMN (Sébastien Felmann) · Scala Group Spa (Katja Lehmann) · Kosuke Shimamura · The Walters Art Museum (Laura Seitter) · Yukio Yasuda

"Books to Span the East and West"

Tuttle Publishing was founded in 1832 in the small New England town of Rutland, Vermont [USA]. Our core values remain as strong today as they were then—to publish best-in-class books which bring people together one page at a time. In 1948, we established a publishing outpost in Japan—and Tuttle is now a leader in publishing English-language books about the arts, languages and cultures of Asia. The world has become a much smaller place today and Asia's economic and cultural influence has grown. Yet the need for meaningful dialogue and information about this diverse region has never been greater. Over the past seven decades, Tuttle has published thousands of books on subjects ranging from martial arts and paper crafts to language learning and literature—and our talented authors, illustrators, designers and photographers have won many prestigious awards. We welcome you to explore the wealth of information available on Asia at **www.tuttlepublishing.com.**

Published by Tuttle Publishing, an imprint of Periplus Editions (HK) Ltd

www.tuttlepublishing.com

Original edition:
Spade e Armi Giapponesi Dei Trenta Più Gloriosi Samurai
© Nuinui SA 2023
Editorial Director: Federica Romagnoli
Graphic Design: Clara Zanotti

ISBN 978-4-8053-1838-6
Library of Congress Cataloging in Process
English edition © 2024 Periplus Editions (HK) Ltd

Front Cover
Top: Katana "Ishida Masamune," pp. 136–137; **Center**: Katana "Nakatsukasa Masamune," pp. 130–131; **Bottom**: Itomaki tachi koshirae, pp. 86–87.

Front Flap
Leather armor of the Ō-yoroi type, p. 83

Back cover
Top: *Tsuba* attributed to Miyamoto Musashi, p. 155; **Bottom**: Katana "Soza Samonji," pp. 98–99.

Distributed by
North America, Latin America & Europe
Tuttle Publishing
364 Innovation Drive
North Clarendon, VT 05759-9436 U.S.A.
Tel: 1 (802) 773-8930
Fax: 1 (802) 773-6993
info@tuttlepublishing.com
www.tuttlepublishing.com

Japan
Tuttle Publishing
Yaekari Building 3rd Floor, 5-4-12 Osaki
Shinagawa-ku, Tokyo 141-0032
Tel: (81) 3 5437-0171; Fax: (81) 3 5437-0755
sales@tuttle.co.jp
www.tuttle.co.jp

Asia Pacific
Berkeley Books Pte. Ltd.
3 Kallang Sector, #04-01, Singapore 349278
Tel: (65) 67412178; Fax: (65) 67412179
inquiries@periplus.com.sgwww.tuttlepublishing.com

Printed in China 2406CM

28 27 26 25 24 10 9 8 7 6 5 4 3 2 1

源頼光